THE
DAFT
APETH

DEFINITION: *DAFT APETH – A PERSON WHO DOES SILLY THINGS, BUT WE LOVE THEM REGARDLESS.*

ACHIEVE SUPERHUMAN RESULTS WHEN YOU
DREAM, ACT, FEEL, AND THINK WITH PURPOSE

First published in 2023

© 2023, Jeremy Chiappe, United Kingdom

The Daft Apeth, Jeremy Chiappe

ISBN: 9798375771236

Produced in collaboration with The Book Shelf Ltd:

Project manager: Ameesha Green

Cover designer: Niall Burgess

Typesetter: Kyle Albuquerque

e-book creation: BookEmpress

For J, L and O...

my three reasons

CONTENTS

1.2 Desires

Sometimes we need help to get that thing that is deep within us out

Make me whole again

Philosophically speaking

Reach for the stars

Caveat emptor

Cave vendor

Cave canem

Life is in the balance

Tell me what you like, and I'll tell you who you are...

1,3 Dopamine

We are animals and respond to chemical cues subconsciously

The Third D will dominate and dictate...

1.4 Novelty and Risk-taking

As animals our survival is our priority, then our curiosity...

Falling to Earth or to Earthworms?

Struggling for stimulation?

Struggling for motivation?

It's never too late, but why wait?

What we say or think or feel don't matter if we don't act

The man (or woman) with two brains

Are you as Sphexy, or what?

The sacred gift

No feeling, no fun

Are you competent enough to fail yet?

First impressions lead to great expectations

What do your muscles remember?

How much emotional leakage do you display?

Sphex lessons

Coordinated improvement – making it stick...

Our feelings guide our decisions

Primal thinking, primal screaming

Chapter 4: Thoughts 143

We can shape our thoughts to meet our desires

Chapter 5: Biased Beyond Belief 165

We are the survivors but we are still just animals

5.1 Attention seeking

Our attention is limited, our desire for other's attention not so much…

5.2 Pattern-finding

Our survival instincts mean we find simple patterns to reduce complexity.

5.3 Erroneous reasoning

Brain work drains our energy banks - shortcuts helps us survive.

Hiding behind a lemon juice mask

The Dulles Brothers knew best

What have flat earthers and Mayan end of the world'ers in common with you?

The bias cascade flushes away the Spanish homework...

5.4 Temperamental

We are unique, yet our moods fall into patterns that we can manage.

We are our choices

How aroused is your amygdala? What is your base threshold?

Feedback – it's what older people eat for breakfast...

5.5 Hypersensitive

We deeply fear threats to our survival - and exaggerate our responses.

Our judgement is flawed

So are our senses...

5.6 Simians

Thousands of years of evolution do not rid us of our animal ancestry.

Yes, you are the Apeman...

Improvement action plan:-

Smell the Bread

What would you tell your twelve-year old?

Listen to the experts

PART 2: MENS REA

We can take steps to improve – first we must understand...

Chapter 1: Meaning, Purpose and Well-Being

This is what it feels like to be us...

Find out what is beyond the broken pencil

What show is playing at your inner theatre today?

The hopes and fears of all our years

Reasons to be fearful

Reasons to be cheerful

Improvement Actions:

Take note

Take control

Take care

Take action

Take two

Take a reality check

Take stock

Take the right medicine

Take mind and body as one

Reframe, Reframe, Reframe

Look after your body and it will help you look after your mind...

Oil the chain

Get a grip

Stretch the point

Improvement Actions:

Do some

Sit on a goldmine not a timebomb

Find a pattern that suits you

The not-so surprising impact of what we eat on our body and mind...

$S=I+Z-E$

The nutritionist's model

Do you eat like an animal?

Hungry? It's all in the mind.

Fasting and furious?

Improvement Actions:

Manage your diet

Have a personal plan

Eat well

A few key takeaways

Sometimes it's helpful to recognise that we need external assistance!

A short story

By Oscar Chiappe (Age 3 ¾)

There was once a bird who was very sad because he couldn't fly.

So he got a jet-pack, and then he was happy.

The end

We all do silly things, but those things do not define us, they merely add to our human charm...

INTRODUCTION

Who hasn't had their car jump-started then immediately proceeded to drive to a fuel station only to fill the diesel tank with petrol? It's no big deal – the tank can be drained, and it only wastes a few hours and it's no great shakes, in the scheme of things, is it?

Who hasn't sent an email to their boss, asking if their boss has lost the plot, only to find you sent it directly to their boss by mistake? It's not the end of the world; your boss's boss will probably forgive you, one day, won't he?

Who hasn't been onion ring hunting in Ohio, taken a U-turn and got their wing clipped by a personal injury attorney? Just me then?!

Those deep-fried onions in crispy golden batter may have been precious, but even Gollum might have balked at the cost. One ring to rule them all, six rings to break the bank – yes, the settlement of £180,000 amounted to £30,000 per ring – one of my more costly mistakes!

As Paul McCartney put it, we are all on a long and winding road. The road is littered with obstacles, only some are deep fried in batter and cost their weight in gold, but we all have our own examples, don't we?

Let's try again…Do you ever try to enlarge the print in a magazine with your thumb and forefinger, open your front door remotely with your car key, or look for your phone when you are actually using it? Then you are in good company.

If, like me, any of your unaccountable actions make you sometimes feel daft, dumb, dopey or dense, then you have come to the right place.

As I again put the butter in the bread bin and the milk in the toaster, I curse myself with various choice expletives – and in doing so I ignore my own advice - 'don't talk to myself in a way I wouldn't want others to', and 'don't say *don't*, as our brains struggle to process negative requests'.

If I'm being particularly kind to myself, I might say 'I'm as daft as a brush...and half as useful'; deploying the old Yorkshire expression of dubious origin.

Perhaps the gentle insult derives from the poem *The Flowers of the Forest,* in which a brush has been 'daffed a great deal' – that is to say that it has been prodded until the bristles have splayed, making the brush 'daft' in the way a person unable to direct their concentration properly might be?

Perhaps it refers to the poor Victorian child who fell head-first down the chimney?

In the Yorkshire villages and towns, most people have been labelled as 'Daft Apeths' at one point or another. It really is a term of endearment. We do stupid things and people love us anyway. Perhaps doing stupid things makes people love us more?

So, hands up if you don't think this applies to you....

Right, you class-room swot, you can go now, but before deciding to do that, you might want to take a look at the studies by VS Ramachandran (see Youtube). It might not be **your** hand that's up at all. We are perfectly capable of confusing rubber hands for our own, we can assume ownership of fingers far beyond the reach of our hands, in fact even a table can be assimilated into our body image due to the curious nature of the sensory mechanisms within our brain.

The Daft Apeth club accepts you as a member; even Groucho Marx couldn't refuse to join. An 'apeth of course is short form for an old ha'penny, or half a penny. The traditional Daft Apeth may then be 'daft as a brush but half as useful'. The twenty first century Daft Apeth may be daft but we refuse to be half as useful.

We are meant to be this way. Daffed or daft, what really matters is what we do with this skill. For that is what it is. Sure, getting petrol out of a diesel engine is not the best use of our resources, but arguably it's the less visible errors that need the most attention.

Our immense skill in maximising the use of our limited energy banks can drive actions with many favourable and adverse consequences. My DAFT model will help you to add the boons, subtract the banes and achieve amazing results.

Our Daft Apeth of course nods to Desmond Morris's *Naked Ape*. By the end of this book, you will see how to be an even more amazing human, despite all the flaws reasonably expected of a featherless biped, one that has survived the perilous tides of the gene pool. You will see that you often do the right things for the wrong reasons and that you, equally often, do the wrong things for the right reasons. Most importantly, with greater awareness you will see that we all have it in our power to decide to do more of the right things for more of the right reasons. This simple power can yield phenomenal results.

If you are ready to embrace your DAFTness, and move from your starting point, whether you feel half as useful or not, onto your chosen path to success, this book is here to help you. My background demanded that I bring together the works of innumerable experts in diverse scientific fields to support this journey.

Perhaps we all have something of Mary Shelley's Frankenstein about us, as we gather 'body parts' and then add that mysterious spark to breathe life into the monster. Perhaps all I am trying to do is to understand a little more of what it means to be human. Victor Frankenstein finally concluded that we should 'seek happiness in tranquility and avoid ambition'. In bringing my Daft Apeth to life, I didn't seek that conclusion, rather hoping to regain my sense of purpose and achievement. Perhaps reading this book will help you in the way you want most. I hope so.

To start the journey of a thousand miles, we need a simple first step. My first step is a look under the bonnet – lifting the lid to consider the organ itself. What is the brain and how does it work? As it informs why we think the way we do, why we make the mistakes we make and consequently how to make the changes we want to make. This seems a sensible starting point to me, where it ends is up to you. I trust you will find this book interesting, informative and enjoyable to read; whether it changes your life will be determined by you. By your actions.

My accompanying book of cognitive errors, *Some Other Substantial Reason* provides a handy reference to many of our common failings, which our awareness will help us to address. After completion of this book, I became aware of the Million Copy Bestseller, The Art of Clear Thinking, by Rolf Dobelli, who argues that we should follow the 'Via Negativa' – eliminate all our weaknesses and what is left is our strength. Having spent many years in industry, this directly reflects the 'Lean' approach to business, where focus on waste elimination continually improves performance. This is most certainly effective in the workplace, however in terms of human performance I will show you why it is not always to be recommended.

The journey towards being our best (our long and winding road) is not without obstacles, but that's the fun of it! Stay the course and you will benefit personally, and perhaps more importantly, you will be able to improve the lives of those around you.

We may or may not push ourselves. We may or may not beat ourselves up. Others may or may not join in. The fact remains, we can only ever do Our Best. The great news is that Our Best is always enough. When we embrace our DAFTness, we stand tall and proud, shoulders square and hands on hips, in a superhero stance to make Amy Cuddy proud, and say 'I am a DAFT APETH.'

'I am the best damn DAFT APETH I can be!'

PART I

DAFT (and Biased Beyond Belief)

We need to think holistically
if we want to live wholeheartedly

We need to think holistically if
we want to live wholeheartedly

Why DAFT?

Why DAFT? DAFT defines us; it is all that we are and all that we do. And what is more, we love acronyms. They help us to remember. They help us to understand. Our **Dreams** drive us and shape our **Actions, Feelings** and **Thoughts.** Our thoughts and feelings create our Dreams and we go full circle. In bringing these four 'elements' into harmony, achieving the perfect balance, we master our DAFTness.

Desmond Morris gave us his seminal text on evolutionary biology more than 50 years ago. His was the start of a move away from the prior tendency to focus on primitive tribes, on the outliers rather than on normal run of the mill humans, like us. As he put it, 'we put the cart before the horse when studying human behaviour'. Since then, of course, the nature of experimentation, the liberalisation of the world, and developments in technology have enabled big data, imaging techniques and advanced thinking to be applied to the analysis of us (humans), and our understanding has inevitably sky-rocketed.

Of course, we now know so much more of what goes on behind the Wizard of Oz's curtain, with myriad new names for the similar number of new fields of neuroscience, yet underneath we haven't changed so much; the later data really only reinforces Morris's observations, and those of earlier scientists, like Mr Darwin, Wallace et al.

As Stephen Covey in his ubiquitous *Seven Habits...* said, 'seek first to understand then to be understood'. Of course, this makes perfect sense and applies equally in all matters, especially where thinking is required, or even thinking about thinking. Sometimes to understand how we think, or more aptly how our brain works, it helps to go back to first principles, which means taking a step back into history, and in this case not just one small step, but a giant leap, or two.

Can we fully understand our brains? It is oft said that if our brains were simple enough for us to understand them, we would be too simple to do so. That certainly applies to me, and (unless you are a quantum physicist) it probably applies to you too. I sometimes take comfort in the life the writer Daniel Keyes imagined for Algernon (in his classic, *Flowers for Algernon*), who swallowed a genius drug and ultimately found out that he was probably happier as a rather simpler fellow, like me.

Algernon was science fiction, but similar things have been developed in real life too, in mice at least. Dr Joe Z Tsien altered a brain receptor gene, resulting in a new strain of mice, (named Doogies, after the fictional TV Comic Doctor of superior intellect, Doogie Howser MD). These mice learned faster, consistently out-performed the normies on a water maze test and were more curious about new toys. Tsien explains their better memory and intelligence, arguing that you are what you can remember, which is unfortunate for me, and yet, as Algernon learned, not necessarily advantageous to him. There are numerous examples of people with truly photographic memories. Imagine the burden of holding so much data in your head; quite onerous, as the infamous Patient S[1] (a man who was simply unable to forget) would testify, if only he could have shifted his focus away from his bulging knowledge bank to share some useful intelligence.

Of course, the developments in imaging technology and Artificial Intelligence have moved the dial from possible to certain that our brains will be fully understood, if not by us, certainly by our future digital overlords. For the same reason that Stephen Hawking, in predicting the end of the Universe, advised stockbrokers it was too early sell, thankfully the exhaustion of the Sun's fuel supply and the evolution of man do not happen fast. But our technology and understanding have accelerated exponentially, reflecting Gordon Moore's Law as it applies to microchips[2]. The rapidly approaching reality makes it more important than ever that we meet the future half-way. By which I mean we build a strong foundation by better understanding our past.

So much is written about our hunter-gatherer ancestors, how we developed to protect ourselves from tigers or other deadly enemies in the deserts or jungles of bygone times, but going back to first base, to understand how, or why our brain works means going back much further than these recent friends. With a little more historical context, we can better understand our current brains.

And then, as with technological change, so with each of us as individuals – a small amount of change on a frequent basis can lead to a dramatic overall impact, so somewhat like the tortoises in Roald Dahl's Esio Trot, a tiny change on a regular basis can have us creatures growing dramatically over time, and yet unnoticed. As James Clear calculates in *Atomic Habits*, a 1% improvement on a daily basis means a 38 fold change over the course of just one year due to its compounding effect. The key for us is to take charge of as much of that change as we can so that the outcomes happen for us rather than to us.

THE DAFT APETH'S PRIMARY TOOL

To appreciate the DAFT model, we need to think a little about our primary tool, the common or garden brain.

There's nothing common or garden about my primary tool, thank you very much!

Jorge Tejada, pathologist at Harvard Brain Tissue Resource Center at MacLean hospital in Massachusetts, has sliced up over 10,000 brains[3]. The giant, spongy walnut; an amorphous mass of tissues, proteins and fats, weighing in at around 1.5kg is a magical mystery that conceals a million secrets. Weighing one in his hands, he says, 'it is hard to comprehend that this is what makes a person think, jump, talk and do everything – how is it possible that these cells and tissues make such a wonderful machine?'

How indeed?

The basic ingredients may be common or garden but put together in the right way and there be magic.

Of course, all models are wrong, one size does not fit all, but some models are useful nevertheless. The DAFT model is no exception, drawing upon the popular simplification model of the brain; psychologists call it the Triune brain.

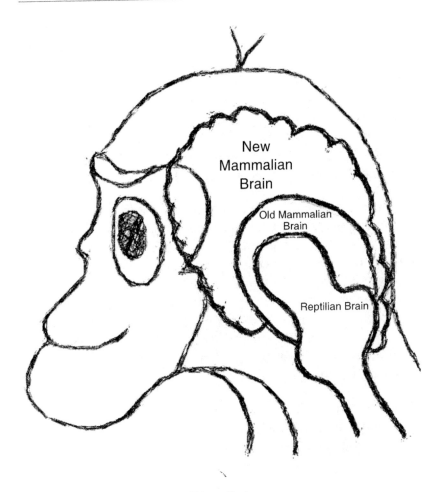

Triune Brain

In this model, our current 'whole brain' is described by reference to three distinct ages, layers like the kind seen in geological studies of rocks. We see a 'reptilian' layer, surrounded by a 'mammalian' layer, and an outer layer being the 'new mammalian or human brain' merged together like a fine cocoa-based confection.

Having left the ocean, and stretched our toes on dry land, we never looked back. Our reptilian base had the primary function of survival, with millions of years condensed into a portion of one sentence, before we branched off into a mammalian strand of the Tree of Life; our limbic system, eventually giving rise to our ape-like forebears, who arranged for that core, the reptilian brain stem to be wrapped in a blanket of emotions and feelings, enabling suffering and joyous desire. Our ancestors took this still primitive dual-layered brain, and enrobed it, with a new mammalian coating. This luxury layer bringing executive function, the ability to think and to think about thinking, and to think about thinking about thinking (and to think about chocolate).

This luxury coating saw our high-quality brains having to make step changes, despite our fine eyesight, efficient grasp and even some social organisation, we needed to shift again in order to improve our hunting prowess; our sense of smell was too weak, our hearing not sharp enough. As Desmond Morris explains, 'as we became more upright, we could move faster, developed improved grip to hold weapons and our brains added a layer of complexity to enable faster, better decisions.' There was almost a tipping point at which we 'plunged into our new role with great evolutionary energy'[4]

However; our body and brain development didn't happen at a consistent rate; our reproductive systems raced ahead whilst brain development happened at a much more leisurely pace, in much the same way as our population has expanded leaving our food supply playing catch up.

Speculators on our future brain evolution recognise the limitations on our brains placed by our birthing method, although it should be said that Neanderthal heads and presumably brains were about 20% larger than our own. We do now know that size is not everything. It was not so long ago that people believed differently; paying good money to have their lumps, bumps and cranial humps felt and fondled as the phrenologists profited from our human ignorance. Whilst not entirely eradicated this thinking has certainly been pushed into a corner by superior science.

Now our simplified model shows the three layers of our brain growing progressively – if we were creating a luxury confection inside our cranium, the base layer must be established before the second and third. Desmond Morris points to our 'differential infantilism'[5]. We are born with just 23% of our adult brain compared to 70% in monkeys. On the other hand, our brain continues to grow rapidly, for the next 6 years and then the outer layer continues to develop until about 23 years old and at very variable rates.

It is worth reminding ourselves of this, as I do often, when frustrated with the 'swooshing' behaviour of our young monsters; Oscar, my three-year old's brain is blossoming primarily in the doing and wanting parts; the thinking part will come later, much later!

> **Swoosh**
>
> In honour of the Greek Goddess of Victory, Phil Knight paid just $35 to create the Nike 'swoosh'. It aptly represents speed of action, a particularly dominant feature of the growing brain.

Given this past, and with recent survival being most likely for those able to tell the best stories, in other words, to best communicate the whereabouts of the enemy tribe or the traitor in the camp, or the berries that made Ug vomit for several days as his body churned in paroxysms of pain, I propose my DAFT model.

The DAFT Cycle

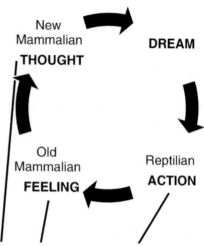

New Mammalian **THOUGHT**

DREAM

Reptilian **ACTION**

Old Mammalian **FEELING**

DREAMS define us, provided our Actions, Feelings and Thoughts toe the line. In this section, we look at our dreams and desires and the precious role of dopamine.

ACTIONS are nestled in the Reptilian Brain. The unbridled brain will 'Just Do It' with a swoosh of instinct.

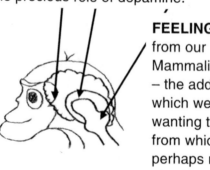

FEELINGS emanate from our 'Old Mammalian Brain' – the add-in, from which we can start wanting things, from which we are perhaps no longer simply coils of DNA.

THOUGHT - a comparatively new enhancement and still fairly flawed. The New Mammalian Brain, (AKA neo-cortex or cerebrum), represents the core of our 'executive function'.

These DAFT elements combine to define us and give us the illusion of our unique existence.

The Dream Team

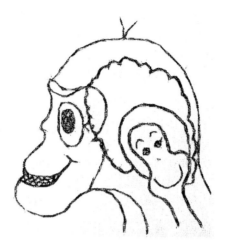

The Dream team is a harmonious one; a high performing team, one with a rich diversity of abilities, with Action, Feeling and Thought trusted to take their unique role in making the whole the best it can be. As in any team, when the balance isn't right, performance suffers, and changes should be made!

UNDER THE BONNET

Even if nothing is broken, it certainly helps if we understand a little of what makes us tick along, smoothly or not so smoothly. Dr Daniel Amen, a clinical psychiatrist who has studied over 83,000 brain scans, observes that there is only one area in which we attempt to cure an illness without looking at the organ we are trying to fix[6]. Psychiatrists persist with resolving mental illnesses by reference to 'system clusters', and treatment so based is like 'throwing darts in the dark'. Imaging technology now shows that the exact same symptoms can occur with radically different brain activity.

With greater understanding of individual brains and with the benefit of Functional Magnetic resonance imagery, many of the troubled brains (of criminals, like the school-shooters of Columbine and others) could be treated more effectively. And, following an acceptance that repeated head collisions in American Football can cause brain injury, NFL brain damaged players might undergo a 'brain smart programme' to improve their brain function, memory etc...

Medical interventions can suit the injury and with greater insight they can change the damaged brain and change lives. The good news is that this doesn't just work for criminals or NFL players; we can all do the same; not necessarily having personalised brain scans, although that will no doubt come, but by understanding what's beneath the bonnet. By doing so, we can react accordingly.

If you don't really care what goes on beneath the bonnet, and just want to drive fast, that is fair enough. Treat it well, keep it well rested and fuelled and you can hope to avoid the need to visit your local mechanic!

If we do open the bonnet, the first thing we can expect to see is 'grey matter' - this outer layer is the new mammalian brain, the cerebral cortex. This cortex is a blanket of neural tissue, about 3mm thick, containing about 75% of all our neurons.

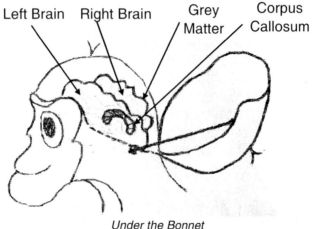

Under the Bonnet

PILIN' ON THE MYELIN

Next, we find 'white matter', our axons are white due to myelination. A fatty tissue (like lard) coats our axons to insulate and accelerate our vital signals.

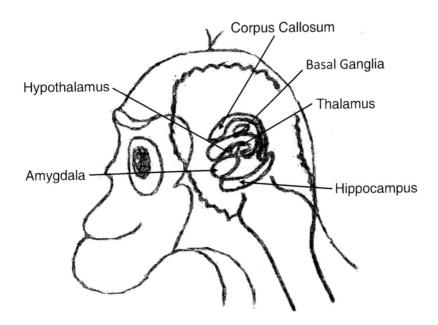

Axon traffic gives rise to myelination, so more use means more myelination, means a faster signal. Hence, 'cells that fire together wire together'. In fact, these vital signals travel 200x faster with full myelination than with none, racing from 2mph up to 200mph. The 00mph is added by regular use!

Behind the closed door of his brain, by the age of two, my son, Oscar had built the foundation of his myelination. Prior to this he 'enjoyed' 'right brain dominance'. In his current phase, between the ages of 2 and 4, his two hemispheres are in constant communication. By his next Birthday, aged 4 his corpus callosum, the bit in the middle connecting the two hemispheres, will be almost fully developed.

The two hemispheres are different but, of course, equally important. The left hemisphere will ultimately be more tightly packed with neurons than the right making it the main decision-making area of the brain. As we know, we thank our left hemisphere for making us logical, analytical, temporal, sequential, verbal, practical, factual and concrete. To our right we owe our intuition, and spontaneity, and our holistic, visuo-spatial, sensory and metaphoric faculties.

When Oscar looks to right, it suggests his left brain is actively processing, looking for logic and facts. More often he looks to the left as he is calling on his right brain for visual learning, creativity and story-telling. Some children tend to look straight up, with a tendency to be tactual learners. Some do swing both ways.

Look left and right

Paul-Pierre Broca, the French surgeon and anthropologist, was the first to associate speech with a region in the left hemisphere, and to the right hemisphere he spotted our spatial awareness bias. It was his early work that revealed that we experience opposing body side control.

There is much debate about right brain/left brain differences, with a growing school of thought that we might profit from a shift to upper/lower brain thinking. In reality, the brain is so complex and interconnected that both schools undoubtedly have some merit and a holistic view is needed if we want to approach a decent understanding of the whole.

The basic structure is not in doubt. Within each hemisphere, we have four lobes to our thinking brain, labelled by the skull bones.

THE FOUR LOBES OF THE NEOCORTEX

Frontal lobe - plays a central role in our speech, planning, emotional expression and empathy

Parietal lobe - critical to our pain response, spatial awareness and sensory screening

Occipital lobe - plays a key role in processing sight

Temporal lobe - central to processing sound and to short-term memory

THE FIVE SENSES

With just a dozen pairs of nerves, (neurons on a stick fibre or bundle of fibres), our brain manages our basic senses and all that we need to service our primary bodily functions. From our Olfactory nerve giving us the sense of smell, our optic and oculomotor nerves giving the sense of sight to our vagus nerve guiding our vital organs, breathing, heart rate, and everything down to our digestive processes.

I maintain that there is no sixth sense, although many disagree, with Guy Harrelson in *Think* collating a number of reputable surveys which show that 41% of Americans, more than 100 million believe in Extra Sensory Perception, and even more

(42%) believe in ghosts. I am not American and I am not one of the 41 or 42%!

In addition, 41% of Americans believe in Miracles. I am not one of them either, although I do believe there is an almost miraculous power within each of us...

THE POWER WITHIN

Our brain is very demanding. It uses more than a quarter of the energy we create, estimated at about 25 watts of the 95 watts that the whole body runs off. This energy powers the 86 billion brain cells (in an average brain), which provide chemical messages, triggered by electrical discharges to send signals racing at up to hundreds of miles per hour. And of course, ours is not an average brain; at least 99% of us know that our brains are above average, in the same way that we are all better than average drivers and so much better looking!

By the Restak reasoning, our brain is 'bigger' than 12,000 universes; a substantial multiverse by anyone's reckoning!

> **Mind the gap**
>
> Gerald Edelman, Nobel prizewinning neuroscientist is famed with the highly practical observation that if we counted out our synapses, at a rate of one per second, it would take us 32 million years.
>
> Richard Restak MD estimates that the neuronal connections (circuits) would amount to an inconceivable 10 with a million zeros. To put that in context, all particles in the known universe amount to 'just' 10 with 79 zeros.

Each nerve cell or neuron is like a mini power plant - a fulfilment centre if you like. Every single neuron has three basic parts; a cell body, an axon and dendrites, which form a production line organised to create, package and send parcels (messages) to their required destination. It is rather like a seed, stem and branches. Imagine a dandelion once it has shed its yellow flowers, leaving just its blowball, the white whiskery sphere ready to blow its seeds into the wind, (or to be plucked and blown by an innocent child, using only their primitive brain function and quite unaware of their own powers of seed dispersal).

The Axon (or stem) acts as a transmitter using its long fibres to send major signals from brain to the selected delivery addresses, via the Dendrites (whiskery branches) which break into even thinner sprouts to act as the receiver, with the gaps between known as synapses or synaptic clefts.

Chemical 'neurotransmitters' send the messages (electrical impulses) between the neurons at these synapses, playing pass the parcel until the music stops and the delivery arrives in the blink of an eye at its target.

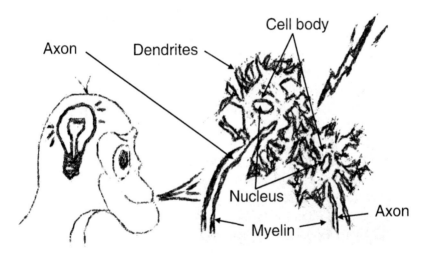

Blow balls

Each neuron may have up to 10,000 points of contact. Let's imagine two of those dandelion blow balls colliding. Now consider 86 billion such 'blowballs' smashing together inside our rather small skulls. And make sense of the trillions of ways we struggle to understand ourselves...

Neurotransmitters, the brains chemical messengers, come in hundreds of shapes and sizes (all rather small!!), sending, boosting and dampening a multitude of signals, with various categories of these small organic molecules performing different functions, and with new discoveries, categorisations, and interactions confounding and exciting the world's neurobiologists every day.

A small handful of these Neurotransmitters are worthy of mention; Glutamate, Oxytocin, Noradrenaline, Acetylcholine, Dopamine and Serotonin. These chemicals inhibit or excite, relaying signals between neurons and triggering our **hormones** to regulate the body's vital functions.

History may remember CATO as Julius Caesar's most formidable, infuriating enemy, his equal in eloquence, in conviction, and in force of character, a man equally capable of a full-volume dawn-to-dusk speech before Rome's Senate and of a 30-day trek through North Africa's desert sands. He made his life a life of purity, refusing to yield to pressure, to compromise, a politician with morals (it'll never work). Cato was pure of thought and mere human emotions were beneath him.

Unlike Cato, few of us are so pure, but CATO may help us recall the key hormones triggered by our neurotransmitters; namely Cortisol, Adrenalin, Testosterone, and Oestrogen. These chemical messengers course the blood stream telling our organs and tissues what to do, in a non-compromising way, keeping the body well-regulated throughout.

When Cato the elder was the Censor at Rome, he persuaded the senate to send the Greek philosopher, Carneades, packing. On the subject of administering justice, one day Carneades would argue for a motion, and the next day against, with equal passion, conviction and credibility, convincing his audience to swing violently one way and then swing back with equal force the next. The destabilising effect was potentially enormously destructive. And so with our hormones; clear instructions and a harmonious balance are vital to our well-being.

CHANGING THE DREAM TEAM

The subject of nature v nature, genes v environment, even the field of epigenetics (how your actions and environment change the way your genes work), leave widely different views about the range of impacts of genes and environment on the different elements of our selves. All agree however that we are product of both. It is not necessary to know what the percentages are to realise that we are never 100% victims of birth. There are always some elements that we can control.

Our physical characteristics and personality traits are described or influenced by our genes. Leaving aside our physical attributes, the likes of height, eye and hair colour, our inherited personality traits might attempt to pigeon-hole us, based on the so-called 'big five' personality types - Curiosity, Conscientiousness, Extroversion, Agreeableness and Neuroticism.

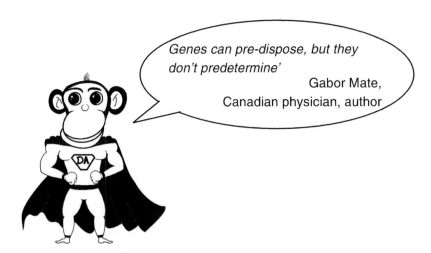

Genes can pre-dispose, but they don't predetermine'
Gabor Mate,
Canadian physician, author

At birth we may be pre-disposed to fall into the low extroversion box, but it doesn't mean we have been disposed of in there - we can climb out, if we want to, or be pushed in later, even if we don't. That box need not determine our fate, any more than the fact that our parents don't speak Chinese will mean that we shan't either.

Of course, we are more likely to be satisfied with our lives if we are able to focus most of our efforts in the areas where we have the most natural ability, so an eternal internal battle is probably not the best use of our limited capacity. Our success does tend to follow our pleasure and excitement. It can indeed be a frustrating life attempting to be something which takes you too far from your natural traits, as admirably captured by Bronnie Ware in her classic work on deathbed regrets. The greatest regret of all is not having been more authentic; having spent a life attempting to please others rather than being true to ourselves.

It is good sense to bear in mind the advice in Reinhold Niebuhr's 'serenity prayer'; accept the things we cannot change, change the things we can, all the time seeking the wisdom to know the difference.

This is certainly not encouragement to give up on our dreams.

Not just a succession of images, ideas, emotions and sensations

1.1 Dreams: It starts with something deep within us

1.2 Desires: Sometimes we need help to get that thing that is deep within us out

1.3 Dopamine: We are animals and respond to chemical cues subconsciously

1.4 Novelty and Risk-taking: As animals our survival is our priority, then our curiosity…

Chapter 1:
DREAMS
(Desires and Dopamine)

1.1 DREAMS

I have had dreams and I have had nightmares. I overcame the nightmares because of my dreams.

Jonas Salk

Who are you? What is your destination? Are you going in the right direction?

This chapter will look distinctly at the three D's - our Dreams, Desires, and Dopamine, the three D's of Dream fulfilment. We'll consider the interaction between the three 'D's, and conclude by circling back round to consider the impact of the powerful human need for novelty.

But first, a quick quiz...

Quick Quiz

Do you know what are your life's big dreams, your purpose or your passions?

If the answer is 'No', then you do not know your life's big dreams, your purpose or your passions.

Read on...

When measuring the circumference of a circle (or size of a head), you have to start somewhere. I start this book and the DAFT model with our dreams, because we all want our dreams (our passions and our purpose) to provide the driving force for our lives. Of course, these dreams are a function of our thoughts so, in the DAFT model, as in life, the beginning and the end are not so far apart.

Some of us know exactly what we want to be *when we grow up*. The YouTuber, **Dream,** knew by the age of fourteen what he wanted to do with his life. By following his hero, influencer and YouTuber, PewDiePie, he reverse-engineered the skills to build his own fan-base. Within seven years he accumulated 38 million subscribers and can boast 2.8 billion views of his on-line content. His video channels are all self-built with the support of his 'Dream Team'. This team has exploited the compelling appeal of gaming sensations like Minecraft. And Dream hasn't looked back. ☺A nine-year-old boy just appeared on my LinkedIn feed; he is already approaching established CEO's in his quest to become a robotics engineer. He is surely setting himself up for similar success.

Sigmund Freud once suggested that our dreams were fulfilment of our deepest wishes. Whilst sleeping some of us are able to invoke a lucid dream state – do you know you are dreaming and somehow have the power to guide the dream, to go wherever you want? Can you fly off to a palatial home and a perfect family if you want to? Lucky you! Can you do the same in real life?

Most of us remain at the mercy of our astonishingly, apparently-random unconscious whims until we wake up. And even then, many of us blunder along, waiting to see which wall of the pinball machine we'll smash into next and whether it will grant us an impressive point score and a sound and light show, or send us in a slippery spiral to a dark pit, a holding bay before we start the process all over again. Too many of us spend our lives in this infernal game, bashed from pillar to post, experiencing ups and downs, in a random walk, dependent on the luck of our birth and our environment.

Were you an obliging child, not causing trouble, just getting on with it - one of the 'other ten kids' who the teacher had to frantically look up in the class list before your parents' visit? Then, you probably hadn't yet ignited the spark. Have you now? If not, you are at risk of not reaching your potential.

If you haven't yet found your unique niche, Ken Robinson, the international educational advisor, has provided helpful hints for finding your element, handy for those of us in the 'not-sure', 'don't know', or 'not particularly good at anything' categories. By following his questionnaires in *Finding Your Element*[7], we can find what lies dormant and, if you are in the latter category, there is much that can be done to tackle those beliefs which are holding you back.

Robinson describes your two worlds. First there is the world outside you, which exists with or without you - perhaps the very idea of a world surviving without you makes you feel small and insignificant? Perhaps not. In any case, it is better to focus on Robinson's second world; your inner world. This is the place reserved uniquely for you. This is where your thoughts and feelings determine how you act. This is where your DAFTness lies.

Our genes account for a lot, but they do need to be switched on. Many of us have latent skills that, due to circumstances, are never exposed. Some of our genes are never expressed. Many of us never find what we are looking for, many of us never find our sweet spot. I recently decided that my hidden skill was avoiding emergency vehicles on the road in a smooth and unobtrusive manner, but this seems to be of limited benefit and unlikely to pay, so I'm having to look further afield. Hence this book; we can all look forward and take choices, or remain in the darkness, only looking back to provide more evidence for Bronnie Ware.

How many hours?

Choosing is difficult. Accountancy is a solid career, pays reasonably well and is near the top of the first page in the Careers list. Too many of us choose our careers based on financial returns - what will make us the most money, rather than what really energises us, what ignites our passion.

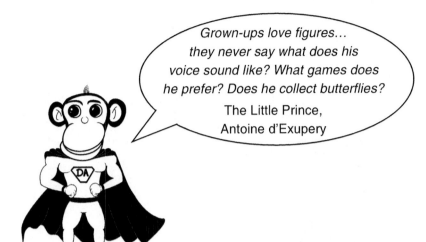

*Grown-ups love figures...
they never say what does his
voice sound like? What games does
he prefer? Does he collect butterflies?*
The Little Prince,
Antoine d'Exupery

Antoine d'Exupery died young, an author and pilot killed in action during World War II. He saw things from a higher perspective in his short life than most of us do. He was the antithesis of your typical, traditional career adviser. Many school careers advisers are somewhat narrow in the scope of roles they consider appropriate for us; they rarely stretch us to think in wider terms, probing for what might ignite our latent passions.

Does what you are doing fill your energy banks, or drain them? Last evening, when Oscar was tucked up in bed, the last story read, in his last fighting breaths before succumbing to sleep, he asked, 'how many hours is it 'til morning time?' If you are not asking this question, eager to bounce out and make the most of every waking moment, have you found your Dream, your passion?

From Oscar's age, my mother knew that she wanted to be a nurse; it lit a spark inside her. Lawrence Preston Gise spent many summers with his grandson on the family ranch in Cotulla in Texas during which the young Jeff Bezos's passion for entrepreneurship was similarly ignited[8], and then provided with rocket fuel. Unlike these characters, or the fictitious Dr Hfuhruhurr..., I was one of the 'other ten kids'....

'...When I saw how slimy the human brain was, I knew what I wanted to do with the rest of my life'

Steve Martin as Dr Hfuhruhurr – 'World's leading Brain surgeon' - The Man with Two Brains (Warner Bros, 1983)

As Robinson says, if you don't know if you've found your element, you probably haven't – keep looking! Seek help of course, people will guide you based on their experiences and will share their wisdom, but only you will know! Matthew Lee knew what he wanted the first time he tried magic. He dreamed of being a magician entertainer and fought against the strong cultural pressures of his Asian heritage to answer his calling. When Matthew practised magic tricks, he lost all sense of time 'it can be very Zen, suddenly you look out of the window and its morning'[9].

Antoine d' Exupery said that '*If you want to build a ship, don't drum up men to gather wood, divide the work and give orders, instead teach them to yearn for the vast and endless sea*'. Even if we absolutely know our dream, it'll never be plain sailing. As The little Prince's alien friend observed '*I shall have to put up with a few caterpillars if I want to see butterflies*'. Antoine d'Exupery was right - if our passions are excited, it is amazing what barriers we can overcome.

But what if the very idea of an endless sea makes you positively queasy? Keep looking. It's not easy!

There are many on-line tools to help.

Our self-imposed limitations though, really do not reflect fear of failure but fear of success. Schwartz concludes that 'people will rise to the level of success their self-esteem can absorb'.

Need help?

There are many experts who can guide you. As an example, Dr Schwartz, Dean of the Institute for Talent Management in Beijing, has created SuccessDNA, which takes a holistic approach, combining traditional personality profiling with autobiographical appraisals, shifting focus to what kind of person you are and a more expansive view of your possibilities. We tend to express limiting ambitions and then we mask them as fear of failure.[10]

How much success can your self-esteem absorb?

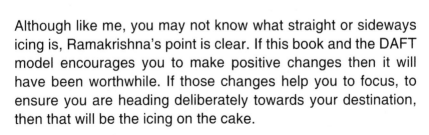

There are many paths we can follow to reach our destination. Whichever we choose, we should follow with whole hearted devotion...'One may eat a cake with icing straight or sideways. It will taste sweet either way'

Ramakrishna

Although like me, you may not know what straight or sideways icing is, Ramakrishna's point is clear. If this book and the DAFT model encourages you to make positive changes then it will have been worthwhile. If those changes help you to focus, to ensure you are heading deliberately towards your destination, then that will be the icing on the cake.

REFLECTION TIME

Mens Rea – Actus Reus

When determining if a crime has been committed, there are two constituent elements - ***mens rea*** – intent and ***actus reus*** – action - both must be present. The Latin terms can be dated to 16th century writings of Sir Edward Coke.- '*actus non facit reum nisi mens sit rea*'

Guilt requires both thought and deed *(as does achievement)*.

Rhesus – a monkey with a genetic likeness to us and with whom we share a red blood cell protein, aka the D antigen.

Dreams		
Mens Rea	Actus Rhesus	Guilty? ☑
1. Know your dreams, your passions and your purpose	Note down your thoughts in the space below. *(Return to this after reading on, if unsure...)*	☐
2. Know what you want? What are your desires?	Note down your thoughts in the space below. *(Return to this after reading on, if unsure...)*	☐

1.2 DESIRES

In the middle of the three D's comes our desires. Let's explore.

> *The trick to doing anything is first cultivating a desire for it.*
>
> Naval Ravikant, entrepreneur, co-founder of AngelList

What do we mean by desires?

> **Desire**
>
> "To want something, especially strongly"
>
> Cambridge Dictionary.org

Where do our desires come from? Why do we want anything and why do we want some things 'especially strongly'?

Perhaps we should separate the physiological from the emotional. We want especially strongly that which we do not have yet need for our survival. After that, things get more complicated. As with our dreams, we do not always know what we want. Or, even if we think we do, it may be because we have not considered why we want it. We might say we especially strongly want chocolate but do we have a physiological need? Or are we trying to satisfy a neurochemical deficiency? We all know, to a varying degree, that our *'future us'* is often not rewarded by the all the immediate actions of our *'current us'*.

To meet our physiological desires, we need to give adequate attention to nutrition (alongside exercise and sleep) and we will turn our attention to this 'holy trinity' later. The desires we are concerned with here though, are those which help us to fulfil our dreams. Such desires are likely to extend beyond the next bar of fruit and nut (although I don't rule that out entirely).

Let's look at what motivates us and start at our beginning. Our earliest motivations stem from our automatic response to sensory stimuli. As babies we have reflex actions, and after these actions we have recognition and desire to repeat a pattern of stimuli.

In the beginning we learn intentionality. With every 'peeka' and 'boo', the joy is reinforced. The new surprise 'peek' reflects the desire for novelty, a kind of novelty that fits with what has already been learned. At this stage we want novelty especially strongly. This desire for novelty provides the incentive for learning. Our cognitive development demands it. As Desmond Morris, primarily a zoologist of course, describes, apes (other than man) are equally inquisitive, exploratory in early years, but in humans, we continue beyond that initial excitement – humans and apes are both delighted at first seeing a pen make a line on a piece of paper. Only humans progress to a circle, then a couple of legs, then an enigmatic face...

Desire first occurs during a 'mirror phase' of baby development. As a baby, you saw in the mirror an 'image of wholeness', which formed a desire for that being. This narcissism manifests as a desire to make us 'whole'.

Jacques Lacan. psychoanalyst and psychiatrist

You may be familiar with the very useful goal-setting and problem-solving tool, GROW. This model encourages us to identify where we are now and where we want to end up and then to take steps to fill the gap between these two points. GROW is an acronym for Goals, Reality, Objectives and Way forward.

Jacques Lacan has identified the G (Goal), but suggests that our R (Reality) is so primitive and the O (Obstacles) simply too great for us ever to find the W (Way forward). For Lacan, the goal is unreachable. For this reason, he suggests that the desire stays with us as long as we live.

Perhaps this idea of an unquenchable desire to be made 'whole' again is disturbing and comforting in equal measure.

(And perhaps Atomic Kitten were onto something with their earworm song, '... Baby you're the one...?!)

Philosophically speaking

All animal movement is guided by their desires

Aristotle

PHILOSOPHICAL DESIRE

*Aristotle taught Plato who then advised us that 'individual desires must be postponed in the name of the higher ideal'. Spinoza said that 'human desires are beyond our own free-will' and Hume that 'our desires and passions are non-cognitive, automatic bodily responses'. Probably explains why reacting well to childish outbursts is easier said than done!

Following the reasoning of Aristotle, one of the fathers of philosophy, you might check yourself before criticising your young offspring for 'behaving like animals'. Easy to say when our little loved ones seem to be sent purely to challenge us. Not so easy to do, as I so often find*. As the 18th Century philosopher, David Hume put it, when describing our desires – 'reasoning is merely an afterthought'.

It was the 17th Century Thomas Hobbes who recognised that the 'fundamental motivation of all human action is the desire for pleasure'. Our youngsters reflect this desire for pleasure in the curiosity displayed in their wildest play. And this curiosity helps them to grow and develop long after all other animals have reached the end of their growth and cognitive development phase. In fact, 'neophobia' and 'neophilia', the fear and longing for novelty, are key human traits that drive us forward (or hold us back).

And we are really no different from our children. When our efforts produce surprising feedback, (like a Mona Lisa emerging from an imperfect circle with two random dots for eyes) we feel most satisfied.

Some of us are guided by religious teaching. Hindus describe desire (karma) as 'the first seed of mind.' Christians warn that unfulfilled desire leads to despair or greed - one of the seven deadly sins. Buddhists on the other hand describe desire or 'craving' as the cause of all suffering. They state that ultimate happiness, or Nirvana, comes from the elimination of all craving.

Roman Catholics of course proffer seven virtues to overcome the sins; humility, charity, chastity, gratitude, temperance, patience and diligence and even Buddhists don't advocate elimination of all desire; with certain skilful qualities seen as liberating and enhancing. Tantric Tibetan Buddhism for example, celebrates the power of self-awareness and choice; to create desire rather than being created by it.

Whatever path you choose, you will recognise that your motivations extend beyond your physiological needs.

Motivation

Desmond Morris noted that from a motivational perspective, in animals, the act of feeding is too remote from the act of killing, so new motivational desires have developed, for example; the act of catching prey became a reward in itself. The sequence of events in hunting animals, from wanting to having, is so lengthy and arduous, that the fulfilment of that ultimate desire is subject to further subdivisions.

Feline motivation

Researchers into cat behaviour identify four independent motivational systems. Cats separately celebrate their success at catching, at killing, at preparing and then at the time of eating the innocent dormouse.[11]

We humans are certainly at least as complex. Indeed, in terms of our eating habits researchers have spotted several distinct appetites. Clearly satisfying our need for carbohydrates will not guarantee satisfying our body's need for protein, or indeed our desire for chocolate. Holistically we may think we are hungry when one of our appetites is not satiated. Unfortunately, we are not always smart enough to know which one, and we may indulge in junk food, when all we needed was a bowl of lentils. Whilst it now appears that the appetite for protein dominates, our multiple appetites serve as a reminder that our desires can be complex, the signals confusing and in just this one area, rich with opportunities to make the wrong decisions.

We fare no better in other areas.

Our physiological desires seek a rewarding stimulus like food or an attractive partner, or alcohol. Imaging technologies enable us to see our sensation of pleasure from positive reinforcement via neuronal activity in the 'reward' areas; particularly the nucleus accumbens, and basal ganglia, an area also part-responsible for long term storage of memories. Our emotional desires are far more complex so we are even more susceptible to errors of judgment.

FMRI imaging allows us to 'see' what the brain is choosing to put into memory. Our subconscious brain filters the millions of inputs, encoding in long term storage only the data we might want (or need) later.

Reaching out

Charles Andrew suggests that a more reliable neuroscientific measure for desire involves the parietal region of the brain. This area has an association with physical movement, specifically the desire to reach out to something in the visual field.[12]

These processes are exploited by 'neuromarketers' who to see our buying behaviours being created; our desires translated to something profitable (for them).

In essence, the idea is that desires are the things we reach for and our memory of the joy making us want to repeat the experience.

Desire initiates and pleasure sustains

D Apeth

This motivational desire is straight forward positive reinforcement. However, our desires are far from straight forward. They are not constants and it is worth being aware of times when others might be attempting to influence them for their own ends. As the Little Prince says, grown-ups do love figures.

Marketers are using imaging technology to study those reactions, the ones normally hidden 'under the bonnet' to chase sales. It is worth being aware of this.

Caveat Emptor (Let the buyer beware)

How do you sell life insurance to people who expect to have many decades left to live? Life insurance companies try to expose or even create a gap, to expose or create a desire by asking leading questions' (What will happen to your young kids, if you die suddenly? Who will feed them? How will their care be paid for?)

Marketeers of course recognise and thrive on this gap - the human appetite for an object is a keen topic for businesses, who want to sell their product (or service). Marketing theorists call this desire the third stage in the hierarchy of effects – the point where their product will satisfy our need.

Though the complex drivers of desire can easily be misunderstood, advances in neuroscience-based research reveal a lot. Steady State Topography (pioneered by Professor Richard Silberstein, and delivered by his company Neuro-Insight), has been deployed for marketing purposes, measuring neural responses in real time. Whilst you look at a picture, watch a film, or listen to an advertisement, neuromarketers watch and learn as our brain responds before their eyes.

In *Buy-ology*, Martin Lindstrom introduces the Nuns of the Carmelite Order, who succumbed to neuro-imaging and when asked to relive their most profound religious experiences, showed a flurry of activity in an area typically associated with serenity, joy, self-awareness and love (the caudate nucleus, part of the striatum)[13]. The power of thought alone elicits those feelings, and then the power of those feelings floods the body with the chemicals as if those experiences were happening naturally. This is probably why Tony Robbins, the leviathan of leadership, incites his audience to re-live their most heightened positive emotions in what might seem to the outsider a rather bizarre, almost cultish performance.

Marketers know that neither Audio or Visual saturation alone will increase desire. Far more effective is to infuse their products (or services) with positive associations, exploiting all the senses, invoking those emotions.

Smell is a popular one. The most desirable fragrances are those that relate to babies. Can you recall the fresh bread smell of your baby's head? Of course, and this is the reason some large shops have in-store bakeries, or even more effectively suffuse the store with such aromas, as if they did.

The strong connection to babies, aided by the bursts of oxytocin during childbirth and during the overall baby-bonding phase provides the evolutionary compulsion to tend to our youngsters. The same neurochemicals invoked affect our mood, and then our willingness to spend. Vanilla is another favourite - being a constituent of breast milk and evocative of those safe and cosy times seems to make it a popular choice.

The fact that aromas influence our desires and our behaviours unconsciously has been shown many times. In one test, students were split into two rooms, one fragranced with cleaning scents, one without. The unaware students who had spent time in the scented room were demonstrably tidier when later given an 'extremely messy', crumbly cookie to eat!

Molecular Reaction

Neuroscientists, Dr. Eva Mishor and Prof. Noam Sobel's at Weizmann's Brain Sciences Department of the Azrieli Institute for Human Brain Imaging and Research have discovered a molecule present in baby's scalps, Hexadecanal (HEX), that unwittingly plays a significant role in adult social decision-making. Indeed they have seen gender specific response with diffusion of male aggression and actually increasing female aggression, both believed to be for protective reasons (stopping men hurting the baby, and allowing women to hurt anyone who might try!)

HEX has no perceptible odour, but smelling it affects our behaviour nevertheless.

We know that our desires are complex. In simple blind tasting tests, we select our wines and waters not on taste but on a range of other factors, including price. We routinely and perhaps disappointingly show that we enjoy our purchases more because we paid more; with the

Fragrant exploitation

Unconscious influences on our desires are not confined to supermarkets, even the likes of British Airways waft 'meadow grass' into their business lounges, to simulate the great outdoors.

same wine presented at once cheap and later as expensive illuminating the image scanners with a much deeper flurry of activity in the cortices associated with perception of pleasantness, based solely on price.

Many big names, especially luxury brands, rely on this with products, like cars, watches, fine wines and perfumes selling because of their price, and providing the thorny challenge for their owners to keep increasing sales without eroding brand value.

Cave Vendor (beware of the seller)

Neuromarketing is as complex as our desires - it is as easy to drive people in an undesirable direction. We probably all know Howard Bloom's famous Coke versus Pepsi test which induced Coca Cola to spend millions reformulating their beloved coke to compete with Pepsi, only to do an about turn when the 'new improved coke' had zero impact on sales in some markets and a negative impact in others. (The Board of Coca Cola also applied logic that may have been even further flawed due to the nature of the test, as the initial extra burst of sweetness of the Pepsi also distorted the findings with taste preferences changing with duration of the experience.)

Nokia at one time had the 'most ubiquitous ringtone on the planet'. Surely a marketing dream, right? Wrong! We all hated it; it was associated with intrusion, disruption and evoked feelings of annoyance (rather like Microsoft Excel's ultra-helpful paperclip, if you are old enough to remember that inane, little pest!). As Martin Lindstrom, who writes extensively on the subject, predicted in *Buy-ology,* the bell did toll on Nokia's ringtone, as it did on Nokia as a whole. The intrusive tone was perhaps a contributory factor. (In any case, the Nokia management failed to respond to the shifting mobile telecommunications market or perhaps suffered what Clayton M. Christensen described as the Innovators Dilemma, where newcomers justify doing things that established players do not.[14])

Satisfying our desires by seeking the most of what we want, without detriment to others seems fair and logical, but more of the same soon loses novelty value.

Cave Canem (beware of the dog)

The dog that barks loudest is usually not necessarily the largest. When we are deciding what to do, how to live our lives, it is wise to take a measured response to the loudest voices – and to balance those with the whispers in our ears.

Our infantile play patterns actually create our play-rules for adult life. We investigate the unfamiliar until it becomes familiar, repeat it until we are adept, vary our approach to the activity in as many ways as possible, choose the best ones and develop those further at the expense of others, mix and match these developments, **and do all of this as an end in itself**.

> **Get the Balance Right**
>
> Achieving the optimal balance of neophilia and neophobia helps us lead our best life.

Whilst **big bonuses** might bark loudest, following this simple cycle of improvement is what **intrinsic motivation** is really all about.

A warning about getting the balance wrong

If we indulge in anti-exploratory behaviour, we repeat one pattern of behaviour enough times that we generate a feeling of safety due to its 'super-familiarity'. An excess of 'neophobia' can give us the feeling that instead of 'nothing ventured, nothing gained', we prefer 'nothing ventured, nothing lost'. We might choose the safe path. Perhaps we'll avoid new situations, taking risks, pushing the boundaries.

How do you know if you are allowing your neophobia to outweigh your neophilia?

Do you twiddle with your moustache or stroke your hair, make jerky movements or rock in a chair? Perhaps these nervous tics are an early warning? Perhaps not. One thing is for sure, you may not suffer neuroses, but if you always 'play it safe' you will not expand your comfort zone. Playing it too safe will very likely have an adverse impact on your desires, and whether they are allowed to guide you towards your dreams.

Our desires are affected by among other things our values, our aspirations, our beliefs and our cultural programming. And most of this 'desire' happens unconsciously. We often decide we want something before our conscious selves become aware of it. What is more, we struggle to identify why we want it, as if our subconscious brain has done all the calculations but doesn't want to show us the workings.

Identity

If our desires aren't leading us to our dreams, or we don't know what our dreams are then it may help to cultivate our desires at a holistic level - by defining who we want to be.

If we have an overarching picture of the kind of person we want to be, this will filter our daily decisions, pointing us in the general direction we want to go. It will start to shape our desires, to formulate our dreams.

An 'identity-first' approach to cultivating our desires increases our intrinsic motivation as it is self-imposed. We will do what we want to, above all else. What is more, if we define who we want to be, then our habits become easier to maintain.

James Clear in *Atomic Habits* recognised the importance of identity when we want to change our habits. And, of course, if we change enough habits, we change our selves. In the words of the afore- mentioned Tony Robbins, if I say 'I haven't smoked for x days', then I am still identifying as smoker.

When I declare 'I am a non-smoker', I give myself a different identity.

Who are you? You decide

To become the best version of ourselves means continually editing our beliefs, this way we can upgrade and expand over time and stay out of a limiting cycle. There is no reason we cannot move from identifying as a cagey fighter to becoming a cage fighting champion, if we want it enough!

We are always looking for the next thing. It is our neophilia that keeps us going. Our brain chemistry reinforces this pattern. Too much of a good thing makes the good thing mundane. This applies to the tangible, the intangible, to fun or to infungibles. As Shakespeare observed, our sweetest joys are our most seldom pleasures. And, as Victor Frankl, the inspirational Auschwitz survivor put it - we do well to seek purpose rather than happiness or pleasure.

A search for pleasure finds something 'as fleeting as the wind - as soon as we feel it, it blows over, breathing in us a new desire'.

Seeking pleasure is tied up with our hunger (or is it thirst?) for the neurotransmitter, Dopamine. In the next section, we explore the third of the three D's, but before digging deeper, now might be a good time to reflect on who you are, or perhaps who you really want to be...

REFLECTION TIME

Desires		
Mens Rea	Actus Rhesus	Guilty? ☑
1. Who do you want to be?	Define your identity. Note down your thoughts in the space below. Can you act like that?	☐
2. Are your desires guiding you towards your dreams?	Note down your thoughts in the space below. Are you aware of the dopamine effect? Read on...	☐

1.3 DOPAMINE

The final element of the three 'D's of Dream fulfilment is the Dopamine effect. This neurotransmitter is so powerful that it is scary. We should treat it with respect.

Many studies over the last few decades have shown its power. Dopamine affects many parts of our brain. Opioid and dopamine systems stimulate the cortices of our new mammalian brain in ways which we experience as pleasure, maybe even euphoria. Dopamine gives us more pleasure than fine dining and, yes, even post prandial activities.

Let's think about James Clear's *Atomic Habits*. He describes four steps in his 'habit loop'[15], broadly summarising that all our behaviour is driven by a desire, a desire to solve a problem. His steps are the cue, the craving, the response and the reward. His cue or 'problem' would be our Dream – how we want to be identified, what we want to be and what we want to do. His craving aligns with our desire, and his response and reward is the outcome and the trigger. This is where the neurotransmitter, Dopamine, steps in...

A bit of history is useful here (see box):

Electrical stimulation of the ventral tegmental area (VTA) is now known to trigger the release of dopamine in the nucleus accumbens, in the same way that all our pleasures do.

Multiple research studies on mice and rats have shown that the levels of dopamine in the extracellular fluid increase when rats are injected with addictive drugs such as cocaine, heroin, nicotine, or alcohol.

> **Skinner Box**
>
> In the 1930s, the psychologist B. F. Skinner devised the 'operant conditioning chamber', or 'Skinner box," in which a lever press by an animal triggered either a reinforcing stimulus, such as delivery of food or water, or a punishing stimulus, such as a painful foot shock. Birds and rats placed in a Skinner box rapidly learn to press a lever for a food reward and to avoid pressing a lever that delivers the shock.

Olds and Milner's rats became addicted to pushing a lever to release dopamine and stimulate their nucleus accumbens. In fact, the desire to receive this dopamine reward was so strong that they would press the

> **Olds and Milner**
>
> The 'pleasure centre' of the brain has been the subject of relentless scrutiny ever since, with the infamous experiments on rats back in 1954 by psychologist James Olds and postdoctoral fellow at McGill University, Peter Milner. Olds and Milner stumbled on the pleasure centre after implanting electrodes into the septal area of the rat.

lever and neglect the needs of themselves and their dependents for basic care and sustenance.

It is said that 'where your mind goes, energy flows'. In the first experiments, the rats' minds returned repeatedly and regularly to the quick fix rewards and their efforts focused solely on more of the electrical stimulation. Subsequent experiments revealed that rats chose dopamine over food, water, sexual partners and pain. Females would even abandon their new-born nursing pups to continually press the lever, sometimes self-stimulating up to 48,000 times a day, to the exclusion of all other activities (rather like the computer game addicts who lock themselves away in their bedroom and neglect to eat). As mum or dad has to drag their teenager out of their room, so the scientists had to unhook the rats from the apparatus before they starved themselves to death.

Olds and Milner refined our understanding of the pleasure centre, prior to the advent of advance imaging techniques, identifying a group of interconnected structures deep within the brain, distributed along the midline to comprise the 'reward circuit'.

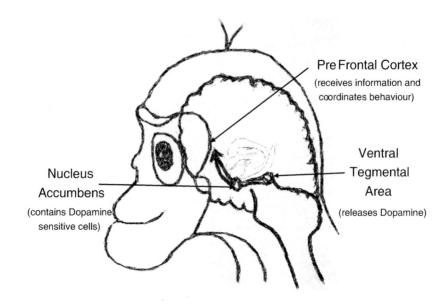

Pre Frontal Cortex
(receives information and coordinates behaviour)

Ventral Tegmental Area
(releases Dopamine)

Nucleus Accumbens
(contains Dopamine sensitive cells)

Dopaminergic pathway – as for many other drugs, e.g; opiates, methamphetamines, nicotine...

When dopamine is released, it causes feelings of pleasure. The pleasurable reward or indeed the anticipation of a reward drives addictive behaviours. As in rats, so too in us humans. Increased levels of dopamine have been observed in the extracellular fluid of the nucleus accumbens when human test subjects experience the rewarding rush of sex, drugs, or hitting the jackpot when gambling.

The creature of 'Habit' fame, James Clear, emphasises the anticipation effect, charting the dopamine released ahead of an expected pleasure and conversely the rapid exhaustion of dopamine if the anticipated reward is not delivered[16]. The Olds and Milner rats provide a dopamine driven feedback loop. Without dopamine, desire died, without desire action stopped. Dopamine is released as pleasure is experienced or anticipated. The anticipation effect is consistent with the 'mirror neuron' observations of Dr Rizzolatti's students as they watched chimpanzees' neurons firing; noting that it was as if they had experienced a pleasure (ice cream), simply by witnessing such pleasure in others[17].

For this reason, in his description of motivation, James Clear, concludes that to make something happen, we need to make it attractive. If we anticipate a pleasure, we will be moved to realize it. Clear provides data that shows that the dopamine spike, or surge, which at the first encounter happens at the time we act, next happens when we expect to act. The spike is as high for the anticipation.

You may be dismayed to learn of the distinct disconnect between 'wanting' and 'liking'. The wanting (or anticipation) shows more neural circuitry. We have but tiny pockets in our brain for enjoyment or liking ('hedonic hotspots'), but large tracts for wanting or desire. As Frankl said, the pleasure from a satisfied desire is as fleeting as the wind.

Perhaps surprisingly then a cocaine addict will get some of their boost when they see the cocaine, not, as you might expect, after they take it. The boost, the surge of dopamine comes from seeing the thing we have defined as 'attractive'. By inference then, the 'attractive thing' provides our urge to act. This is why, as non-cocaine users, we should make our habits attractive – that is what promotes the dopamine production, which then motivates us to act.

In the case of drug takers, if the cocaine is not then supplied, there is a dip, which is then only remedied by the actual drug-taking act. The same dip will apply to you if you take off your running shoes without showing them the road.

We can make Dopamine our friend, a very powerful and loyal one at that. It is also known to help us to update information in our memory and to aid focus. It is often described as the novelty neurotransmitter and it certainly helps us have fun. The Dopamine Effect certainly helps to explain why we tend to enjoy things we are good at; our desire is met so we get a dopamine fix encouraging us to do more. And, in doing so, we get better and better at that thing.

Beware of this novelty neurotransmitter though. It can easily lead us away from our dreams and desires…if we are not careful. What is more, we'll need more each time we repeat a task if we want the same effect. With this knowledge, and sensible personal planning, we can design our lives to ensure that we get the right doses at the right times, the doses we need if we are going to be our best, the doses we need if we are going to keep on getting better and better…

REFLECTION TIME

Dopamine		
Mens Rea	Actus Rhesus	Guilty? ☑
1. Do you want it?	Note down your thoughts in the space below. Have you made what you really want attractive enough to you?	☐
2. Are you aware of your need for Novelty and Risk?	Note down your thoughts in the space below. Read on is you are unsure...	☐

1.4 NOVELTY SEEKING AND RISK-TAKING

When we first stood upright yet didn't know where our next meal was coming from, we sought instant gratification. The tendency to gorge is an almost inevitable urge in times of scarcity, and this is certainly not always beneficial. Many victims of enforced starvation, like the WW2 concentration camp survivors, have repeatedly demonstrated this. Of course, this urge was even more powerful in a less developed pre-historic brain.

The ability to delay gratification, which in recent times has received much attention for its suggested ability to predict those of us who will succeed in life (see Walter Mischel's Stanford University Marshmallow experiment[18]), probably secured its place with the agricultural revolution as we succeeded by using our ability to store food for later consumption. We have now identified a dopamine receptor gene, DRD4. And this DRD4 which is associated with novelty seeking and risk taking[19] will play its part in our propensity to wait or our urge to proceed.

Psychologists Robert Yerkes and John Dillingham Dodgson have studied performance effect and found that they can improve a rat's maze-running ability by prodding them with electric prodders. Up to a certain voltage their performance improved, but then rapidly declined in line with the classic 'n' shaped curve with arousal (or stress) set against performance.

This curve applies in humans but varies by person (and other conditions, and time of day) on a spectrum with some, like astronauts needing much more arousal than rocket scientists. Hugh Laurie, the actor and comedian, and notoriously not an astronaut, recognised he had a mental health problem (since diagnosed as depression) when flying through the air at a demolition derby left him feeling 'stirred only to boredom'. Neither Hugh Laurie nor those astronauts are technically flying of course - they are really falling towards the Earth with a speed Charles Darwin would probably have avoided. He famously and happily committed 25 years of his life to the study of earthworms.

So-called 'adrenaline junkies' who fly at hundreds of mph though tunnels or sky dive **into** aeroplanes (yes, really!) no doubt think librarians are a little dull, but these extremes remind us that diversity makes all our lives that much richer. At the extremes, the need for dopamine can put the user, like the obsessed rats, in peril and of course has brought many to an early end.

Stimulus Struggle

Traditionally we looked forward to a long and happy retirement, putting our feet up and 'taking it easy'. As Desmond Morris points out in Human Zoo, we abandon the stimulus struggle at our peril[20]. Without an 'optimal level of stimulation', we wither and die.

NOTE: If we do not find sufficient stimuli, we have a tendency to create artificial ones, like the zoo-bound gorilla who regularly ate his food, regurgitated it and ate it again, simply to relieve his boredom.

Maintaining Novelty

As our life proceeds, there is increasing risk that what we do doesn't continue to give us the buzz we got when we first started, when putting our boat on the river at 5am on a frosty winter morning motivated us. Our neophilia stays with us and demands that we avoid boredom by finding novelty and challenge. Achieving peak levels of desire means staying motivated and expert opinion demands that we work on tasks that are of 'just manageable difficulty'.

To be realistic, we almost need to learn to love boredom too, in the sense that to continue to flourish we need to be able to continue to focus on our self-improvement. It is said that 'loving the hard work is what makes the champion'. Carol Dweck's work on mindset helps define what plays a big part in determining which of us continue to grow, with the 'fragile perfects' amongst us less likely to cope as things get tough [21].

This is recognised by high performing coaches, who see that imaginative thinking is essential to avoid complacency by its star performers. The LA Lakers basketball team Head Coach

Pat Riley noticed a tailing off of performance of top talent as they eased into their roles, so he established a Career Best Effort programme. The CBE programme recognised that chasing effort is more effective than chasing results, especially when you are already part of a successful team.

The great long-distance runner and world record holder, Eliud Kipchoge, despite having broken the two-hour barrier for the marathon (albeit under controlled conditions), still takes detailed notes after every practice run of what he could do better. His feedback loop enables him to continue his fine-tuning and to stay at the top of his game.

The great news is that there are ways for us all to stay motivated and even if 50% of our dopamine demand is genetic, the other half will make all the difference. It is up to us to decide how to satisfy our desires, live the life we want to and satisfy our dreams.

Rewardless motivation?

Freud's pleasure principle stated that we are motivated to do that which brings us pleasure.

Yet somehow we find motivation to do difficult boring tasks too.

Maslow brought us a hierarchy of needs peaking, beyond pure pleasure at self-actualisation, at reaching our potential.

Edward Tory Higgins' self-discrepancy theory describes each of us as lots of selves – what we want to be is the 'ideal self' based on our goals, biases and priorities. The 'ought self' is how to get there.

The Richard M.Ryan and Edward L.Deci's self-determination theory suggests we seek 100% intrinsic motivation, warning that any reward can reduce motivation as it is an extrinsic push.

Maintaining Motivation

When we come to the autumn of our years, we instinctively understand the transitory nature of our desires, our dopamine driven impulses. Abraham Maslow's 'hierarchy of needs' is generally presented as a pyramid, with needs from the bottom rung taking precedence over the higher, 'smaller' needs.

They may be smaller needs, but they are not small. In a world where for most people basic survival needs are met, as Josiah Royce, the early twentieth century philosopher explained in *The philosophy of Loyalty*, being housed and fed and safe do not cut it. To feel we are leading a worthwhile life, we need to seek a cause 'beyond ourselves'. Be it small or large, caring for a pet, or saving the climate. It is this 'cause' or 'loyalty' which gives our lives meaning.

Throughout our lives, it serves us well to serve others, and to keep finding new ways to do so as we progress through what Joseph Campbell described as our 'hero's journey'[22]. Our life will surely follow a meandering course, with myriad failures, successes, and more failures and our best life will be made up of one 'hero's journey' after another, as we grow, like the universe, in an ever-increasing spiral.

Atul Gawande in *Being Mortal* attributes the rapid decline of so many of us in our twilight years to the absence of a cause or meaning[23]. The really great news is that, even if you haven't found your dream, your cause or your meaning yet, it is never too late – Ray Kroc 'founded' McDonalds in his fifties, and his counterpart, Harland Sanders of KFC was in his sixties. Adding a bit of seasoning, Mohandas Ghandi was 61 before he led the 240 mile march, a journey from his religious retreat to the salt mines at Dandi on the Arabian Sea, leading the way ultimately to the liberation of India from British rule. Joe Biden went through innumerable tragedies and challenges on his way to winning the US presidency at the age of 78, the same age as Grandma Moses when she started painting and, of course, Sir Captain Tom, the hero of Covid resilience, didn't reach his peak until the age of 100.

If a little dreaming is dangerous, the cure for it is not to dream less but to dream more, to dream all the time

Marcel Proust

REFLECTION TIME

Dreams, Desires, Dopamine, Novelty and Risk taking		
Mens Rea	Actus Rhesus	Guilty? ☑
1. Do you seek novelty?	Note down your thoughts in the space below. Find ways of making the old new...	☐
2. Revisit Dreams, Desires and Dopamine	Have you taken time to define your dreams, passion and purpose? Do you know your identity? Do you Act Like That? Are your desires guiding you to your dreams. Are your desires attractive enough to you?	☐
You are never too old to dream		

THE DAFT CYCLE - **ACTION**

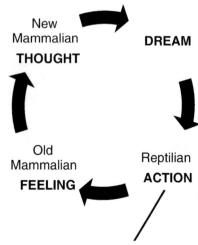

New
Mammalian
THOUGHT

DREAM

Old
Mammalian
FEELING

Reptilian
ACTION

DREAMS define us, provided our Actions, Feelings and Thoughts toe the line. In this section, we look at our dreams and desires and the precious role of dopamine.

ACTIONS are nestled in the Reptilian Brain. The unbridled brain will 'Just Do It' with a swoosh of instinct.

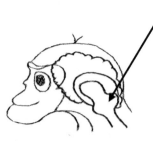

FEELINGS emanate from our 'Old Mammalian Brain' – the add-in, from which we can start wanting things, from which we are perhaps no longer simply coils of DNA.

THOUGHT - a comparatively new enhancement and still fairly flawed. The New Mammalian Brain, (AKA neo-cortex or cerebrum), represents the core of our 'executive function'.

What we say or think or feel
don't matter if we don't act

Chapter 2:

ACTION AND THE REPTILIAN BRAIN

This pre-historic brain incorporates the-upper brain stem, the reticular activation system, the mid brain, the basal ganglia and some of the hypothalamus; all of which are

> **ACTIONS** are nestled in the Reptilian Brain. The unbridled brain will 'Just Do It' with a swoosh of instinct.

about receiving sensory inputs and doing what is necessary to survive.

The Cerebellum too (otherwise known as the little brain), rests it's two wings like a butterfly, across the two hemispheres, controlling coordination and balance. It connects to the brain stem at the mid-brain, pons and medulla and monitors voluntary movement.

'*...Ladies and Gentleman,
I can envision a day when the brains
of brilliant men can be kept alive in the
bodies of dumb people*'

Dr Hfuhruhurr, The Man with Two Brains
(Warner Bros, 1983)

Perhaps the visionary comic doctor was right. Perhaps it was ever thus!

Let's take a look at a few more of our inner workings before we go on:

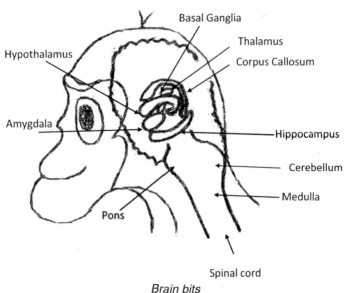

Brain bits

The Medulla, at the base, links the brain stem to the spinal cord and monitors many reflex actions like blinking, coughing, sneezing and swallowing. The Pons is a white matter bridge to the brain stem and the cerebellum, and then there's the RAS...

The Reticular Activating System (R.A.S)

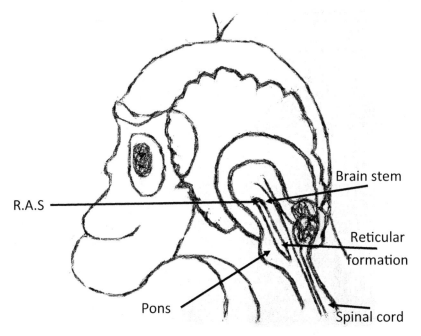

Reticular Activating System (R.A.S)

The Reticular Activation System (RAS) sits, like a fingertip sized hot dog in the brain stem 'bun'. This rich micro-chipolata of neurons acts as a dimmer switch controlling the speed that signals are sent to the spinal cord. RAS influences our alertness and acts as a filter passing on selected data to our new cortices, so shaping our conscious brain. When we are bombarded with over 2 million bits of data, choosing what to focus on is quite important. It's the RAS's job to decide what gets through, calling for help from above, from our 'new mammalian' brain layer.

[83]

Our RAS obeys our thinking brain's demands – which is why we should be careful what we wish for.

Whatever is going on in your mind, you are attracting to you

Rhonda Byrne,
The Secret

A little simplistic for sure, Ms Byrne, but think about it, what you focus on is what you are most likely to get. Want to flunk your interview? Keep thinking about all the ways it might go wrong. Want to do that restoration project and become a surfer dude, daydream about a battered VW camper-van. Your RAS will scan the roads, obliging you by passing you all the relevant images until you take the action to make your project a reality. Of course, if you dwell on your partner's myriad irritating habits, your RAS will find those for you too!

Perhaps Henry Ford put it best, when he observed that 'whether you think you can or think you can't, you are right.'

Of course, this section is about Action, not about thinking. Let's first consider briefly what happens when we act without thinking.

In his book *Blink*, Malcolm Gladwell gave us a lesson in valuing ancient Greek artefacts[1], sort of. To cut a long story short, a marble statue had been identified as a 'Kouros' and accordingly, after many months of painstaking research it was valued for a sale in 1983 at almost $10m. An expert visited and giving it one sniff declared 'it's a fake!', instantly discounting all that extensive research. In describing his reasoning, he and another similar expert were not be able to give a definitive explanation. The first just felt an 'intuitive repulsion'. For both, the 'knowledge' came from a deep-seated place – from the pattern-noticing sub-conscious brain, known as the 'adaptive unconscious'. They were right of course; it was a fake, albeit a pretty creditable imitation of the real article.

This adaptive unconscious is what cognitive psychologists term 'fast and frugal' thinking, This is definitively not the same as action without thought.

So, how effective are our actions when we take them without thought? What about the actions we take without feeling? What difference does it make when we think about our actions? Can we over-think? Can we over-feel? Let's explore this Action wheel, spoke by spoke....

Action without thought

It would be a knee jerk to suggest that intuition leads to thoughtless action. Sometimes we may struggle to explain our actions; we feel it in our guts and know what we are doing is right, but ask for an explanation and our left brain goes into overdrive looking for supporting data, which it may even invent in an attempt to achieve DAFT harmony. Sometimes we may not think that we are thinking but we are, and very fast; so fast that even we don't know we're doing it. Sometimes neural imaging has shown that our actions appear to precede our thoughts. And then we move into the territory of questioning our free-will.

Benjamin Libet conducted the famous tests to discover our awareness of our intentions. While spots were randomly moving on a clockface, his subjects were asked to note where the spot was at the precise time they were aware they had made the decision to stop the spot. Brain activity, as measured by electrodes on the scalp was seen to have started 300-700milliseconds before this awareness point. The findings have been confirmed by Hawker Lan deploying FMRI, and later with multi-voxel pattern analysis, which make an even more convincing case for some decisions being made before we are aware[2]. Let's consider everyone's favourite enemy, the humble wasp...(Sphex Ichneumoneus...see right).

> **Do you think you're Sphexy?**
>
> The digger wasp, sphex ichneumoneus, demonstrates that in some cases what we might think of as a choice is merely a path dictated by pre-existing factors. The Sphex wasp can be seen to continue the identical routine of stinging its prey and placing the victim at the opening to her burrow, checking for blockages, then bringing prey in. If the prey is moved (for example by a devious research scientist), Sphexy goes back to the blockage-checking process and repeats that step before moving on to the next one, i.e; bringing the prey into her burrow. She doesn't only do this once, but, with a devious enough researcher intervening, will repeat this step ad infinitum...[3]

Of course, you may be a determinist, believing all actions are determined by prior events, or a fatalist doomed to proceed according to the will of others or a believer in chaos in which the flap of a butterfly's wing somewhere in outer Mongolia will dictate your life. We instinctively know that there are simpler times, when, like Sphexy, we do not think at all; we just do. Our reptilian brain simply gets on with it, a gulp here, a sneeze there, all in the line of keeping us alive. And a person who doesn't ever blink is a serious cause for concern.

In more complex matters, we leap to time saving conclusions. As psychologist, Timothy D Wilson states in his book, *Strangers to Ourselves*, we toggle back and forth between our conscious and unconscious modes of thinking, dependent on the situation. And it is questionable which elements would be described as thinking at all. Of course, the ability to think rapidly boosts our overall efficiency. Indeed, taken to the extreme, we couldn't function at all if we had to deliberate over every action, every time, regardless how many times we had done it before. Imagine having to think before taking each breath; sleeping would be deadly, and if I had to run through all the steps needed to make my coffee in the morning, I would give up and go back to bed.

Indeed, we would be dead already. James Lovelock in *Novacene*, reports that recent measurement shows how we respond to danger within 40 milliseconds; way faster than conscious thought[4]. When you step aside to dodge the collapsing floor in the burning building, 'you are saved by instinct not by rational conscious thoughts about the danger'.

Our intuitions though are often just plain wrong – we think we know more than we do, we make snap judgements which are simply wrong (see *Some other Substantial Reasons*). Gladwell in his book, *Blink*[1], is guilty of that other cognitive error – survivorship bias - he sees the times we succeed due to that intuition. He doesn't identify the myriad times our intuition has put people into hot water rather than getting them out. He doesn't mention the aircraft engineer, who walked through a moving engine blade, which should have shredded him, only to realize his mistake and reverse back into the safe zone, immediately securing his demise.

Yet, Lovelock and Gladwell are right that we shouldn't denigrate intuition. In spite of the case of the engineer above it is fair to say that 'without it, we die'.

'The intuitive mind is a sacred gift and the rational mind a faithful servant. We have created society that honours the servant and has forgotten the gift

Albert Einstein

This sacred gift is of course not strictly action without thought. We have evolved such that it is not possible, or indeed desirable to separate the two. Yet, as our 'fast and frugal' thinking happens at a sub-conscious level, it certainly may feel that way…

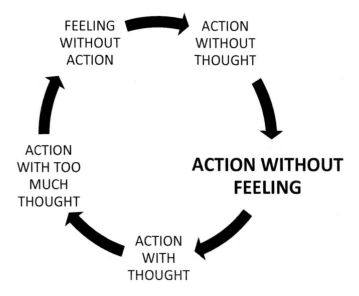

Action without Feeling

A few unfortunate individuals do not experience their emotions in the same way as the rest. For some of those alexithymics, their brains are not cluttered with the normal complex emotional interference. This is not common and, whilst we are all aware of occasions when our emotions have got the better of us, not experiencing emotions is far from desirable.

Apart from those autonomic functions, and unless you are one of those unfortunate alexithymics, you may be surprised how little we could do without feeling or emotion.

The Insular Cortex

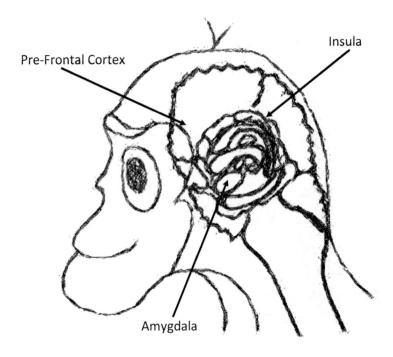

Insular cortex

Whilst our Insula or insular cortex holds our awareness of the body unconsciously, our amygdala, the seat of our emotions, works eagerly with our prefrontal cortex to make our vital choices.

Reductio ad Absurdum

A popular approach to arguing a point is to take it to the extreme. If no-one believed this to be effective then the expression would not exist at all. It is in the extremes that we learn about the rest.

As stated earlier (see philosophical desire box), Plato suggested that 'individual desires must be postponed in the name of the higher ideal'; to reason well and to make the optimal decisions demands that we set aside our emotions.

Let's take it to the extreme and visit the case of Elliot, the alexithymic, as described by UCLA neuroscientist Antonio Damasio in his book *Descartes' Error*. The impact of a brain tumour damaging his frontal lobe and consequent loss of parts of the brain associated with our emotions, has shown us that an otherwise extremely competent and intelligent person is rendered incapable of making the simplest decisions. He might spend an entire afternoon trying to determine how to categorise his papers – by date? By size? By relevance to a project? Damasio finally moved from studying Elliot's perfectly in-tact intellect to take a more holistic view. Elliot proceeded to give a detailed account of his life. Despite the tremendously emotional journey he portrayed, he showed total disconnection, as if he was describing someone else, as if he was an impartial bystander. In fact, Elliot demonstrated a complete loss of the feelings of pleasure or joy. In short, his brain damage left him with an absence of 'drive'. Cases like this have convinced neuroscientists and psychologists that our emotions drive our behaviour.

Nobel prize winning economist, Daniel Kahneman explains that the rational and the logical follow the emotional. Feeling, for him, is the primary mode. Without emotion, we have no drive. Without intervention, we would then be condemned to the fate of Buridan's ass.

For the same reason, your computer might freeze if it is given two possible paths and has programmed no basis for following one or other. We all suffer this indecision from

> **Buridan's Ass**
>
> In conception of free-will, Jean Buridan introduced this philosophical paradox. The donkey stands equidistant from, on the one side a tasty bale of golden hay and on the other, a bucket of delicious, fresh drinking water, both of which it desires equally.
>
> The Ass cannot decide between the two and therefore dies fixed to the spot.

time to time, but with the emotional centres lost, the problem is paralysing.

For those of us with (relatively) healthy brains, the impasse is resolved by a simple coin toss - whilst the coin is in the air we always decide. If you find yourself saying, as the Grim Reaper does in the humorous 1990's movie, Bill and Ted 2, 'best of two from three', you will have your decision. This all may prove of little consolation to Buridan, the philosopher, who ended his own life in the fourteenth century, (long before we knew what it was to be 'sphexy'), tied up in a bag and drowned in the Seine like an unwanted kitten. Here's to the fools who dream.

Action with Thought

The case of the experts knowing, but not knowing why they know, (like the Kouros spotters above) conforms to what David Robson has dubbed 'the intelligence trap'. It seems that the smarter you are, the more you know, the more likely you are to rely on what you might call gut instinct; yet, the more vulnerable you are to the downside of your labour-saving subconscious intervention.

Once our memories have been processed and reinforced to the point of unconscious competence, they are stored 'like macros' in the basal ganglia, so they run without the need for energy-demanding conscious effort (we like it, we do it, we get the reward signal, we do it again, etc… until a pathway is etched into our basal ganglia; the 'macro' recorded). We then do it without conscious thinking, like riding a bike or driving a car or playing piano, using what some refer to as 'muscle memory'. This small but precious brain part, its rat-like shape evoking for me Basil, Manuel's pet rat, in the old but classic sitcom, *Fawlty Towers*. Our basal ganglia keeps our favourite programmes running, like a 'Siberian Hamster' in our running wheel.

The journey to competency

There are four basic stages on this journey.

Stage 1: unconscious incompetence – we don't yet know how little we know!

Stage 2: conscious incompetence – we now know and it's almost embarrassing! If we knew then what we know now, we never would have got started!

Stage 3: conscious competence - with hard graft and focus we edge slowly forwards.

Stage 4: unconscious competence – we can do it 'with our eyes shut' – just press the 'play' button in the basal ganglia.

As Frederike Fabritius et al, in their book *Neurohacks to Work Smarter, Better, Happier*, observe, pleasure and attention inform our brain's ability to 'wire', 'unwire', and 'rewire'[5]. The first memory of an event that is stored in the hippocampus leaves the strongest mark; continued later experiences reinforce and, whilst it is true that 'neurons that fire together wire together', it is also true that nothing replaces that first impression. Each later experience has an increasingly smaller impact.

Our brains have evolved such processes to minimise energy consumption. We make endless cognitive shortcuts, many in the areas we think we know best. We then do not always make the best choices (see *Some Other Substantial Reason*).

It is well known that we tend to form an opinion of another person within a few seconds; perhaps fewer. As an interviewer, it is extremely hard to shake off that initial impression no matter what we later learn about the suitability of the candidate's skills. For the job candidate, a series of high quality interview responses and an impressive resume are over-shadowed by a stray shirt flap!

First impressions

FMRI imaging of sheep in labour has shown heavy bursts of the neurotransmitter oxytocin in second and later births but not so much in the first. The initial memory is strongest and the extra oxytocin is needed in later births as a boost to ensure a bond.[6]

This is perhaps why humans who say 'never again' manage to repeat the process, sometimes even several times, once the pain has gone!

With our initial memories sticking fast, it is perhaps easier to understand why the 'rewiring' process is rather difficult. As we can't just unsee an un-savoury image, so we can't just un-learn a 'fact' that we have 'learnt' – we are not able to 'strike that comment

---

Seeing the unexpected

In a study by Anna Floyer-Lea and Paul Matthews in which subjects learned to apply forces with their forefinger to follow a bar on screen, it was seen that over time and with practice they learned a repeating sequence. As the sequence was learned, FMRI imaging showed more activation of the cerebellum, at the base of the brain and less use of the pre-frontal cortex. In other words, visual cues were no longer being demanded. As we learn, with our hunger for the novel, we start to look for prediction errors, and respond strongly where things are not as we expect. In John O'Doherty's experiment in the anterior striatum, subjects are trained to expect juice or money as a reward for performing actions. When the subject was not rewarded as expected, the subject's anterior striatum lit up, in effect demonstrating a 'prediction error'.

---

from the record' - it is only by creating a stronger alternative impression that we can overlay a new opinion.

It is indeed hard to erase that image of our would-be employee showing up for their first interview with their shirt hanging out or their fly undone!

Roald Dahl understood that our brains respond to novelty. Hence the phenomenal success of his *Tales of the unexpected.*

And what of the lack of surprise from the *Pink Panther's* Inspector Clouseau when pounced upon by his hired help, Kato? Of course, Clouseau had trained himself to 'always expect the unexpected' so he never experienced greater activity in his cerebellum, nor in his anterior striatum when he didn't receive his just rewards!

For the same reason, we are unable to tickle ourselves.

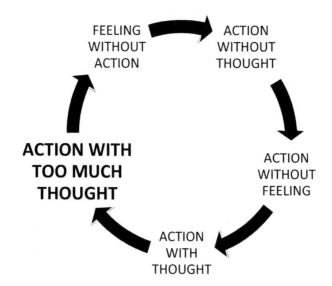

Action with Too Much Thought

Our 'muscle memory' of course, is really just a quick thought - pressing the 'macro' button and the recording being played, which is why sometimes snapping out of subconscious mode, like interrupting the macro, can corrupt our effort – 'You have a great backhand, how do you do that?' Sports psychologists will confirm that praising your opponent's technique can see a run of form grind rapidly to a halt as their conscious brain can't help but interfere with the well-oiled subconscious machine.

'You lose flow'. As Schooler explains, 'there are certain kinds of fluid, intuitive, non-verbal kinds of experience that are vulnerable to this process'. Generally, the motor tasks, those we run in the 'hamster wheel', perform best when we do not engage the higher thought processes.

When I hired a small digger for my own construction project, a wayward swinging scoop and a smashed corner to the shed roof gave me a clear lesson that you cannot operate effectively if you have to think too hard about the to's and fro's, left to rights and ups and downs for the smallest of acts.

If we want to improve any of these processes though, we do need to think about deconstruction and reconstruction of our technique.

Perhaps with the exception of childbirth and hangovers, with the right mindset, we will learn from our mistakes. Our mistakes and daftness are a good thing. In fact, we learn most from our mistakes. In the areas where we have lesser knowledge, we are forced to make extra cognitive effort, to place extra demands on all our experience, and to draw on all the information we can access. In doing so we critically pause for thought and challenge our initial assumptions. A sense of humility, knowing our infallibility, increases the likelihood that we will do this.

Carol Dweck in *Mindset* introduces a US Footballer who wasn't paying attention to the game and so seized the ball and 'scored' only to find that he had run the wrong way down the pitch[7]. Of course, he was mortified, he knew this impression would live with him for a long time, but he decided not to wallow. He recognised that everyone fails sometimes, indeed the best people fail their way right up to the top of their game, (as Michael Jordan notoriously boasts). So, he briefly admonished himself for his crushing stupidity, and resolved that the show must go on…

Feelings without Actions

Clearly, we have emotions which don't manifest as any kind of action at all. I can't begin to list them all so I feel that this will be a short section!

On the other hand, it is worth briefly mentioning the times when we have emotions that we would prefer didn't spill out into our actions. Whether we are a poker player or not there are often give away signs of our underlying feelings, however hard we try to suppress them.

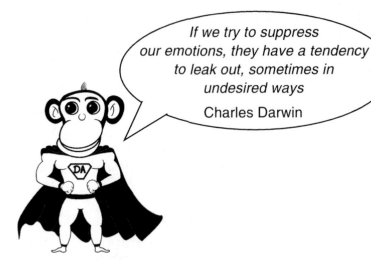

If we try to suppress our emotions, they have a tendency to leak out, sometimes in undesired ways

Charles Darwin

We know it is in most cases impossible to act without deploying our emotions. Antonio Damasio has shown us the patient who had suffered brain damage to his emotional centres and was unable to make any decisions. This led him to his **'somatic marker hypothesis'**[2]. In Elliot's case, there were no markers, no tension, no sweaty palms, no fluttering heart; Elliot was deprived of **the normal neurological feedback loop**; feeling with actions in accompaniment.

Like most area of life, we sit on a spectrum – from Damasio's unfeeling

How much are your actions influenced by your feelings?

What Carl Jung started, Mother and daughter team, Isabel Myers and Katherine Briggs developed into the world-renowned personality assessments methodology, Myers Briggs Type Indicators (MBTI).

After a lengthy self-assessment your scores are filtered to four scales, which in turn provide 16 personality types. This, the world's most popular profiling tool says that we are either Introvert or Extrovert, Sensing or iNtuiting, Judging or Perceiving and Thinking or Feeling.

Broadly speaking, if your decision making tends to be based on facts and data, you are classified as a Thinker. If your decision making is based on emotions and other people, you are classified as a 'Feeler'.

Myers Briggs' Feelers sit at the opposite end of the spectrum to Damasio's patient, Elliot.

Elliot at one end to the hero of Stephen Spielberg's tear-jerker, ET, at the other. Some of us are better equipped to suppress our feelings, the somatic markers expose our feelings, but they do not measure their intensity.

We tend to lean in certain directions, but with self-knowledge and application we can choose our direction, or we can allow ourselves to sway in the wind.

***

It's match point, the crowd are on the edge of their seats, I stand behind the baseline, bounce the ball three times to help me concentrate. I bend my legs, arch my back and thwack... The ball hits the frame and soars way above the court, and over into the trees on the other side of the fence. There's nobody watching really, except my opponent and an even more disinterested pigeon, and as I start the 100 yard march around the court to the overgrown fields beyond, I contemplate the game-ending double-fault and really, I was only a couple of millimetres off at the point of contact with the racket. Compounded by distance and demonstrated over the short time it took to blow the point, I realize how small changes can have significant impact.

As stated earlier, we become 38 times better per year if we make a one percent improvement daily. The same applies in reverse of course; a couple of millimetres for a hundred yards. I laugh it off knowing that if I were to do the deliberate practice, identify the 1% improvement I could make each day, every day, and put in the hours, who knows what kind of a tennis player I might be. If I had done this when I was younger, rather than indulge in idle whack-abouts, perhaps trophies could have come my way! We'll never know.

Our Dreams keep us going, they provide our motivation. It is our Actions that do the leg work. Improvement requires awareness of the dream but focus on the systems, not on the goals. When swimming at sea, I get back quicker when I focus my efforts on my front crawl technique, for the time being setting aside my dream of sunbathing in a deckchair with an ice-cold corona.

Everyone wants a cold beer, don't they? It's not the beer that drives improvement. Usually, winners and losers have the same goals – who doesn't want to win their next match, their league, parade the glistening cup through the streets? As David Brailsford recognised on his way to turning around the fortunes of the British Cycling team, one minor improvement at a time, it's not the goal that gets you there, it's the cycle of endless refinement and continuous improvement. Indeed, it's your conscious commitment to the **process** that will determine your **progress**.[8]

Until you make the unconscious conscious, it will direct your life, and you will call it fate.

Carl Jung

Sphex Lessons

First, we learn, then to improve we must re learn.

To learn: Fitts and Posner, psychologists in the 1960's, defined three stages in acquiring a new skill: cognitive stage (intellectualising the task and strategies to become proficient), associative stage (less concentration, fewer errors, more efficient), finally autonomous stage (you've got as good as you are going to get. You can now run on autopilot, with the non-thinking parts of the brain take over the task. i.e You are now 'unconsciously competent'.

Psychologists call this phase the 'ok plateau'. There was a time when they would have called it your peak.

Not now. To go beyond that peak, we must re-learn. To re-learn, we must go back to stage 1

A professional golfer improving their swing will deconstruct every aspect of their play; their mental preparation, position of feet, hips, thighs, shoulders, grip etc......... and re-learn, then practise, practise, practise until the re-wiring has taken place and autonomous stage is returned. Until the next time a step change is required.

We reach a physical and mental wall which we cannot with any education or exertion overpass

Francis Galton,
Hereditary Genius - 1869

Nowadays the myth that 'talent is all' has been blown apart by the likes of K. Anders Ericsson, whose 'deliberate practice[9]' has provided more relevant and helpful thinking. He has advocated we focus on bolstering natural ability with focused hard work. In this way we deliver what some might term our 'spare capacity', for which Ericsson contends we know no upper limit. Ericsson explains that the best amongst us find conscious ways to stay out of the autonomous phase.

As we take the steps to move through the various stages of incompetence to unconscious competence, we do well not to stop there or we are perhaps no better than the Sphex Ichneumoneus.

Unconscious competence leads to sloppiness and complacency

Frank Devine,
leadership guru

It is in our quest for continuous improvement that we prevent our unconscious competence from spilling over into sloppiness and complacency. Let's not allow ourselves to overstate our knowledge or capability based on what we were once proved capable. As Intel's famed former CEO, Andy Grove put it, "Success breeds complacency. Complacency breeds failure – only the paranoid survive". And, after all, a little paranoia never hurt anyone!

Improvement Actions

A step change requires taking steps. Whatever rung of the ladder you want to reach, there are certain steps you must take to get there. In John Kotter's organisational transformation change programme, he proposes eight steps starting with 'Increase Urgency' and ending with 'Making Change Stick'[10].

The process is not so different for us personally. 'Increasing urgency' means defining your 'Why change' in a way that shows you that you mean it. It's your response to your dream or vision. If your dream means you want X, then to reach that end, you will need to do Y.

Now that you know why you are embarking on a change programme, it is helpful to break Y down.

Kotter's main steps are to communicate and empower action, remove obstacles, create short term wins, and don't let up.

1. Clarity of aims (Communicate)

The key to making improvements is clarity. Do you have your X and Y well defined?

Now your Cartesian coordinates are set, break Y down. Your $y1$ and $y2$ should be near and easy to reach. You don't ned to see the whole staircase. You will choke to death if you try to swallow your elephant in one bite.

2. Easy steps (Empower Action)

Make $y1$ really obvious. Set the time, the location, do it.

We easily rationalise little exceptions, so have a plan which prevents this, stepping you through the process, with stepping stones and small interim rewards to keep you focused on the path rather than dwelling on the end goal. Look too far ahead and you justify allowing yourself to stop and pick daffodils. (There are numerous on-line apps, like Duolingo, language learning that have absorbed this lesson and embedded it within their learning programmes).

Work back through the steps if necessary – I work best in the morning, so let me make it easy for myself:

- I need 8 hours sleep so if I want to be working by 7am;
- I need to be asleep by 10;
- To be asleep by 10, I need to start shutting down by 9.30;
- I always feed the fish before I go to bed;
- The fish like to be fed with the light on;
- I set the timer for the fish tank light to switch off at 9.35.

If I don't follow my routine, I have to take extra effort to illuminate the fish tank, or get a net to scoop the weakest one out of the tank.

3. Environment (Remove obstacles)

Of course, perseverance, grit and will power are all essential to success, but we help or hinder ourselves by our preparation for action.

Behaviour is a function of the person, in their environment

Kurt Lewin

We make that environment and we make our improvement actions easy by shaping our environment to help us promote good and avoid bad habits with minimal conscious effort.

Before you start that amazing diet, putting a picture of yourself in a prominent place on the fridge door may prevent you looking in the fridge and seeing the alluring chocolate cake. A calendar showing your training success and a place for your running kit beside the fridge may induce you to pick that up instead!

4. Temptation management (Remove Obstacles)

When Taiichi Ohno initiated what has become LEAN, (referring to the Toyota production system[11] and not the dangerously addictive Purple Drank), he described a way of working which principally focuses on the elimination of waste, the removal of all obstacles; what James Clear describes as 'addition by reduction'. This widely adopted management and manufacturing philosophy is consistent with the premise that habits are easiest formed where the process is most simple with least distractions to its success.

Clear's 'Cue-induced wanting' happens unconsciously - the advert for chocolate might send you to the fridge subliminally triggering the desire. The sight of your running shoes can have a similar triggering effect. The Premack's principle, named after David Premack, psychology professor, states that more probable behaviours will reinforce less probable behaviours, so Clear suggests linking them, as Amazon bundles some products so the less likely to be purchased are made attractive by association, in the same way that streaming services bundle their movie offerings. This 'temptation bundling' fits with habit stacking; if I do this which is quite easy, then it will lead onto me doing that which is quite hard. If I do 5 minutes on my exercise bike, then I will be in my gear and will go for that 20 minute run.

5. Spiral of improvement (Create wins)

James Clear describes the Diderot effect: Diderot was once a poor 18th century French philosopher and a grafter. In those innocent, pre-Wikipedia times, he found that selling encyclopaedias gave him a sudden surge in success and wealth which led to his wedding in a magnificent scarlet robe. The robe was conspicuously too sumptuous so as not to fit with the rest of his humble dwelling. This led him into a spiral of 'justified' consumption in order to bring the rest of his living standards up to the level of his sumptuous robe.

Events can easily spiral with this Diderot effect in a negative way as well as a positive. As an accountant I learned first-hand one evening. Weary from a long day of budgets and bean-counting a quick snack dinner was all I could think of. The bread was safely in the toaster when the tin wriggled out of my tired fingers. A chipped kitchen worktop needed replacing. And of course, the new worktop couldn't sit on old cupboards or an old hob, and the boiler needed to go when the supporting wall had to be knocked down to enable the adjoining room to be redecorated in the same style!

That was an expensive tin of beans and I was counting the cost for quite some time. This spiralling effect can though be used to our advantage; in what James Clear terms 'habit stacking', we can make one small step, which will make the next step easier, one small domino can this way demolish the house (assuming that is our desire!).

6. Recognise our winning ways

We love to succeed, hate to fail and don't like to be bored – If we do a challenging thing for two minutes a day, that is better for us and more effective than failing to do ten minutes! Short tasks may retain our interest until we find other motivation. Our improvement actions are most effective if we reframe them as habits, and changing our habits is most effective if we understand some of our less apparent motivations.

We have a deep-seated desire to be like those close to us, to be like most people and to be like powerful people, who we respect. We like to fit in. Often, we'd rather be wrong with the crowd than right on our own. We want to associate with other smart people, like us. Steven Pinker, author and cognitive psychologist places our desires into two categories, those that we want for ourselves and those that we want in order to identify ourselves with a particular group or culture[12]. Research has demonstrated that our judgement itself is impacted by our allegiances with evidence supporting our tribal position readily received and contrary evidence much more easily challenged. For this reason, changing our habits to fit in with our tribe is so much easier than to go against it.

If your tribe doesn't do what you want to do, find a new tribe that does!

7. Keep it going (Don't let up)

When training for my first triathlon (of just two – I am a fair-weather athlete), I used the Jerry Seinfeld approach – he wrote jokes every day and was generally considered to be pretty good at it. His commitment was 'never break the chain'; write some jokes, every day, without fail.

I started recording my daily exercise on a monthly calendar- a blank space on the calendar stood out and exposed my weakness. A training partner is a great idea, but 'exposing yourself' (not literally) is even more effective. And each record is its own mark of success, a little dab of dopamine every time – yes, even more satisfying than 'closing my rings' on my iWatch!

We humans have a limited resource of internal energy, so, like a trickle of water running down a pile of sand, we will follow our path of least resistance. We do this not because we are lazy, but because we are smart. We seek to optimise use of all our resources. If my training shoes are by the door, I will put them on and run. If they are in a jumble in a shoe rack this represents slightly more effort and is consequently much less likely to happen!

We can make deals with ourselves - a Ulysses pact if you like. By committing to an act in advance in the way Ulysses tied himself to a mast so he could resist the enchantments of the sirens, you can lock it in whilst your will power is strong. If you find an 'accountability partner', that can be even more effective - knowing that someone else is watching, someone from your tribe, provides an immediate cost of 'failure'.

It almost always happens that when the immediate consequence is favourable, the later consequences are disastrous

Frederic Bastiat,
Economist

Improvement actions are not easy. We can design our process so we are less likely to eat that chocolate cake if we are going to regret it later. But the occasional slip is not the end of the world. We can do like Dweck's football runner and pick ourselves up and run back to the right end. One own goal should never determine the outcome of the entire match.

Ramakrishna advises that we savour that cake with its sweet icing. Thich Nhat Hanh in his Art of Communicating, suggests a daily habit which includes, being grateful (expressing appreciation by metaphorically watering the flowers), apologising when we err, politely explaining when others hurt us and, when a child reminds its parents about a 'cake in the fridge'[13], it provides a gentle way for them to curtail destructive behaviour, creating an environment for calm reflection. And, as my old Granny used to say, 'a little bit of what you fancy never did any harm'.

REFLECTION TIME

Action		
Mens Rea	Actus Rhesus	Guilty? ☑
1. Do you want to get closer to your dreams?	How are you going to change the way you act? Note down your thoughts in the space below...	☐
2. Change is chaLLEnge made simpler	Take **Little steps** on **Light feet**, **Everyday**. We can tiptoe past our amygdala and humbly achieve greatness. What little step will you take today?	☐
Our Actions are not truly effective unless they gel with our Feelings...		

THE DAFT CYCLE - FEELING

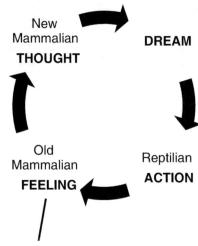

New Mammalian **THOUGHT**

DREAM

Old Mammalian **FEELING**

Reptilian **ACTION**

DREAMS define us, provided our Actions, Feelings and Thoughts toe the line. In this section, we look at our dreams and desires and the precious role of dopamine.

ACTIONS are nestled in the Reptilian Brain. The unbridled brain will 'Just Do It' with a swoosh of instinct.

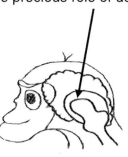

FEELINGS emanate from our 'Old Mammalian Brain' – the add-in, from which we can start wanting things, from which we are perhaps no longer simply coils of DNA.

THOUGHT - a comparatively new enhancement and still fairly flawed. The New Mammalian Brain, (AKA neo-cortex or cerebrum), represents the core of our 'executive function'.

Our feelings guide our decisions

Chapter 3:
FEELINGS AND THE OLD MAMMALIAN BRAIN

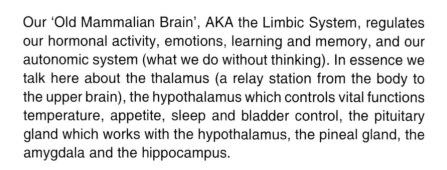

*You're face to face
with greatness, and it's strange.
You don't even know how you feel.*

Dwayne Johnson
(as Maui from Moana – talking about
himself but this applies to us all!)

Our 'Old Mammalian Brain', AKA the Limbic System, regulates our hormonal activity, emotions, learning and memory, and our autonomic system (what we do without thinking). In essence we talk here about the thalamus (a relay station from the body to the upper brain), the hypothalamus which controls vital functions temperature, appetite, sleep and bladder control, the pituitary gland which works with the hypothalamus, the pineal gland, the amygdala and the hippocampus.

The amygdala, an almond shaped cluster (one in each hemisphere) features heavily in the provision of our emotional world. Harmonising our Actions, Feelings and Thoughts (AFT) will require focus on this small marvel. As the 'emotional centre', it is no surprise that our Freeze, Fight or Flight reflex activates in this region in times of danger or threat.

If we find ourselves confronted by a 'hostile face', we may experience inner conflict, as our emotions egg us on at the same time as holding us back. Mostly a show of force from either party brings things to resolution as we expose our position of dominance or submission, our anger or fear take the form of a reddening or whitening of the face for example, and we, or they 'climb down'.

***

Public speaking, which, in a fine example of our 'DAFTness', many fear 'more than death', may stem from an internal confusion. An attentive audience or a confrontational 'threat-stare'? It is sometimes hard to tell the two apart. Our emotional confusions abound. With the reverse effect, children are frequently bitten by animals as they assume the snarling pit-bull is flashing them a toothy grin!

> **Primal Trigger**
>
> Eye contact is a primal trigger of emotional thoughts.
>
> To counter his primal trigger, Nassim Nicholas Taleb consciously averts his gaze to prevent him getting enraged by the stupidity of others![1]
>
> It's one approach to anger management!
>
> Another is the primal scream (see Part II, Chapter 1, Meaning. Purpose and Well-being, Improvement Action No.4)

The Hippocampus, or hippocampi as again there is one in each hemisphere. is the central point for our short-term memory, working alongside the amygdala to process the emotional impact of those memories as they are sent onwards or discarded, sometimes to our great frustration.

The hippocampus is so named as shaped like a seahorse. Let's imagine it as a giant miniature hippopotamus due to its weighty impact. It is worth keeping it particularly healthy as it can absorb a lot of informational nourishment. It can process all this information effectively and spray the good stuff, the memories we want to keep to the relevant parts of the brain for long term storage. This information, these memories, are spread throughout our vast network of neurons, enabling interconnections to be formed. The hippo' can also reject the superfluous information as waste and repeat the cycle continuously throughout our waking lives and indeed during sleep.

We neglect our hippo at our peril; tiredness or distress can affect data digestion. Memory selection becomes flaky and we may remember the telephone number for the call centre we'll never ring again, but forget the appointment to have our head examined.

***

When neurons fire together they release BDNF (brain derived neurotrophic factor), a protein that consolidates that network, triggering Acetylcholine production and the myelin we want to 'pile on' if we are to further embed the memory.

***

This demonstration of neuroplasticity is encouraging for us all. And luckily, keeping our hippo in good shape is relatively easy, in theory. As always, Nutrition, Exercise and Rest are the 'holy trinity'.

Oh, and the hippo is rather like the Incredible Hulk - it is not at its best when angry - an angry hippo straightens its tail and flaps wildly, fanning its excrement as far and wide as it possibly can. Whether you upset a hippopotamus, or your hippocampus, the sh1t really does hit the fan!

***

Use it or get lost

London taxi drivers, with the famous 'the knowledge' have clearly superior spatial awareness. They show an enlarged posterior hippocampus. In a study by Professor Eleanor Maguire over a period of two years, taxi drivers' posteriors were seen to grow, whereas bus drivers (who travelled a limited, predetermined route) showed no such change!

We have seen what happens when we feel but do not act. Can we feel without thinking? And how does thinking help?

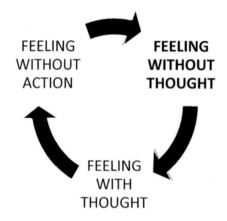

FEELING WITHOUT ACTION

FEELING WITHOUT THOUGHT

FEELING WITH THOUGHT

Feeling without Thought

> *We are what we do, not only with our body but with our words and our mind. This is the essence of Karma; to have a feeling is to produce a thought, to produce a thought is to act.*
>
> Thich Nhat Hanh

We instinctively know, that our feelings and thoughts are inseparable acts. To feel is to think about feeling, but...

'How aware are you of your feelings?'

Your level of awareness of your feelings or interoception, will determine how well you can guide your actions to align with your thoughts.

The good news is that all of us are on a spectrum of 'in-touchness' with our 'markers'. The even better news is that we can make positive steps along that spectrum, if we want to - if we want to enough.

Interoception

A useful measure of our 'interoception', or sensitivity to our body feelings, can be gained by measuring how accurate we are at counting our own heart rate by feeling it beat in our chest.

Stop for a moment and estimate your BPM?

Now do you have a means of measuring it. How close were you?

Try again Tomorrow.

Because practice makes perfect!

The more 'in touch' we are with our markers, the more we understand how we feel.

Yet we must take care as these markers are as flawed as we are. It is surprising how easily any background feelings can be unwittingly incorporated into our decisions. This 'affective realism' is responsible for many of the less exemplary decisions that we might make during the course of our days, weeks or lives.

Affective Realism

Sometimes we take false readings. Studies show that if it was raining when you interviewed that candidate the first time, you are less likely to have picked them for the job* (regardless of their state of dress)!

*if you live in the desert, presumably another day of sun would have the same effect.

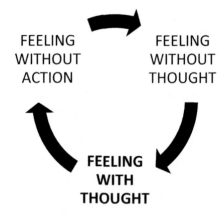

FEELING WITHOUT ACTION

FEELING WITHOUT THOUGHT

FEELING WITH THOUGHT

Feeling with thought

Let's cast our minds back to early thinkers and specifically the philosophical works of Aristotle. In *The Nichomachean Ethics*, he challenges us to **manage our emotional life with intelligence.** How on earth do we do that?

Sigmund Freud, in *Civilisation and its Discontents*, said that society has had to enforce from without, rules meant to subdue tides of emotional excess that surge too freely within. Rules like the Ten Commandments, the Mongolian Yassar code, the off-side rule, are all devised to harmonise our daily lives. Clearly the law breakers test this harmony, and none of us, except perhaps the Dalai Lama and maybe Robin Sharma's Monk who *sold his Ferrari*, are exempt from some emotional excesses. We have already established the vital role of emotional inputs to our daily functioning. Physiologically, emotion prepares us for our different responses, for example; in anger, blood flows to the hands making it easier to grasp a weapon, in fear to the large skeletal muscles like the legs accompanied by a flood of hormones to put the body on general alert ready to flee or fight, in surprise, at the very least a lifting of the eyebrows as the eyes widen to take more of the light in.

Psychologists describe two minds, the rational which is able to ponder and reflect, and the emotional. One thinks and one feels, and they operate in tight harmony, for the most part – amazingly well coordinated - until our passions surge.

As Daniel Goleman observes[3], Erasmus of Rotterdam in the 16th Century wrote that we have passion to reason in the ratio of

$$24:1^*$$

'Reason shouts herself hoarse repeating formulas of virtue, whilst anger and lust bid her go hang herself and are increasingly noisy and offensive until at last...reason surrenders'.

Sound familiar?

*1 hour of reason in every 24.
That would be a great day!

DAFT Apeth

Before Daniel Goleman's *Emotional Intelligence* was published in the late 1990's, we lacked a comprehensive appraisal of the importance of our emotions to our overall greatness, and it's strange indeed that such an analysis of the relative importance of emotions to our success has been so late coming. In the manner of much of our recent learning, the curve of knowledge has been exponential. Even since Daniel Goleman's seminal work, less than three decades ago, further leaps in technology have seen imaging capabilities enabling the interaction of our thoughts and feelings to be studied real-time (see **desires**). Indeed, our emotion-rich memories can almost be seen to move from the hippocampus to the outer layer of the brain, the neocortices, like the memories pulled from Albus Dumbledore's pensieve. They cannot quite yet be *'siphoned from one's mind, poured into a basin and examined at leisure'*, but our understanding of patterns and links between memories is certainly improving all the time.

In the beginning

It is worth looking at how our bonds are formed after birth. As a rule of thumb, it is believed that 90% of an emotional message is non-verbal; in infants as young as three months old, moods can be seen to be directly dependent on the moods of their mother. Babies are highly sensitive to that relationship. When things go wrong, emotional neglect can dull empathy and emotional abuse can make kids hypersensitive to the emotions of those around them.

Babies tend to be mothered on the left, which is (usually) where the heart is. They draw comfort from their comparable heart beats. In adults incidentally, a notable rocking or bobbing of people in situation of discomfort, for example when preparing to make a speech, stems from this activity – (One of my legs used to bounce crazily, in tutorials – I never realised that the fear of exposure of my lack of grasp of the Modigliani and Miller theories had this origin. This fear of being found out, a classic 'fixed mindset' manifestation explains my nervousness but also my silence on the subject).

Desmond Morris even suggested that it might account for our musical preferences with folk music notably displaying such rhythmic qualities[4]. (At the time of the Naked Ape, back in the mid 60's, the teenagers may have been becoming more liberal, but the music scene was rather more limited than today - it would be interesting to learn if his suggestion of teenagers choosing music 'that takes them back to the safety of the womb' might still hold true). Of course, he observes that the squealing and wailing of the fans of such as the Beatles was really a show of communication to the other fans, (akin to the crying of children for the comfort of their mothers), and not really demanding the support of the band member idols themselves.

Morris observed that communication became more critical as these connections enhanced our hunting effectiveness as we could coordinate better with our tribe. In fact, laughter evolved from crying, which then led to smiling and then to the frown[5] as the smile was 'turned upside down' to convey an opposing message as part of learning to communicate. Laughter and smiling both evolved as a means of conveying a fear of social contact and a means of displaying attraction and acceptance. For a mother, the smile is the ape's clinging substitute – her reward for protecting the infant. Despite restricted facial movement, babies, he observed, seem particularly acute at assessing incongruity between the face and the mood. When a smile is not genuine, the eyes don't lie (see former PM, Gordon Brown's attempt to smile when he was unhappy for a clear demonstration of this!)[6].

It is in the incongruity between our words and our actions that we show ourselves. Parents may ask their children to do as they say, rather than as they do, but the majority of our actions are a result of our 'imitative absorption' during our early years. It doesn't matter what you tell us to do, we emulate, we base our values, and we base our beliefs on what we see. Showing is far more effective than telling, as a parent, a teacher, and a boss. We are programmed to notice and detest inconsistency and hypocrisy from those who set the rules but believe themselves to be above them.

As Morris puts it 'Man still clings to his home-based habits and prejudices...it is a cross we have to bear if we are going to sail through our vital juvenile 'blotting-paper' phase of rapidly mopping up the accumulated experiences of previous generations'[7]. From our youth, we become attuned to tiny movements, postural changes, and vocal tones and it is not just humans, the animal kingdom shares this instinct, which is why 'Clever Hans' (the incredible counting horse), by reading the cues from his keeper, Wilhelm Von Osten, was able to convince people back in the 1890's that he could really count. The magnificent beast convinced many of his generation that, among other things, he could 'count' by tapping his hoof the right number of times to respond to a simple sum! Thus originating what psychologists now term the 'Clever Hans phenomenon', in which any of us may be guilty of unconscious cueing, which is really the equivalent of unconscious emotional leakage.

By learning more about our feelings and emotions, we can adapt our behaviour to optimise our connections and relationships and make a difference to our lives and to the lives of those around us.

The coordination of such moods is akin to the mother-child alignment. It is the essence of rapport. It is also why you should choose your friends wisely!

> **Mood makers**
>
> It is surprising how quickly emotions can pass between people, often subconsciously.
>
> Tests with pairs of people quizzed on their moods using 'before and after' checklists demonstrate *a striking tendency over a very short time towards the mood of the most emotionally expressive.*[8]

Indeed, this kind of emotional entrainment is exploited consciously or unconsciously by speakers, politicians and all other kinds of leaders, as the exertion of influence.

Our sweet and sensitive, little almond of delight, the amygdala, is poised like the first emergency service, waiting to send police, fire or ambulance whenever it is called.

In effect, the bypassing of the neocortex that was identified by LeDoux shows that the amygdala can and does support emotional impressions and memories that the neocortex may never even be aware of.

> **The High Road**
>
> Joseph LeDoux has shown that sensory signals from the eye or ear travel direct to the amygdala. A second signal travels to the thalamus and the neocortex. We can see that the feeling brain can respond before the thinking brain knows anything about it.
>
> His early work on rats where their auditory cortex had been destroyed showed that they feared a tone which accompanied an electric shock, even though they could not register the sound.[9]

Memory jogger

Joshua Foer, the one-time US memory champion (in a feat he accomplished within a year as an interesting diversion from his normal journalism role), describes how we store our memories and embeds his logic in the very title of his bestseller, 'Moonwalking with Einstein'. Prior generations may have preferred to drum facts and words into storage by the force of repetition, in what he terms the old 'drill and kill'. Now we understand the way we store information, we can appreciate the more elegant 'memory palace' technique of remembering through visual associations, and links with our emotional inclinations.

The Rhetorica Ad Herennium, a Latin text from maybe 80BC advises on the construction of a so-called 'memory palace', in essence, by using exaggerated imagery. In a loose translation of an extract 'the petty, ordinary or banal, we generally fail to remember – because the mind is not being stirred by anything marvellous or novel...but the exceptionally base, dishonourable, great, unbelievable or laughable we will remember for a long time'.

That we commit to memory when we are 'stirred by something marvellous or novel' was known by the wise over 2000 years ago, yet appears to be understood by few in recent times and was not taught in schools until, well, ever.

The visual imagery requires conscious effort, to think in a way that attaches emotion to facts, to link the amygdala to the neocortices. As we know, Desmond Morris said that we are instinctively neophilic – the newness of the images helps arouse us to commit to memory. LeDoux showed that the higher the emotional arousal, the stronger the imprinted memory. As LeDoux says, the minor brain system in mammals is the main brain system in non-mammals and offers a very rapid way to turn on emotions, but it's a 'quick and dirty process'; the cells are fast but not very precise. In his *Emotional Brain*, LeDoux points to the connections from emotions to neocortex, observing that they are stronger than the reverse – in other words we feel it, then think it. As Antonio Damasio put it, emotions are the 'lubricants of reason'.

Emotions may lubricate our reason, they also cement our memories, working in tandem with the neocortices. For disturbing emotions, the left pre-frontal lobe appears to play a part in the decision whether to commit to storage. It is said by some that the amygdala proposes, the pre-frontal lobe disposes, although most argue that in a battle between thoughts and emotions, emotion wins every time, and the more disturbing the emotion, the more significant the mark it leaves in our neocortex.

It appears that the ability of our pre-frontal lobe to diffuse the storage power of undesirable emotional experiences can be significantly affected by our sleep patterns, with REM sleep playing a particularly significant part in softening the edges of emotional memories[10]. Matthew Walker, the sleep-obsessed neuroscientist, describes this effect in his compelling investigative commitment to *Why We Sleep*.

Memory Walker

Psychologists recognise that the Hippocampus has limited capacity, but the involvement of our emotional centres, partially explains the 'Baker/baker paradox' – when shown a man's face and told he is called Baker, your chance of recalling that name a week later is rather low. If you are shown the same face and informed that the man is a baker, then your prospect for recall is dramatically greater. With the description comes a vast network of facts and emotions, whereas the name is just a series of five letters. Incidentally, our short-term memory for numbers tends to fizzle out at just 7 digits*, with a range between 5 and 9 digits covering the majority of us. The Hippocampus holds this in a 'phonological loop', i.e; in the voice in our heads. Foer demonstrates various techniques to push that data into longer term storage cortex including 'chunking' in the manner of our phone and credit card numbers.

*The so-called magic number of 7 comes from a famous paper by George Miller, a Princeton University psychologist, back in 1956 titled 'The magical number 7 plus or minus 2'. He was referring to Scottish philosopher William Hamilton, who threw marbles on the floor and stated 7 was the number that could be counted without confusion. Some neuroscientists dispute this saying it is more like four for most people, before we need to employ techniques like chunking to manage larger numbers, like telephone numbers. I happen to have eight tetra fish in my fish tank and a couple of pairs of guppies. When I do an inventory, it's like counting children in a playground – impossible; but I can tick off the two pairs of guppies and then have some success sometimes catching the tetra's four by four. As for the marbles, they are easier to count once you disregard the ones that have rolled under the sofa.

Actions for improvement

There is a limit to how much we can improve that which we do not understand. So how do we improve our understanding?

1. Learn how to use our intelligence wisely

Remember that old spelling aid: **E before I, except after C?** But...but...that's not right....

It is now! First there was **Intelligence Quotient**, then the value of **Emotional intelligence** was recognised and now...

IQ tests were introduced to provide the right help where needed, misunderstood to be a ranking system, then recognised as flawed for various reasons. Many alternatives have been proposed and tested.

All have their flaws and, in the end, we follow easy paths, stick with heuristics as anything else is impractical on a grand scale. Emotional Intelligence has gained status over recent decades and the impact of our emotions are more widely understood and more readily accepted.

IQ

When Alfred Binet devised the original IQ Assessment tool back in 1908 alongside Thoedore Simon, he was acutely aware of its limitations and certainly did not devise it as a means to rank children, rather to promote the French ideal of egalite, to enable children to be given maximal opportunity to develop. He never intended it to be taken up and used as a purely quantitative method of classification.

Rather like King Cnut, who placed his chair on the beach in order to demonstrate that he could not control the tides, Binet's work became rather misunderstood and when adopted in the United States by Lewis Terman, it was rapidly developed into a 'one size fits all' evaluation of the 'mental worth' of an individual, with Terman's own children being ranked according to their IQ score. The lower scoring family members were virtually discounted in his mind, as it appears that he, somewhat perversely, loved them in proportion to their test score.

In a rather classic example of Carol Dweck's fixed mindset, combined with the more recently understood placebo effect, Dunning and Kruger effect and confirmation bias, it all started when Terman was given a rather flattering personal assessment of his own intelligence by a visiting phrenologist. Of course, Terman didn't believe in such techniques. Craniologists and phrenologists were largely discredited professions by this stage, but his ego was boosted nevertheless by the generous assessment of his intellect. (No assessment of our 'worth' is valid unless it flatters us!). This newly inflated confidence was sufficient to steer him to Stanford University. The power of flattery really should never be underestimated! (See Some Other Substantial Reason). It was at Stanford that he became passionate about Binet's IQ assessment tool.

The formula, revised by Terman, is still in use today. We went from limited reliance on any intelligence assessment tool to a near total reliance on IQ as a measure of 'general intelligence'.

The use of IQ as a single unitary construct is a 'deplorable verdict

Alfred Binet

Binet would have turned in his grave if he had been alive to see his tests, devised to help with the development of underperforming children, deployed for Terman-style ranking purposes.

IQ and the Flynn Effect

Even today, we tend to think that the abstract reasoning skills reflected in IQ scores translate to better judgements and higher quality decision-making abilities in all areas of life. The Flynn effect is a direct challenge to this.

James Flynn showed that improvements in IQ scores had risen by over 20 points on average in just 40 years. Yet no-one would dare suggest that we are really that much cleverer, would they?

Flynn's data dissection shows non-verbal reasoning increasing somewhat, but verbal and numerical reasoning not really budging. Whilst we do learn new ways, it is clear that our overall average intelligence can't rise that fast. In other words, Flynn shows us that it is dangerous to read too much into IQ scores alone.

EQ

Carl Jung said that all emotional shades derive from just four - are you mad, sad, glad, or scared?

Daniel Goleman further shifted the dial and for the most part, we have moved a long way from the pure IQ approach as we now understand the importance of Emotional Intelligence, and 'why it can matter more than IQ'.

Goleman categorises our eight basic emotions. Satisfying these emotions could be linked to Maslow's famous 'Hierarchy of needs'. The first five emotions are about survival and rely on the Autonomic Nervous System. They are fear, anger, disgust, shame, and sadness.

The next two are for attachment. These are love and enjoyment.

And finally...BOO!! - the 'potentiator' – the emotion of surprise, bringing good news and/or bad.

The good news is that we didn't stop there. We now have a richer understanding of the wide range of 'intelligences' that help to define a person, include emotional intelligence, intellectual humility etc.

CQ

When Howard Gardner, Harvard University psychologist wrote his 1983 book Frames of Mind, he recognised that the 'IQ way of thinking' which declared that a 'single kind of aptitude determining your future' was the kind of thinking that permeated society. He strongly refuted this approach, introducing the 'theory of multiple intelligences' and noting that the core of interpersonal intelligence includes the 'capacities to discern and respond appropriately to the moods, temperaments, motivations and desires of other people'. Alongside that, our intra-personal intelligence demands that we can access our own feelings, have the ability to discriminate among them, and can draw upon them to guide behaviour.

The eminent psychologist Robert Sternberg choked in his (IQ based) SATs and as a result believes he would have succumbed to the self-fulfilling frame of mind of the dumb person the test said he was but for intervention of one insightful teacher.

He has measured the leadership performance among platoon, company and battalion commanders, communicating mission goals, dealing with insubordination etc... and has devised a number of test tools which better assess ability to perform in various situations. He has proposed a mid-ground 'triarchic theory of successful intelligence' - practical, analytical and creative, addressing concerns about educational focus and better influencing decision making in a diverse range of cultures and situations. This is perhaps a more useful measure of 'the ability to achieve success in life'.

Psychologists now tend to take the wider view. As an advocate of this wider view, Daniel Goleman references the works of Robert Sternberg and fellow psychologist Peter Salovey of Yale University, who defined five domains of emotional intelligence; knowing one's emotions, managing them, self-motivation, recognising emotions in others and handling relationships.

His work may have inspired the Cultural intelligence revolution, and the work of Soon Ang, Professor of Management at Nanyan Technology University in Singapore, inspired by ineffective teamworking of cross-global IT workers on the 'Y2k' problem. Her measure of cultural intelligence, (abbreviated as CQ) extends prior works to consider sensitivity to different cultural norms.

For example, if I, a Brit, proposed a solution to one of my Japanese colleagues and they did not get back to me promptly: As a person of low CQ, I merely assume they are not interested in my idea, or in me. If I were a high CQ individual, I would know to ask directly for feedback, as a lack of response is the cultural norm.

The bad news is that we still have a way to go and perhaps always will. The easy path is always the most followed. The US SAT's (Scholastic Aptitude tests) and worldwide GRE's (Graduate Record Examinations) feature heavily in candidate assessments and have a close link to the original Terman-promoted IQ tests. Widespread adoption of alternative assessment methods remains a challenge. IQ still wins on ease of application, in the same way that Sales or Stock Turns remain primary metrics for a business leader where Employee Engagement and Innovation might be so much more useful. Away from all the measures, in practice **using our intelligence wisely** is what really matters.

2. Learn what do we do with our Emotions?

If we have the ability to capture in our thoughts our feelings, then we can start to regulate them.

We have varying abilities to know our own emotions. When we have a high level of awareness, we may achieve what Sigmund Freud described as an 'evenly hovering attention'. If we can view whatever passes through with impartiality, as an interested, yet unreactive witness, then surely we can tick this box.

Quick Quiz - What are you like?*

Do you understand your emotions? Do you refuse to languish in an emotional state for long? You sound like you fit into the Self Aware category.

Do you often feel engulfed by your emotions? Do you sometimes feel swamped by them? Do you feel that there is not much you can do to escape your bad moods? You sound like you fit into the Engulfed# category.

Do you allow yourself to have a strong response to your emotions, positive or negative, yet for your own reasons, you prefer to be that way? You sound like a good fit for the Accepting category.

Do you love going to parties? You sound like the party-going type.

*John Mayer, psychologist at University of New Hampshire categorises us as S E or A.[11]

Engulfment is probably the largest category – perhaps a classic symptom of what Dweck calls 'fixed mindset', in which we place the problem beyond ourselves.

Clearly in John Mayer's style of categorisation, most of us would prefer to be in the Self Aware category most of the time. The more effort we put into understanding our emotions, the easier life becomes. If we can describe our feelings, we can help to regulate the emotions they induce.

Feldman Barrett even suggests learning or inventing new words to describe specific emotions, like 'hangry', or the Japanese, doki doki, 'the feeling of great anxiety when someone is about to do something very nerve wracking', or 'sonder' the new (in 2012) English word meaning 'profound feeling of realization that everyone, including strangers, has a life as complicated as your own'. This enables us to process more emotions and enrich our emotional sensitivity perhaps in the same way that Eskimos find it useful to have more words to describe snow.

3. How to manage our emotions – to take arms against a SEA of troubles

The better we can regulate them the greater our powers of differentiation, the greater we can become, in line with the Buddhist teaching of Nirvana, which requires total attunement with our emotions. It is why mindfulness and meditation are considered by so many people to be such powerful tools.

Temperamental genes?

Our temperament is to some extent genetic, but does that make it destiny? Jerome Kagan, a Development psychologist at Harvard university, proposes at least four temperamental types.

Which one are you? Timid, Bold, Upbeat or Melancholy?

Of course, as always, we are somewhere on a spectrum.

Our nervous system is calibrated with a base threshold for amygdala arousal. Focusing on 'timid to bold', reflects our ease of being frightened, our sociability and our curiosity. In Kagan's analysis, 20% of us are timid, 40% mid-range and 40% bold. He speculates that the timid amongst us may have inherited abnormally high levels of neurochemicals, like norepinephrine, which activate the amygdala and lower our threshold of excitability.[12]

If a careless lorry trundles too close to the pavement and soaks your new sneakers with the filthy, oily water amassing in the gutter, it helps to be able to 'step slightly away from the incident', as if hovering above and looking down on yourself. Your physical steps are accompanied by raised heart-beat, hot cheeks and cold fury and an immediate desire to show the lorry driver the hand-signal best reflecting your ire.

John Mayer points to the example of a child, who is told not to hit another – even when physically restrained, the emotion of anger remains. The child who manages to say to themselves 'I am angry because he stole my toy' has shown self-awareness and is less likely to wallow in that anger. If that child wrestles free of his adult captor and seeks retribution, his style will be less easy to determine!

We can all be subject to 'flooding' where we experience anger or contempt, causing adrenaline and the CATO of hormones to flood the body. This pushes the heart rate up by maybe ten beats per minute and causes a swamp of toxic feelings making others' perspectives impossible to recognise. As a child we are primed by our parents with our emotional habits. We may over-react to a perceived slight, or shut down at the first sign of confrontation.

With our adult awareness box ticked, we may be able to resist the angry signalling to that lorry driver for soiling our stylish footwear. If not, perhaps we can gauge the mood of the lorry driver who has now stopped and is rapidly approaching. Perhaps we can hover above ourselves now, to avoid being too immersed in an emotional interaction? Perhaps we'll even see that the driver is apologising? And perhaps we'll hear that he swerved to avoid hitting an escaped puppy we didn't observe on the opposite pavement? Perhaps, perhaps perhaps.

Dolf Zillman, a psychologist at University of Alabama defines 'rage' as a 'limbic surge, with dual effect'. First we feel a rapid burst of energy, ready for our fight or flight, then an 'amygdala driven ripple, creating a general tonic of action readiness lasting much longer'. Mitigating information, like the sight of the puppy in the arms of our frantic neighbour, allows us to reappraise the situation. It provides a 'balm for our anger'. The window of opportunity for de-escalation is however, fairly short, after which the mitigation will no longer penetrate our 'cognitive incapacitation'. The less aware of our emotions we are, the more powerful our surge may be, and lesser awareness of our heightened response reduces the likelihood of managing our emotions and ensuring a rational reaction.

When we can perceive our anger, we can monitor and in doing so control all the physiological responses. If we remain angry, like the second child, we can use distraction as an extremely effective mood-altering device. Every parent knows that it is impossible to stop a child being angry but much easier to make them interested in something else, with the same desired calming effect.

Some amongst us believe in the so-called ventilation fallacy. We may even teach it to our kids? 'You've got to fight back – at least it makes you feel better'. Although this cathartic anger may have worked for Michael Douglas in 'Falling down', or Russell Crowe in 'Unhinged', the idea of giving vent to rage has been proven to be one of the worst ways to cool down, as it has a tendency to 'pump up the emotional brain's arousal…'.

> **Ventilation Fallacy**
>
> When Chogyam Trungpa, a Tibetan teacher, was asked how to handle anger, he said 'don't suppress it. But don't act on it.'
>
> And we do well to remember Ghandi's advice; '*if you are right, you have no reason to be angry; if you are wrong, you have no right.*'

Some studies however do show that anger can actually reduce the cortisol induced by stress, consequently reducing the potential harm. Miguel Kazen at Universitat Osnabruck traced neural brain activity with more in the left hemisphere encouraging you to approach your conflict and more right bias advising backing off, (fight v flight) as if we actually do have an angel and a devil, one on each shoulder[13]. It is believed that a short-term display of anger can give a sense of control, which we know is good for our mental well-being.

Displacement

Of course, if we dwell on it, the cortisol can build back 'greater' ending with 'displacement' response, the proverbial straw breaking the camel's back - and perhaps, an over-the-top four-letter tirade, like the fantastic example portrayed by Tamsin Greig in the car park at the end of an exhausting episode of the BBC series 'Episodes', in which her character finally snaps giving an innocent parking attendant the full sense of her day's extraordinary series of disasters.

Mastery of the emotional domain is difficult as it requires learning at times of heightened emotion. Daniel Goleman identifies schools that train children in emotional expression in ways that do not spiral into aggression[14]. It is interesting to see how children so schooled are able to express their emotions with a greater self-awareness. In these cases, confrontations that, in more normal environments would lead to fights, actually diffuse calmly.

It is possible to tame an aggressive personality, which may result from perceptual biases, as Kagan explains, 'an over-excitable amygdala can be tamed provided the brain experiences the right emotional lessons. Parents who engineer gradually emboldening experiences for their children offer them what may be a lifelong corrective to their fearfulness.'

In one test, when bullies and non-bullies are paired up to watch videos where benign acts have been judged to be hostile, the bully justifies the aggressor's actions reflecting their own tendency to judge the actions of the other party. Bullies tend to have a low threshold for upset which affects their rational judgement. These tendencies are embedded at a young age and can manifest in violent outbursts. As a result, the child becomes disliked and he falls into a slippery spiral. The child who says 'that boy is angry, and he needs to learn to manage his anger' remains a rare find.

With self-awareness, it becomes easier to consider impulse control; we know the difference between feelings and actions, and as in the Serenity Prayer, we can make better choices.

4. Can we choose or accept?

Perhaps you are one of an elite group of 'unflappables'[15]? Do you show 'perennial cheerfulness' in the face of disturbing feelings? It happens to about 1 in 6 of us. Can you repress negative emotions? Is it a physiological response not an emotional one? Although the emotional response is effectively 'tuned out', you 'unflappables' will still experience some underlying agitation, that may betray your veneer of calm. Unless of course you are in the alexithymic camp and do not consciously experience emotions at all?

Clearly some of us generally inhabit a more cheerful inner world than others. Richard Davidson, University of Wisconsin psychologist has pinpointed relevant brain signals and shown that people with more left or right frontal lobe activity have a greater or lesser propensity to cheerfulness respectively. So, if we aren't born cheerful, (or as categorised by Jerome Kagan 'upbeat'), with high left frontal lobe activity, does this mean we are doomed?

Surprisingly, not at all. Change is quite possible and for people who Richard Davidson suggests don't 'gravitate towards the positive pole', our environment plays a significant part, and so do our choices

We can all learn to make better emotional decisions by controlling the impulse to act and identifying the alternative actions and consequences before acting. It is not of course an overnight, big bang process.

Good schooling of emotions means small impact, delivered regularly over a number of years. The strengthening of pathways, creating good neural habits to apply in times of duress, frustrations, hurt etc...

If we want to veer more towards that 'positive pole', reframing is a highly effective tool. We can represent (to ourselves) our responses to emotional triggers, for example, a racing-heart and cold sweat could be bad; 'I am nervous' or it could be good; 'I am excited; so excited that I can feel I am getting an adrenaline rush to help me perform'.

Framing is everything

Mark Rober's very interesting TED talk demonstrates that how we frame life's challenges has a significant impact on our results. A test to sort lines of computer code to move a car through a maze showed a 16% greater success rate from the half of the 50,000 participants who were not 'penalised' for failure. What is more, in what he calls the 'SuperMario effect', he demonstrates how we think we want our lives to run smoothly uphill to our goals, but in reality, life is only interesting when we experience challenges.[16]

In other words, we need failures, in order to appreciate our success and when we see life's challenges as a game rather than a test, we will pay to play rather than having to be paid to endure a challenge.

As Edith Eger, the psychologist, protégé of Victor Frankl, fellow concentration camp survivor and author of The Choice, explains 'everything can be taken from a person but one thing, to choose one's attitude in any given set of circumstances, to choose one's way'[17]. We all experience some suffering in our lives, thankfully few as extreme as Edith and Victor's, yet our reaction, like theirs, is within our control.

The power of positive thinking

has been linked to our tendency to perform 'pre-motor programming'. If we visualise it, if we 'practise' something in our heads, our brain changes to make it happen. Our frontal and pre-frontal lobes are active in this process.

In injury we can see damage within these frontal and pre-frontal areas which affects abilities which are key to human distinctiveness from the animals, including our sequencing, drive, executive control and what is termed our 'future memory'. Our future memory reflects our ability to imagine, to dream, to see future goals. When Lewis Carrol's Queen of Hearts said that 'it is a poor sort of memory that only works backward', he understood the importance of forward thinking.

5. Remember that you'll be fifty anyhow

Dr Albert Ellis (founder of Rational Emotive Behaviour therapy, the precursor to Cognitive Behavioural Therapy - CBT[18]) taught Eger that repeatedly reinforcing her negative thoughts (her limiting beliefs) determined how she felt about herself and her capabilities and directly influenced her behaviour. These limiting beliefs reinforce and become self-fulfilling.

Eger knew that she was her own worst enemy, amplifying her limiting beliefs. She knew this was preventing her from fulfilling her dream. And what was her dream? To truly help others to transcend their own limiting beliefs. She knew that to help others she would need first to help herself. Frankl's four simply words enabled her to reframe her thoughts. When she asked him, 'how could I help other people transcend their limiting beliefs – I could study but by the time I'm qualified I'll be fifty?', he responded, 'you'll be fifty anyhow!'

Whatever age you happen to be now, the observation works, just change the number. And it's this kind of thinking that can help any of us re-frame other concerns we might have.

Eger's mantra for managing emotions is to 'notice, accept, check and stay', not so different from Sternberg's knowing one's emotions, managing them and self-motivation. This then is also not so different from improvement in the business world. The philosophy of Lean which David Bovis and Philip Holt, the Lean guru describe as an 'emotional journey' applies the 'Deming model for continuous improvement'; a reinforcing cycle of planning, doing, learning and refining.

This 'Plan, Do, Check, Act' business improvement tool is equally useful as a personal improvement tool. Here, the change cycle starts with self-awareness (aware of where we are now and where we want to be) and continues indefinitely seeking feedback for refinement.

With emotions, with feelings, we gain control. As Eger puts it, in order to change our behaviour (our actions), we must change our feelings, and to change those we must change our thoughts. Penny Ferguson, inspirational leadership guru, says that when we change our thoughts, we change our day, and when we change our day, we give ourselves the power to change our entire lives.

Of course, change is easier said than done, and there will be many obstacles on the way, but as Eger's mother used to say, 'when you can't go in through a door, go in through a window'[19]. If you are determined enough there is always another way. Sometimes it just requires a little more thought...

REFLECTION TIME

Action		
Mens Rea	Actus Rhesus	Guilty? ☑
1. Do you understand your emotions?	How can you use this knowledge to change the way you act? Use the space below to note your intial thoughts…	☐
2. Can you control your emotions?	Think of a time when you did not. differently when this happens next time?	☐
Controlling our Feelings to make us even more effective requires Thought …		

THE DAFT CYCLE - THOUGHT

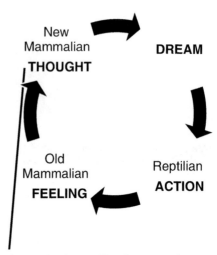

New Mammalian **THOUGHT**

DREAM

Reptilian ACTION

Old Mammalian **FEELING**

DREAMS define us, provided our Actions, Feelings and Thoughts toe the line. In this section, we look at our dreams and desires and the precious role of dopamine.

ACTIONS are nestled in the Reptilian Brain. The unbridled brain will 'Just Do It' with a swoosh of instinct.

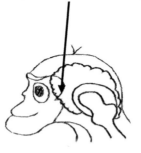

FEELINGS emanate from our 'Old Mammalian Brain' – the add-in, from which we can start wanting things, from which we are perhaps no longer simply coils of DNA.

THOUGHT - a comparatively new enhancement and still fairly flawed. The New Mammalian Brain, (AKA neo-cortex or cerebrum), represents the core of our 'executive function'.

We can shape our thoughts to
meet our desires

Chapter 4:
THOUGHT

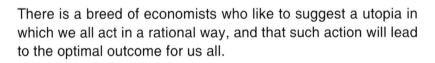

> *If you make someone think they are thinking, they will love you. If you make someone actually think, they will hate you.*
>
> Don Marquis,
> American humourist.

There is a breed of economists who like to suggest a utopia in which we all act in a rational way, and that such action will lead to the optimal outcome for us all.

If everyone acted rationally, like some economists like Rousseau and Condorcet suggest we should, then we could predict the future with certainty. Of course, then we would change it, and in doing so predict a different future, and change that, probably. But we don't and we can't. Robert Lucas, the economist famed for his 'Lucas critique', described the paradox. In effect, predicting the future forces us to change it - prediction not achieved. And so we go round in circles.

You will be aware of what economists call the 'perfect market'. In a perfect market, buying and selling is pure, there is only demand and supply, perfect information and no interference. In theory, theory and practice are the same, in practice this is never the case. The perfect market bears no relation to reality, nor does the 'Efficient Market hypothesis', in which shares are correctly priced reflecting perfect information.

Utopia is not a real place. We do not act rationally. To do so would require us to think and act without feeling. If you hope for this, you are destined for disappointment.

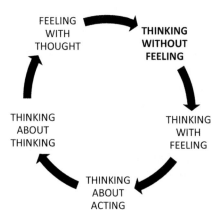

Thinking without feeling

The idea of pure rational thought, or 'thinking without feeling' is easily challenged. From the extreme, we know from the work of Antonio Damasio, it is not that simple. Thinking without feeling seems to make those very thoughts run very dry.

In more recent decades, the works of Daniel Kahneman and Amos Tversky, the experimental economists, have demonstrated beyond doubt that in fact whilst we may profess to rational thinking, our behaviours demonstrate what might be called 'bounded rationality'. Our thinking and decision-making exist in a world of shortcuts, quick and dirty, fast and frugal, flawed thinking, with routine deployment of inaccurate heuristics (rules of thumb).

Bounded Rationality

Perhaps it makes sense to consider a kind of bounded rationality. This is what was proposed by Herbert Simon, the Nobel prize winning scientist back in 1956. His 'satisficing theory' suggests that it is advisable that we do just enough thinking to get by, to get an acceptable result, to reach a threshold of acceptability. If we spend more time and resources trying to make better decisions, then that extra time will constitute waste.

The very attempt to optimise is simply too costly, so we should have a process to determine what is good enough.

The inference from Herbert Simon's thinking is that perfection is unachievable. If you seek it, you will be condemned to a sysyphian struggle, a tail-chasing programme.

You will not find satisfaction unless you settle for excellence, until you recognise that this is perfectly adequate.

Unsatisfied?

The makings of the Rolling Stones hit, 'Can't get no....' reputedly came to Keith Richards in a dream – and was recorded serendipitously on his malfunctioning tape recorder, whilst he dozed.

Having this dream gave the band their first No1 Hit in America, way back in 1965. Arguably they got their fair share over the years!

Perhaps someone should have told this to Mick Jagger and Keith Richards...although, deep down, they probably knew!

Sometimes we don't even appear to follow consistent thinking. I think that I prefer oranges to apples and apples to grapes but I always choose a grape before an orange.

Simple syllogistic fallacies can exaggerate our tendency to apply false logic. Oranges are fruit, so are apples. So, apples must be oranges. All dogs are mammals, so are all cats – so dogs must be cats. Schrödinger should not have been asking whether his cat was dead or alive – rather if it was a dog or a cat. In the quantum world of course, the answer of course would still be ...**both!**

Quantum question finally answered

A Welsh tabby cat, called Lucy reportedly lived to the age of 39 – she holds the Guinness World record.

Erwin Schrödinger put his theoretical cat in a theoretical box with a vial of radioactive poison in 1935. His cat is nearly ninety years old. It is not in the Book of Records.

Conclusion: The Guinness Book of records is alive. The cat must be dead.

Of course, my fruit choices may be more logical than it first seems. My tastes vary depending what is most readily available, what mood I am in and most importantly how the respective fruit has been fermented!

And so, many of our apparent flaws of thinking give us an evolutionary advantage. When we allow our biases to influence our thinking, we think quickly, and we thus conserve vital brain energy. But there is a downside to this dependence on our biases. Our conscious biases may nudge us from the path but it's the unconscious ones that really lead us astray. Our unconscious biases inform our actions unbeknownst to us. That is where some major mistakes are made (see Chapter 5, Biased Beyond Belief).

There is no limit to the follies that can be swallowed if one is under the influence of feelings of this kind. One has to belong to the intelligentsia to believe things like that. No ordinary man could be such a fool

George Orwell

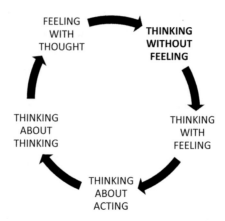

Thinking with feeling

Orwell observed our rational thought veering away from Stanovich's instrumental towards the epistemic rationality*. Our rational thought does not increase with intellect. The great escapologist Harry Houdini spent a lifetime fooling people and declared that the greater the brain, the better educated, the easier a person is to mystify[1]. A perfect defence when you fall for a schoolboy prank! (Or fall victim to a confidence trickster).

---

*Rationality

Cognitive scientists like Keith Stanovich describe two classes of Rationality:

Instrumental rationality – do you seek optimisation of goal fulfilment (get best from your available resources)

Epistemic rationality – do your beliefs map to the external structure of the world (eg do you believe in ghosts and/or fairies?)

Motivated Reasoning

Dan Kahan at Yale Law School examined motivated reasoning with a question on attitudes to gun control. He asked 'Would gun controls increase or decrease crime rates in this city? The Data on impact of gun control were provided as follows:

Cities that banned carrying hand guns in public – 223 decreased, 75 increased;

Cities that did not ban hand gun – 107 decreased, 21 increased.

Of course, he also did a numeracy test and a political affiliation question too which validated raw numerical ability, and in effect asked for participants own views on gun control. The results showed that those who supported no ban reasoned well on this issue, but those who did not, did not. (in this instance it may seem on first glance that a ban is effective, but the maths says otherwise with 25% increase with a ban and just 16% without a ban). When he swapped the results with a different group, he found those who supported a ban reasoned well, and those who did not, did not!

Dan Kahan's test highlights how are reasoning is flawed and how we reinforce our personal 'belief bias'.

In many cases we provide explanations which bear no relation to the underlying reality. In a distant life in a financial role, when auditors would ask me why sales turnover was up in a given period, I would give a perfectly plausible explanation, as indeed I would a few seconds later when they realised that turnover was in fact down! These plausible but useless explanations are akin to stock market traders explaining market movements, where investors tend to focus on the noise rather than the signal. With infinite interactions in the markets minor fluctuations actually have no discernible meaning.

Can R join the Q? Are we even capable of rational thought?

We know the IQ is an inadequate metric. EQ and CQ are improvements, but will they stick?

What about Keith Stanovich's Rationality Quotient RQ? Stanovich has devised a 'Comprehensive Assessment of Rational Thinking' (CART)*, in which he tests our logical reasoning.

For example; can you identify syllogisms? All living things need water, roses need water. Roses are therefore living things?

What about a swimming pool? – you might argue that it doesn't actually need it, but…what then is need?

It has been found, time and again, that our ability to reason and make a sound judgment is dependent not only on our powers of reasoning but also on our beliefs.

An argument is not necessarily logical just because the conclusion makes sense.

*Perhaps this test would have been an appropriate one to properly assess the abilities of Clever Hans!

Robert Shiller's 1981 paper on how society handles information[2] states that there is too much variation, too much volatility – prices swing more than the information which they reflect, which accusation is certainly apparent in the uncertain times like the highly volatile post-covid speculative markets. There is no perfect, efficient market. Our thoughts always have accompanying feelings, although we rarely indulge in thinking about their impact. We subconsciously decide whether to head for the bucket of water due to the temptation for hydration or towards the hay due to the lure of the straw man.

Emotional Valence

Psychiatrists score the impact of feelings on our every thought. This valence reflects a positive or negative feeling at the reptilian brain level – if the valence is high, the emotion is strong. If it is high enough, it influences our moods and over-rides our rational responses.

As Richard Restak describes, some people seem less in-touch with their feelings. They deny feeling angry despite showing the symptoms for others to see. Thinking about feeling for ourselves means being aware of ourselves, our emotions, our markers. Once we have sought to understand, we can react accordingly. We can observe the feelings as if from afar, we can engineer the time to choose and to react better.

When I responded to my wife after being told where in the dishwasher to put Oscar's bamboo plate, I thought I was being calm and rational. It had been a long day, and the baby had been screaming in my ear virtually non-stop since 5 AM. During my evening of silent treatment, I had plenty of time to re-think. With effort and practice our 'observing ego' can become more and more attuned. We can avoid unnecessary friction. We need never even contemplate who would be best at loading the dishwasher in future or where else to shove the bamboo.

Our 'in-touchness' with our feelings can be improved, like most things with conscious effort and practice, and, with experience, our thoughts and emotions may remain separately recognizable, yet woven together into a unified experience. If we think and feel differently, then we will act differently. The wheels will not come off the dishwasher. We will edge closer to Nirvana.

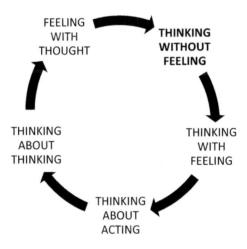

Thinking about Acting

Should we Fake it till we make it?

When Randle McMurphy enters the mental institution, he fakes his own insanity in order to avoid hard labour for his crimes. The Electro Convulsive Therapy he receives (ECT) is the start of a slippery slope which doesn't end well for the increasingly volatile character that Jack Nicholson plays in the Oscar winning movie 'One Flew over the Cuckoo's Nest'. It is said that if you want to win an Oscar, you need to be a method actor and whilst Jack Nicholson gave such a convincing performance and has claimed to understand method acting better than anyone else, unlike some of his compatriots, he is not particularly known as such. Perhaps he is more naturally able to switch in and out character than some, in the way some people appear to be better at 'multi-tasking' than others.

Note on Multi-Tasking

Due to the nature of our brain processing, we are not actually able to multitask in any thoughtful way. Of course. we can breathe and think, our heart will beat whilst we are reading this, but, beyond the autonomous actions to keep us alive, all we are actually able to do is Task Switch, that is shift from one task to another fairly rapidly, with varying degrees of inefficiency and waste in the process. In his book 'Thinking Fast and Slow' Daniel Kahneman shows us a simple demonstration by asking us to walk along with him whilst doing some sums:

When the computation is easy (e.g; what is 5 x 5?), you already know the answers based on prior experience, then you can walk and 'do math' at the same time, no problem. If, on the other hand, your hippocampus is challenged to keep hold of slightly more complex numbers and for messages to be passed to and from your pre-frontal cortices, to manipulate the data (e.g; what is 25 x 26?), then watch your feet grind to a halt as you work!

The fictitious, Randle McMurphy is, of course, not the first to fake his own insanity, the subject was a perpetual challenge for Captain John Yossarian in Joseph Heller's Catch 22; if you can fake your own insanity, you have proved that you are not insane... Indeed Jon Ronson introduces us to Tony, in his intriguing yet by some interpretations light-hearted *The Psychopath Test*[3]. Tony is a patient at Broadmoor Psychiatric Hospital, who battles to prove that he 'faked it' for many years. In the end, we are left, far from certain whether he fits the diagnosis as a dangerous psychopath or not.

A note of caution to be careful what you act for!

10% of us are Psychopaths
Jon Ronson

There are 5 people in my family. There is a 50% chance I am living with one. Gulp... it might be me
Me me me!

The 10% are not faking it. Some of our more unreasonable leaders owe their unreasonableness to the diagnosable medical condition. American corporate turn-around executive, Albert Dunlap, also known as 'Chainsaw Al' or 'Rambo in pinstripes', admits possessing many of the traits. Where he claimed positive leadership attributes, Carol Dweck in *Mindset* attributes the leadership style to a 'fixed mindset', a mindset in which failure was not an option; 'maintenance of his ego was everything and the massive accounting scandal which he engineered at Sunbeam Products was part and parcel of that need to continually prove himself in a way that constrains all people of a fixed mindset.'[4]

'Fake it till you make it' has its origins in Ancient Greece. Aristotle wrote that 'Men acquire a particular quality by constantly acting in a certain way'. It was of course adopted and adapted by Amy Cuddy, the inspirational Harvard psychologist and author of *Presence.*[5]

'Faking it till you become it' is all about confidence. It's not about lack of integrity, but about persuading yourself to do brave things, with expectation of a more positive outcome than Randle McMurphy's. She introduces her superhero pose; standing upright, shoulders tall with hands on hips, in the manner of Wonder Woman, or Hercules before commencing any one of his great labours.

There is of course a plethora of evidence that body and brain act together as one machine, and oiling that machine boosts its efficiency. Cuddy's stance was that this pose, along with the adoption of a positive attitude, can actually create a chemical change within the body. Her research suggested her power pose caused a reduction in cortisol, one of the key stress creating chemicals, and an increase in testosterone, a confidence booster.

In *Some Other Substantial Reason*, we explore the illusion of causality. The chemical changes Cuddy identifies may yet be shown to be correlated to this behaviour rather than caused by it. The observations are still useful. Indeed, the placebo effect has been proven to work, even when we know we are taking a placebo. If you want something to work enough then you give yourself the best chance to make it happen.

Are you a Single Lady?

David Robson, in his BBC article, as a method of combatting stress or anxiety prior to a performance, alludes to the well-worn question, 'what would the Lone Ranger do?'[6]. In what he terms 'the Batman effect', he explains how some extremely successful and famous individuals, the kind you would not imagine having confidence problems, have assumed an alter ego in order to portray that image, at least at first. Whilst a 'single lady', in her mind, Beyonce assumed the character of 'Sasha Fierce'. This bestowed her with boldness and confidence, as she explained to Oprah Winfrey back in 2008. Indeed, she kept this strategy until 2010, when she 'felt she had matured enough to avoid the psychological crutch', or as Amy Cuddy might have put it, she faked it till she became it.

Adele, now a reasonably successful singer, learned of this and became Sasha Carter, an amalgam of Beyonce and Country music star, June Carter.

We might describe embodiment of a fictional persona as an extreme form of 'self-distancing', but it has been shown to help to rein in undesirable feelings, like anxiety. It also increases perseverance, boosts self-control and improves performance. Relabelling yourself in this way is a technique that can be deployed to make small shifts in your perspective.

'Third-party thinking' seems like an effective self-control strategy for anything requiring strong will-power (eg dieting).

Selina Furman a social psychology researcher at University of Minnesota led a study which showed that the third-party perspective made study participants more likely to choose 'the healthy option'.

Professor White, a psychology professor tested a group of six year old children on their ability to complete a boring task (an iPad distraction was thrown in for added challenge). The children were told to think about their feelings. Some in the first person, some in the third person and some as a fictitious person, like Batman. The professor found that the children were 10% more effective when thinking in the third person, and yet another 13% more so when acting in persona. He found gains in concentration and confidence, self-control and general poise.

> **Third Party Thinking**
>
> In one study of a future event, participants were either immersed or distanced, so the participants felt either it was happening to them or that they were watching events from a distance. Those who were distanced demonstrated much less anxiety. In another study, participants are asked to describe real events as if they were are a third party (he/she did this...). Viewing things from an outside perspective was demonstrably effective at anxiety reduction.

Oscar bites a carrot whilst he inhabits the character Peter Rabbit. He smiles as he digs the soil with his bare hands, creating secret tunnels in his mind. It seems to work for him, with the added benefit of improved night-time vision!

This can apply to your job role too. It seems that pretending to have the job you want is probably quite a good idea. If you want to be the boss, it is a good idea to act as you would if you were already the boss - whilst taking care to bear in mind that others will not see you as such!

It is perhaps surprising to note the extent to which some actors are prepared to go to inhabit their on-screen characters and some like Lady Gaga reportedly talking 'Italian' on and off-set for several months whilst filming the House of Gucci, almost out-doing the great Robert De Niro, who merely secured a taxi licence and drove a cab round the streets of New York in his down-time from filming 'Taxi Driver'.

To be clear, I am advocating the use of priming techniques as they are effective method of mood management and confidence building. I am not suggesting that 'faking it' is an effective long-term strategy. Evidence abounds that pretending to be someone that you are not for a sustained period is actually bad for your health. Imagine being an air steward or stewardess, or indeed any customer facing role, where we need to present a smile, when we don't feel it. It can be very tiring! When we pretend to be something that we are not, then we suffer stress, anxiety, adverse impact on our relationships and insomnia (and see part 2, Chapter 4 for evidence of the repercussions of poor sleep). The trick it seems is to make that smile real – finding ways to feel grateful for your 'lot' is a great method. If it remains fake, the strain will be too much. Kahneman's benefit will not last.

Such priming or 'reframing' techniques, where we choose to look at our situation from a more positive perspective can positively impact our confidence, which is good news, particularly

> **Keep Smiling**
>
> Daniel Kahneman's priming effect[7] has a bearing. When considering the relationship between our brain and body, we shouldn't underestimate the value of a smile. If you bite a pencil, holding it horizontally in your teeth to force a smile, after a while you cannot help but feel happier, as your body has told your brain that you are smiling, so it deduces that there must be good reason. It wrks with carrots too!

> **But inauthenticity hurts**
>
> 30 years research by Ute R.Hulsheger and Anna Schewe on US bus drivers showed those who faked their daily happiness suffered all these emotional downsides.

> **Imposter syndrome** is suffered by 75% of us at some point in our lives.
>
> Take comfort knowing that your confidence is often inversely proportional to your competence.

for those who may otherwise suffer insecurity, which is indeed most of us…

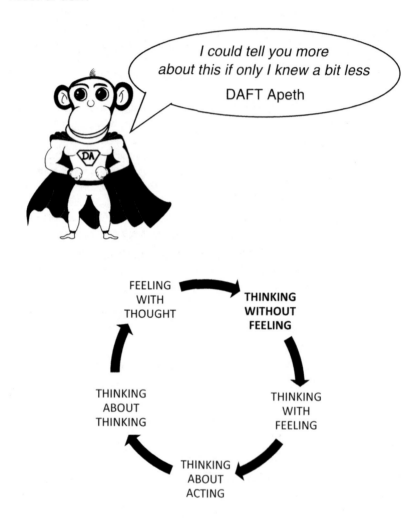

Thinking about Thinking

There are those times when we are prepared to stake everything on our superior knowledge of a fact, or circumstance. And yet we are wrong!

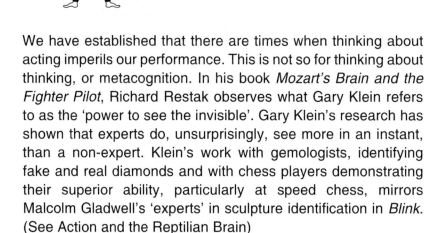

It's not the things you don't know that will get you into trouble but the things you know for sure, but just 'aint so.

Mark Twain

We have established that there are times when thinking about acting imperils our performance. This is not so for thinking about thinking, or metacognition. In his book *Mozart's Brain and the Fighter Pilot*, Richard Restak observes what Gary Klein refers to as the 'power to see the invisible'. Gary Klein's research has shown that experts do, unsurprisingly, see more in an instant, than a non-expert. Klein's work with gemologists, identifying fake and real diamonds and with chess players demonstrating their superior ability, particularly at speed chess, mirrors Malcolm Gladwell's 'experts' in sculpture identification in *Blink*. (See Action and the Reptilian Brain)

Klein provides techniques for improving metacognition and thinking like an expert, becoming acquainted with your memory and its limitations, getting the big picture, self-critiquing your own performance, and effectively selecting the best strategy. It is perhaps noticeable that he focuses on memory, as the starting point of self-awareness. The ability to see our limitations becomes surprisingly harder the more we know, which is why David Robson and others argue that it is essential that we maintain intellectual humility. We know that a downside of superior knowledge, or expertise is a tendency to overstate our knowledge, and overestimate our ability in our specialist field.

Remember the Reticular Activation System (RAS), that magical nano-sausage, filtering the information sent to our neocortex, shaping what we think about? When Leo Tolstoy purportedly challenged his brother to go to the corner of the room and stay there until he could stop thinking of a white bear, he was unwittingly exploiting this device.

Our inability to process a negative is the very reason it is more effective to yell to your infant 'WALK' rather than 'DON'T RUN' when you don't want them to crack their head open at the poolside, or should I say, when you want them to stay uninjured throughout their childhood!

> **The white bear principle**
>
> This psychological phenomenon suggests that whilst our brains can think about thinking, there is no mechanism for 'not thinking a thought'. Indeed, to do so invokes that thought; in that same way you can never win 'the game', you will not knock off the pope's hat or the Monarch's crown.

You lose by thinking about 'the game'. If you have ever played, you just lost, sorry! The best you can do is think about something else. As Professor Wegner, psychologist and author of *White Bears and Other Unwanted Thoughts* says, we have to embrace them and 'escape the tyranny that suppression can hold over us.' In other words, if we don't like our thoughts, we think of something else whilst we smother them with a pillow.

Of course, some of us suffer severely from ruminative thoughts, which can be debilitating, cause or exacerbate insomnia and contribute to many serious medical conditions, thoughts which cannot be smothered lightly or without specialist medical assistance.

Beyond thinking about ourselves though, our ability to reflect on the intentions and feelings of others also involves thinking about thinking. We use our memory, and particularly emotional memory to appraise others. Whilst we do seem to have evolved to look after ourselves and focus on our own best interests above all else, our neocortex, particularly the right marginal gyrus, appears to have developed a place for correcting some of the biases we experience as a result of the self-centred, self-protecting, self-loving DNA.

Thinking is hard work, all those micro-factories steaming away. We don't do it lightly, which is why when trying to learn new skills, it's recommended to take regular breaks and do it in short bursts, when energy levels are high. Practising piano ten minutes a night for a week is more effective than once a week for 70 minutes[8], as we run out of steam rapidly when taxing ourselves and the brain is particularly adept at avoiding such strain. Anyone who has ever studied for anything will know how compelling the trivial becomes when the alternative involves hard thought. Thinking about thinking is harder still.

And yet, I say to Don Marquis who headed up this section on Thinking, 'If you make someone think they are thinking, they will love you. If you make someone actually think they will hate you... *But afterwards, they will thank you...and then love you even more!'*

When Phineas Gage was impaled with an iron tamping rod through the head back in 1848, dramatically changing his personality as a lump of brain was excised, he provided science with a perfect 'before and after' case study. The mild mannered, kind man became bitter, angry and generally unpleasant and the change provided a useful way to understand how our hardware and associated software performs under normal circumstances. In a rather less extreme version, we can explore what happens when our thinking is wrong or flawed in the normal course of life. And indeed, it is because we show so many cognitive failings, that I have compiled *Some Other Substantial Reason* as an accompaniment to this book. Our biases as we'll see contribute substantially to this...

REFLECTION TIME

Action		
Mens Rea	Actus Rhesus	Guilty? ☑
1. Thinking is hard	How do you want to use this most precious resource? Use the space below to note your intial thoughts...	☐
2. Thinking creates your reality	What thoughts hijack your dreams? Can you practise changing those thoughts? Use the space below...	☐
When thinking about thinking, it helps to understand your biases...		

THE DAFT CYCLE – ALL TOGETHER

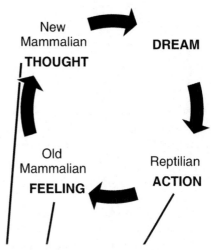

New Mammalian **THOUGHT**

DREAM

Old Mammalian **FEELING**

Reptilian **ACTION**

DREAMS define us, provided our Actions, Feelings and Thoughts toe the line. In this section, we look at our dreams and desires and the precious role of dopamine.

ACTIONS are nestled in the Reptilian Brain. The unbridled brain will 'Just Do It' with a swoosh of instinct.

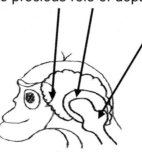

FEELINGS emanate from our 'Old Mammalian Brain' – the add-in, from which we can start wanting things, from which we are perhaps no longer simply coils of DNA.

THOUGHT - a comparatively new enhancement and still fairly flawed. The New Mammalian Brain, (AKA neo-cortex or cerebrum), represents the core of our 'executive function'.

We are the survivors, but we are still just animals

5.1 Attention seeking: Our attention is limited, our desire for other's attention not so much...

5.2 Pattern-finding: Our survival instincts mean we find simple patterns to reduce complexity.

5.3 Erroneous reasoning: Brain work drains our energy banks - shortcuts helps us survive.

5.4 Temperamental: We are unique, yet our moods fall into patterns that we can manage.

5.5 Hypersensitive: We deeply fear threats to our survival - and exaggerate our responses.

5.6 Simians: Thousands of years of evolution do not rid us of our animal ancestry.

Chapter 5:
Biased Beyond Belief

We are DAFT, we are also APETHS.

APETHS are Attention seeking, Pattern finding, Erroneous reasoning, Temperamental, Hypersensitive Simians. APETHS are biased, biased in so many ways that it is hard to believe. Our beliefs, shaped by our environment make it so...

5.1 Attention-seeking

Our brain can process 11 million bits of information a second. The conscious mind can handle 40-50, which is why the filtration by the RAS is so important. Our attention window is variable but small, like looking through a keyhole, we can focus consciously on... not very much. We all know that we have a limited attention resource; we would like to have more. We also seek attention from others. Many of us want more of that too.

When we were babies, we were in a high state of alertness, whilst we were awake. As Friederike Fabritius describes it, babies are always switched 'ON' for learning, due to naturally higher levels of the Neurotransmitter, Acetylcholine[1]. As adults we need to switch it 'ON' for conscious learning, like learning a language or the piano, which require focused effort. The extent of our conscious attention is an area of on-going, substantial, costly research at the likes of Google and NASA; pilot attention to information projected in the cockpit in a Heads-Up Display can be a matter of life and death with overload (in a simulator) shown to lead to incidents of one plane landing on top of another.

The change blindness in the door study* is a result of our attention limits, which is amply demonstrated by another infamous experiment involving a basketball game and a big hairy ape. You have probably seen the 'missing gorilla experiment', which starkly demonstrates the same.

In 1999, Christopher Chabris and the same Daniel Simons show a basketball game and ask participants to count scores by one team. If you haven't seen the video, it is available on all good short video streaming services (youtube)[2]. Warning, Plot Spoiler if your read on.

> ***The Door Study**
>
> In a famous study back in 1998, Simons and Levin conducted research by stopping people at random in the street, pretending to be lost and asking them for help with directions and handing them a map. A person carrying a door strategically steps between them enabling the 'lost' person to switch with another person. The change of 'lost' person wasn't noticed in 50% of cases.

Half the students didn't see the gorilla, did you? The same test has since been replicated multiple times with similar results.

The ones who did the best counting were focused in their attention, focused on the task in hand. But they did not spot the big dark, hairy gorilla who invaded the court and paraded for several seconds before discreetly making his exit. It seems some focus better and are probably hated by their wives as they 'just don't listen', whilst others spread their attention better and their husbands love them for it!

Our focused attention though, is required to reach peak performance, even though we cannot hope to sustain that level. The superstars amongst us reach plateaus which edge nearer and nearer to their peak as they gain competence and self-awareness. They also know how to step up from excellent to amazing when the need arises; on those crucial break points where it is more important than ever to be able to maximise focus and hit the sweet spot of form. The superstar has gained unconscious competence, and all conscious attention needs to be channelled wisely, as focus on the process can cause it to breakdown. Players often 'choke'; a tennis star double faults because they are thinking about the snap of the wrist or the trophy that's theirs for the taking, a golfer gets the yips and blunders that six-inch gimme' putt for the title. In these cases, they would be better served by trusting what they have learned to do unconsciously.

Incongruence test

The well-known Stroop colour-word test shows that our cognitive process falters when we are asked to state a colour which is written alongside a different colour (eg; the word 'green' is written in red). This reveals our inner workings in a way we cannot hide (our brain has to work harder to inhibit extraneous information).

It is less well known that the same applies to our gender bias: Harvard University Professor, Francesca Gino, describes research showing that Harvard students quickly link words related to work and office life to men and home-related words to women, but they show a marked delay when it is the women to whom the work-related words should apply and the men to whom the home related words are most appropriate.

What is more, ironically this particular bias doesn't appear to show a gender bias. Students all appear to show this tendency![3]

What is even more, ten minutes moderate intensity running has been shown to improve speed of processing with increased blood flow to the pre-frontal cortex, as well as a mood enhancement effect[3] (see Part 2, Ch2 – Exercise). At least the benefit of exercise isn't gender-biased!

A less experienced player chastises themselves to focus, screaming 'come on, focus' too often and puts themselves under too much pressure to be alert, without the self-awareness to know when to peak.

Our pre-frontal cortex boosts or attenuates the signals telling us where to place our attention, providing the right mix of neurotransmitters to support the task, which is why it is important to ensure this environment is optimised.

In some fields, like say, neurosurgery, deep focus is at least desirable. In more creative fields, we are most effective when our networks are open to lots of stimuli which spark our connections, so it is ok to be a bit more 'dreamy'. Either way, our attention capacity is limited and most of our thinking still goes on beneath the surface, beneath our superficial attention. As a result, most of our thinking errors, or biases are unconscious.

> **Allostatic Load**
>
> At the extreme, constant alert pushes us towards 'allostatic load'; physiological and neurological overload, a most undesirable state.
>
> Evidence suggests though that rather than intensely focused, most of us get distracted quite easily. One study suggests as much as 50% of the time. If you thought it was just you, take comfort, you are quite normal (in this respect at least!).

Our brains deceive us in many ways. Once we are aware, we can make choices that either free us of our biases or tie us to them. We saw the gun control bias above. We may or may not be aware of this or our other biases, and, even if we are, we may not realize their impact on our judgement. We can get some idea by use of an Implicit Association test (IAT).

There are numerous types of IAT's, each designed to expose different biases, for example, are you Ageist? Sexist? Prone to fat shaming? Simplistically, the tests require you to sort pictures and words and in doing so they show how you associate things and therefore, by implication, your biases. Neuroscientist Calvin Lai, at Washington University St Louis, is on the executive committee of Project Implicit which used, as an example, data from 630,000 people around the world using an IAT to associate gender with science-related abilities. Two out of every three people associated males more strongly with science roles, and the same for females with humanities, which is why many of us even now still stop to think when presented with those lateral thinking puzzles like 'the pilot in a dress'[3]. These tests can tell us about our own prejudices and, in aggregation, they reveal the shape of the unconscious bias within a society.

Eva Telzer, at University of Illinois FMRI scanned children and adolescents. She discovered that the difference in the amygdala response to different faces was not innate but developed over time, a finding which shows that these biases are learned. This is great news, as that which is learned, with effort, can be un-learned. We can un-learn, giving us the space to learn afresh, to learn better.

So, we surely want to optimise our own attention - what about the more traditional attention seeking; the desire for attention from others?

Of course, this occupies the minds of many parents with rising numbers of children (and some adults) being diagnosed with the disorders ADHD, HPD etc…Excessive or 'maladaptive' attention seeking may of course be a core component of a mental health diagnosis. In the majority though, we seek attention of others as a reflection of a simple desire to be cared for, to be loved.

5.2 Pattern Finding

As a debunker of what he terms 'Bad Science', Ben Goldacre decries the lazy reporting and careless use of statistics which mislead us, the public, and undermine good science. He points to the Rules of Thumb or heuristics, made famous by Kahneman and Tversky, and aligns these brain devices with the human need to find patterns. Sometimes the patterns are patterns out of nothing, rather like the images the clouds waft in and out of existence. Clever people can spot 'patterns' in random data as was ably demonstrated (and characterised in the film 'A brilliant Mind'), by John Nash, who kept finding 'patterns' to justify his paranoid delusions.

A great many people think they are thinking, when they are merely rearranging their prejudices.

William James

The classic inkblot analysis psychological test, devised by Hermann Rohrschach uses interpretations of inkblots, to provide a general approach to perception. It is based on our multiple senses and how they merge to make interpretations. Although misused after Rorschach's death, the data from such tests shows patterns of responses which do however provide a reliable diagnostic tool to define personality types.

Note on Rules of Thumb

The use of something convenient to measure something less so…

I know that the distance from the tip of my thumb to the tip of my pinkie is 9 inches, so four hands equal three feet. (Unless I'm lunching in Subway, where feet are shorter*).

The expression has dubious origin. Many commentators suggest that Sir Francis Buller, 18th Century judge, defined it as the limit to the thickness of a stick with which it is acceptable for a husband to beat his wife*.

*No evidence exists that this statement is true.

Our heuristics, which some call 'quick and dirty', are described by evolutionary psychologists as fast and frugal. Gerd Gigerenzer, a cognitive scientist with the ABC group (Adaptive Behaviour and Cognition) says that our adaptations are rational. We have an 'ecological rationality'. In other words, we are wired for optimising probabilistic behaviours[4]. These are, of course, dependent on getting the right inputs. And Taleb highlights many such problems that we face when attempting to make probabilistic assessments. We are vulnerable to the affect heuristic, which means emotions determine the probability in our minds, and so, we often simply get it wrong.

Black and White Swans*

Black swans may be rare but they do exist. Rare events happen all the time. Nicholas Taleb uses the 'black swan effect' to make his living; exploiting the fact that at the extreme we cannot act rationally due to our brain flaws. Even if we have never seen a black swan and we have only ever seen a million white swans, it is wrong to assume that all swans are white. We err by attaching too small a probability that the next swan to waddle past will be black.

Rare events are always 'undervalued'.

*Black and white swans on the other hand do not exist, as far as we know – perhaps what you saw was a badger taking a bath?!

Many of us state that the fact that such a thing has never happened before means it cannot happen. But then it does. And because we do not cope well with our own errors and it is human nature to justify them, we explain away our rare events (like severe stock market crashes) as bad luck, with the so-called 10 Sigma event, (being 10 standard deviations away from the mean and so unlikely as to be 'impossible') created to protect our self-esteem.

We are not programmed to like losses - we'd prefer to lose £10m once than to lose £1m ten times. Indeed, if we lose £1m nine times, and then win £10m once it still feels bad![5]

On a very hot day, I find it hard to believe that I will need to wear socks again tomorrow. It is easy to allow yourself to believe that this pleasant weather is now the norm. It will always be warm, even in England! It is particularly easy to allow yourself to believe that an event can't happen if we have never experienced it before. Unlike Oscar who regularly says that he did something next week and will be able to do that when he is younger again, our adult brain doesn't cope well with non-linearities. We assume things will flow smoothly, which they may do most of the time. And because they often do, it is harder to believe that there will be other times when they don't.

One reason that rare events are undervalued is because they haven't happened yet. When the structural engineer came to assess the decaying Methodist chapel I bought for my home conversion project, they said 'it hasn't fallen over in 150 years', and somehow I was supposed to and (probably actually was) assured that this meant it would continue to not fall down in the future.

So, the corollary of our pattern finding expertise is our similar ability to ignore things which are real but do not fit our hunger for patterns.

As another related effect, we are simply not instinctively brilliant at doing the maths. Who wasn't surprised the first time they heard the so-called Birthday paradox?

We are still surprised to find two people with the same Birthday in a group, even when we now know that in a room of 24 people there is greater than 50% chance that this will occur.

Keep a stiff upper lip

Even the odds of the same person being struck by lightning or winning the lottery twice are not as short as you might think, as long as you don't name the person in advance!

Taleb calculates that the odds quoted of 17 trillion to 1 for the New Jersey lottery second time jackpot, is a rather less unlikely 30:1 with that proviso.[6]

And if we are struck? Taleb recommends stoicism; stress your own personal elegance at your misfortune, learn to exhibit 'sapere vivere' (know how to live) at all times.

Worthy advice indeed, and easy for him to say!

5.3 Erroneous Reasoning

We all get things wrong. We are all guilty of erroneous reasoning. Being clever doesn't exempt you from this. In fact, as Julian Baggini puts it, 'Beware of complacent superiority'. This ultimate fallacy - what he calls the 'fallacy fallacy'[7] is a warning to people who are aware of other misgivings, that they need to take the mote from their own eye first.

Experts list our fallacies (see *Some Other Substantial Reason*) and then attribute them, mainly to others.

Dunning and Kruger demonstrated that people tend to over-rate their abilities, and they do so in proportion to their self-confidence*. Bertrand Russell, in his essay 'the triumph of stupidity', way back in 1933 said that the 'fundamental cause of the trouble is that, in the modern world, the stupid are cocksure while the intelligent are full of doubt'. This long-held view had now gained scientific backing.

Now, in their specific field of study, the educated claim to know more than they do, and that is because they think they do - they confuse their current level of knowledge with their peak level of knowledge. I knew it then (when I was deeply embroiled in study on the topic) so I must still know it now.

> ***'But I wore the juice'**
>
> David Dunning and Justin Kruger at New York University were reportedly inspired by bank robbers who were caught on CCTV making this statement. One bungling robber was mystified that he had been tracked down as the lemon juice (which we all know as a constituent of 'invisible ink') that he had rubbed onto his face was supposed to make him imperceptible on camera! Really!

Shane Snow, Influencer, and author of *Dream Teams*, reviewed the case of the Dulles Brothers: In the 1950's, the US Secretary of state and his brother (The Dulles brothers) and a CIA director formulated a plot to overthrow the Guatemalan government, due to a strong belief that they were in cahoots with the Russians and planned to turn central America into a 'beachhead' for Western Communism. There was plenty of evidence that this was not the case but this was disregarded due to the strength of their conviction. The Dulles Brothers plot was successful and the US placed a president of their choosing. Meanwhile they raided the ex-presidents house looking for evidence (like the WMD of Saddam Hussein). None was found but they were so convinced that they were right that they rationalised planting some. We hear about this all the time in criminal cases where police have similar strength of conviction that it clouds their judgment. As Snow says, myriad smart business leaders have launched company initiatives and, in the face of clear evidence that their strategy was failing, have refused to try something else.

A classic example is the Flat Earthers, all around the world, who remain so convinced that they are right that they find imaginative and creative ways to justify all the evidence to the contrary, (see

2018 documentary 'Behind The Curve'). Another is the 'End of the world'ers'. When the time has been and gone, you might think they would put their hands up and say 'fair cop', but do they? Look at the Mayan calendar; followers predicted end of the world on 21 Dec 2012. It is not hard to find retrospective adjustments to the flawed calculations which previously ignored the impact of a peculiar feature of the Mayan calendar, the 'long count', which with some fancy mental gymnastics makes the actual end of the world date more like 2087, which of course we will have to leave to future generations to explain (away).

World end: Rain serpent (representing 34,000 year 'world periods'), the Tiger Claw goddess (the 'malevolent patroness of floods and cloudbursts'), and the Black God with screeching owl (the 'final all-engulfing cataclysm' – illustration from the back page of the Dresden Codex.

Contrary to most opinions, the Flat Earthers too are often can generally well-educated, nice people, engineers and businessmen and the like, who genuinely want to find the truth. Yes, like all of us, they have a desire for truth, but when we think we know the truth, all our judgements are coloured by that presumption.

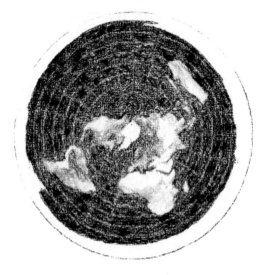

An ice wall surrounds our disk-shaped Earth.

The FBI proved beyond doubt that Mr Mayfield was guilty of the 2004 Madrid train bombings, based on the reliability of fingerprint experts. Despite much evidence to the contrary, including that he had not been to Madrid, (and a determined effort to prove his guilt included misinterpreting his daughter's Spanish homework), it was based on a faulty reading of a fingerprint by an expert, which was then reinforced by another expert, in what Itiel Dror terms the 'bias cascade' with one expert knowing the previous one and therefore unconsciously relying on his knowledge of the prior expert's capability.

The FBI were so sure, the experts were so confident of his guilt, that he could have been on death row based on one error of judgement, compounded by many others who willingly supported that position. Thankfully, the Spanish National Police independently apprehended the actual guilty party.

As Mayfield put it, in court each piece of evidence is like a brick in a wall – the problem is they treat the fingerprint analysis as if it is the whole wall – but it is not even a strong brick, let alone a wall. The finger-print expert, like all experts, suffer from 'earned dogmatism'. This is why we don't see our limitations and we are prone to over-reach our abilities. Our entrenched, automatic behaviours can mean we are oblivious to warning signs of disaster.

This doubling down on our beliefs, known as the Backfire effect can mean that presenting evidence against beliefs leads people, like in the psychopath Catch 22 test, to double down on their convictions, for two key reasons. We don't like to be proved wrong, or even worse, stupid! Secondly, we benefit from our version of reality and motivated reasoning is a powerful driver.

And what is more, the smarter you are, the more you are able to justify a false premise, and therefore paradoxically you are, in fact more likely to believe something that is not correct (where the error suits you!). Of course, with awareness of this fact, and a superior intellect, you can take steps to obviate your own natural genius for self-delusion! David Robson, in *The Intelligence Trap*, describes how intelligent, educated people are less likely to listen or learn from their mistakes and they have a bigger bias blind spot, so they are less able to recognise holes in their logic[8].

In the case of the Dulles brothers, both political and financial motives and the authorised proliferation of fake news allowed them to justify an erroneous position and it has taken a lifetime for historians to unravel the truth.

In the biography of Steve Jobs, his biographer Walter Isaacson refers to Jobs' famous 'reality distortion field', which is impressively described by his colleague Andy Hertzfeld as 'a confounding melange of charismatic rhetorical style, indomitable will, and eagerness to bend any fact to fit the purpose at hand'. It is plain that this tendency, at least the latter third, whilst extremely well developed in this case and even better publicised due to the man's personal profile, is not the preserve of Steve Jobs.

The mistaken use of logic may easily be used to dismiss an argument, rather than a flaw in the argument itself. As Baggini says, looking for bad reasoning from others means you may fall foul of it yourself. We should all check for sloppiness in our own reasoning and be careful not to use rhetorical devices, making up stories, which allow us to delude ourselves and others into believing that our arguments are more persuasive than they have right to be. Easy to say of course, and harder to achieve in an animal that loves to be right. Are you determined to be open-minded? Do you encourage rigorous questioning of your logic at all times? You might then expose those reasoning flaws. You are a rare beast indeed.

Evolutionary psychologists say that we needed brain power to keep track of others feelings, to know who we can trust, who will take advantage and who we need to keep sweet. And once language evolved, we needed our eloquence in order to gain support within our tribe or group and to bring others to our way of thinking. More often than not, our arguments don't actually need to be logical, they just need to be persuasive[9]. This may explain why irrationality and intelligence go hand in hand.

> *Our brains are made for fitness not for truth*
> Steven Pinker

5.4 Temperamental

We know our emotions are brought to bear on our actions, as stated earlier, psychologists describe the extent that this is so as the Emotional valence.

You will recall that Kahneman described his two mental systems, the level 1 or primary system being the 'fast and frugal' or 'quick and dirty'. This is the 'fast' of his book *Thinking Fast and Slow* and reflects the emotional and rapid responses of our more primitive brain segments. This is where most of our brain work takes place to ensure our very survival. The level 2, the 'slow' is the basis of our rather more rational, thought-based decisions. For this we utilise predominantly our neocortex.

Operating at Level 1, which aligns with Dr Steve Roberts' Chimp or Ray Dalio's 'lower Level you', we can perhaps be forgiven for elements of rashness, whereas operating at Level 2, Roberts' 'human' or Dalio's 'higher level you', should know better. Perhaps the most interesting finding of the extensive research is not that level 1 makes errors of judgment, but that level 2 is far from perfect either.

'In the end, we are our choices', says Jeff Bezos, summing up an inspirational graduation speech at Princeton University[10]. If we accept that we are the sum of our choices, our decisions, it seems a good idea that we put some effort into making good ones, especially the big ones, doesn't it?

But, do we do that?

If you believe Daniel Kahneman, which seems sensible given the durability, quantity and quality of his research, the answer is probably an unqualified 'No'. The Nobel Prize winning economist elaborates at great length, based largely on his work with Amos Tversky, revealing some pretty damning evidence, a suite of fallacies and illusions that we employ every day. The good news is that we get by pretty well despite some of the irrational decisions we are prone to make, and the better news is that with awareness we can improve our chances of making optimal choices more of the time.

Jeremy Kagan, the developmental psychologist we met earlier states that we have a 'base threshold for amygdala arousal'. His scoring system reflects our ease of being frightened, our sociability and our curiosity. And we all sit naturally somewhere on a spectrum with 20% of us timid, 40% mid-range and 40% bold.

Nevertheless, we still have some ability to manage the impact our emotions play on our decisions. Robert Thayer, a psychologist at California State University describes four basic moods; calm-energy, calm-tiredness, tense-energy and tense-tiredness and we will see that choosing the timing of our decisions based on an understanding of these moods helps to counter our instinctive level 1 reactions (see Meaning and Well-Being - stress reduction).

As some form of compensation, ageing brings with it a degree of wisdom, a particular kind of wisdom that relates to experience. We have seen it all before, so the intensity of our reactions is tempered by our experience of the impact of whatever circumstances. We learn what to worry about because of the ever-increasing points of feedback. In the field of decision making though we depend on the quality of our feedback – do we even know if we have made good judgments in the past? Have we any way of knowing?

As sponsor of a significant business system implementation, I became aware of the reason so few (if any) such implementation projects deliver to their promise. Invariably unforeseen issues arise, like when digging a car park in a City Centre, so, after removing the bones of Richard III, the timescales and budget are so deformed that compromise is required; when the system meets a basic functional specification, the most expensive, and probably the best consultants are lured to start new projects. These consultants do not see the problems they have left in their wake and with the best of intentions they proceed to make them again in their next assignment. The vital feedback loop is conspicuously absent, as it is with many of our personal judgements.

5.5 Hypersensitive

The greatest enemy of knowledge is not ignorance, it is the illusion of knowledge
Dr Stephen Hawking

The illusion of knowledge is what Mark Twain called 'what we think we know but just 'aint so'. We are all guilty; guilty of the illusion that we are right. And for this reason, we don't like it when others disagree.

We don't like being judged. Sometimes with good reason:

We learned earlier that Cato as Censor banished Carneades from Rome when his arguments persuaded his audience to believe one thing one day and the opposite the next. Judgements are difficult...Judgments made in a court of law, by full time professionals, those we might consider the best at making rational decisions are no less prone to error than us amateurs. Judges are demonstrably more lenient when they are not tired, or hungry, and the size of awards is determined as much by an emotional story and surrounding events as by a clinical, rational assessment of the relative facts*.

---

*Rough Justice

Kahneman's detailed study of parole judgments in the Israeli courts found that judges spent around 6 minutes judging each parole application, and approved around 35% of applicants, released more willingly just after eating, in fact at a rate of about 65% dropping to nearly zero over a two-hour session. So, an applicant seen just before meal time, has virtually no chance of parole, as the parole judge's leniency is impaired by his fatigue or hunger or an unknown combination of the two.

He set up mock juries in Texas, US and found that a child suffering burns would be awarded a dramatically higher award if the case is considered alongside the case of an unscrupulous bank causing a substantial loss for another bank.

He witnessed German judges with average of 15 years experience, no less, determine sentence in months, heavily influenced by the roll of a pair of dice – 9 dots led to the woman's sentence being determined as 8 months incarceration, whereas when the dice showed just 3 dots, the same woman was sentenced to 5 months. That's 3 months in prison on the roll of a dice!

Whoever said life was fair!

Daniel Kahneman, Olivier Sibony and Cass R. Sunstein elaborate in great detail in their book, Noise, with myriad examples of extreme unfairness caused merely by random variability by expert 'judges', which may be even more hard to accept than outrageous bias or straight forward malice!

Indeed, regarding comparative penalties for different crimes set by different agencies, when put alongside each other, you might think them absurd, for example; serious violation of worker safety fine was capped at $7,000, yet violation of the Wild Bird conservation Act could elicit a fine potentially as high as $25,000. It is also known that when fines are capped, the final award tends to be closer to the cap than when they are not capped; so, a low cap is great for the defendant, a high cap virtually guarantees a higher penalty.

Indeed, even within the same agency it is sometimes difficult to comprehend the logic of the available penalties; in the UK Criminal Justice System, the penalty for defacing a statue can be ten-year imprisonment, whereas for rape the penalty may be as little as five.

Given the challenge of providing adequate evidence, the impression you give in court can be paramount. And perhaps it's also not surprising that, whilst it is true that ignorance is no defence, confident people do 'get away with more' as they simply appear to be less guilty. A study by Penrod and Cutler in the 1990's confirmed the Dunning Kruger assertions, with their research showing that juries believe the testimonies of confident and assured witnesses more than nervous and hesitant ones who seem unsure of their claim[11]. Wouldn't you? In fact, I learned from my own experience in an Employment Tribunal that some other people are better at telling lies than I am at telling the truth. Or, to put it more in context, the shameful cowardly c-suite forced their spineless subordinates to present a deceitful corporate spin under threat to their careers. Such defensively confident, coordinated lies then defeated my nervous truths.

Beyond the courts, similarly questionable judgments impinge on the integrity of every field, with financial forecasters, medical experts and flying instructors certainly not excluded. Kahneman, with others, leads us through a vast suite of human errors and areas in which poor judgment is possible, even likely[12].

Due to our hypersensitivity, we tend to react and over-react. We will do most anything including foregoing the positive to avoid suffering the negative (see Prospect Theory). I detail many of these in *Some Other Substantial Reason*. As well as highlighting some of our serious prejudices, which account for much of the injustice in our world, our reactions remain surprising, in some cases amusingly so.

We can suffer from a transparency illusion – we think our emotions are transparent but the other party cannot read all the clues as well as we think. Worse of course is an electronic correspondence where we are vulnerable to typo's or productive testes, and is in any case, entirely deprived of the benefit of emotional clues…

Ben: Did you complete that report?

Adam: I'll do it soon, after looking at the other BS you sent me.

Ben: It's not BS. I just haven't sugar-coated it. If you don't want to work here, you know what to do…

Adam: When I said BS, I meant Balance Sheet! But if you don't' want me here, I'll update my CV!

Now Adam is suddenly one step closer to the door…to be sensitive is to preserve our ego; it is how we   survived on the Savannah, it is how we survive now…well, that's the theory.

Yet we get it wrong all the time. None of our senses is as safe as we might think. There are infinite ways to discombobulate a human being. Consider just a few minor distortions of our senses, of what we see, hear, feel, taste and smell….

The Power of Five

SEE

We all know about the young lady and crone, the rabbit and the duck, Ruben's vase – or is it two faces? Our brains seem to be programmed to see one or the other but we really struggle to see both simultaneously. We don't want to seem two-faced so we tend to stick with either or rather than managing the integrative complexity associated with seeing **both** – the same issue we have when judging other people (or indeed ourselves).

It's all Black and White to me.

Not only do we perceive things wrongly sometimes but we also perceive the same thing in different ways. Perhaps you recall that White and gold dress... or was it blue and black?

HEAR

If a sound (let's call it Hoo.) is made from one side of a room and rapidly followed by another sound from the other side (call it Rah), due to the so-called precedence effect, you will hear both as if one longer sound (Hoorah) and locate it at the source of sound Hoo. You have to turn sound Rah up to volume 11 (actually just 15dB more than sound Hoo) to jolt your senses and remove this effect.

At blind 'violin playing', even violin impresarios cannot distinguish a $10,000 21st century violin from a $10m Stradivarius. Tested a number of times (hidden behind welders' goggles), results show random selection, much to the chagrin of the players themselves and the finest violin makers of today.

FEEL

Put a weight in a matchbox and feel the weight in your hands. Add two empty matchboxes and feel the weight reduce. Isabel Won at Johns Hopkins University, Maryland tested this with 30 students and 90% confirmed this coup de main. Where we have two objects of identical weight, we perceive the smaller one to be heavier - when we expect it to be lighter, the brain seems to over-compensate.

By the way, the mechanical processes of touch and hearing are closely correlated; weakness in hearing is often accompanied by reduced sense of touch. The violinists in the 'blind tests' have extremely sensitive hearing and sense of touch for their beloved instrument, yet, with the smell masked by perfume*, they rely on branding to make the distinction.

TASTE

Like the violinists above, it turns out even professional wine tasters can't tell red wine from white wine with red dye in it, they don't agree on what is good and they can't tell cheap from expensive. Also, we often mistake odour for taste, which is perhaps why we won't eat our packed-lunch at the local sewage plant!

SMELL

Note that smell is the surest means of enhancing an emotional memory – hence the bread baking in supermarkets or the effect of Proust's madeleines. If you have the time to re-live his (very long) life story, these little cakes provided this 'Swann's way' of capturing past memories. This may be because the Olfactory bulb links directly to the limbic system, whereas all the other senses have intermediary connections.

Of course, our sense of reality (what we believe), and that elusive quality, common sense (what everyone should know but most people don't) seem to be even less reliable. When we do come to our senses however, we can start our journey of discovery – we begin to get to know our broomstick and our bristles...

5.6 Simians

Yes, we are all Attention-seeking, Pattern-spotting, Erroneous-reasoning, Temperamental, Hypersensitive, Simians.

The Chabris and Simons gorilla experiment mentioned earlier is notable not only for the fact that half the participants didn't spot the gorilla, but that almost all participants were shocked to learn this – their incredulity is our incredulity – not only are we DAFT APETH, but most of us simply refuse to believe it.

In life, we usually don't see the gorilla, **because that gorilla is US!**

Ray Davies, of the Kinks was partially right in his 1970 classic '*I am an Apeman*', noting that 'the only time he felt at ease was swinging up and down in a coconut tree'. Your risk of being killed by a coconut is much reduced when you choose to live amongst them!

Charles Darwin spent quite a long time studying Men and Animals. He spent quite a long time studying Earthworms too but that is for a different section. In his *Expressions of the Emotions in Man and Animals*, he studies our responses in great detail. He reveals how we give ourselves away, how we show our true colours. He also observes some of the imperfections in our brains, some system flaws which confuse our senses. Try the 'Aristotle illusion':-

Simians, Primates, Anthropoids, Monkeys (SPAM).

That is us. There is a reason that humans are part of the superfamily Hominoidea. Sometimes we don't know what we don't know, sometimes we don't know what we do. Sometimes we have no idea.

A somewhat irrelevant note on SPAM

Spiced Ham was made popular during WWII due to its shelf life and low cost, and purloined for the same reason for general digital use, especially unsolicited electronic messages, thanks to Monty Pythspamspamspam pamspamspamspamspamspamspam spam...

Cross your first and second fingers and touch a marble. Do not look.

Are you struggling to convince yourself there are not two marbles? Have a look or uncross your fingers - there is clearly only one. So, the arrangement of fingers helps send the correct signal to the brain. Muddle your signals, muddle your brain, sometimes in unexpected ways.

With fingers crossed, we can feel two marbles where there is only one. We know that we are Daft as a Brush, but with fingers crossed we can hope to be twice as useful, we can hope to change, we can hope to exhibit more common sense. But that will be an illusion. It is only with concerted effort that we can make it so. As we will see, it is not crossed fingers, but a positive attitude, a sense of humility and a sense of humour that will send us on our way.

Hitler's cryptorchidism

The school playground song has in fact been endorsed by German Medical records from 1923, which show nothing on his right side – perhaps Hitler was as deluded in this area as he was in most others – perhaps he was over-compensating?!

In my accompanying book, *Some Other Substantial Reason* I set out my favourite 35 cognitive failures. These are our built-in biases, energy saving shortcuts, inconsistent and irrational applications of logic and any other flawed reasoning, to which we are all eminently susceptible no matter how smart we like to think we are. You can see numerous examples of those things that we like to think are true, but just 'aint so. You can see numerous examples of how we are unduly influenced by emotional factors, and witness how poor our judgments can be, based on environmental factors, often factors that are beyond our control or awareness.

I'm sure you'll find that light-hearted but deadly serious book to be of great benefit. Every ounce of awareness of the myriad ways our thinking can be compromised by our daftness, is worth a pound of progress towards being the best Daft Apeth we can be.

Improvement Actions- How to make better use of your broom?

> *There is no expedient to which a man will not resort to avoid the real labour of thinking*
>
> Sir Joshua Reynolds, 18th century painter in the 'Grand Style'.

As DAFT APETHs, we all need to check our thinking if we want to make better decisions, to become more useful, to be better leaders of others, to live our lives in our own grand style.

On top of all our unconscious biases, I routinely turn the wrong way on the road when not going to a usual destination, try to go through doors before I have opened them, or turn on the light as I leave a dim room.

It turns out that the light wasn't the dimmest thing in the room. Donald Broadbent describes such lapses as cognitive failures. These cognitive failures only compound our myriad errors of reasoning. Indeed, many of these failings are the classic traits of the absent minded; the stereotypical behaviour of the professor who is so engrossed in his subject that he completely misses the conversation he has just had with his wife. And for which she will no doubt remind him, endlessly, later!

1. Decide for yourself where your broom lies.

We know that intelligent people are at least as susceptible as the rest of us to bias. It is also true that when they become aware of this, their superior intelligence can result in better decisions as they have a greater capacity for thought and can therefore reason better. Of course, in this context, CAN is a far cry from DO. The same conditionality applies to the rest of us, to humanity as a whole.

It is good to learn from the exceptions. David Robson proposes as an example, Benjamin Franklin, the American politician, philosopher, physicist and all-round polymath, who vowed not to allow himself to suffer from 'earned dogmatism'. He banned words which imply certainty from his vocabulary, stating late in life 'for these past 50 years past no one has ever heard a dogmatic expression escape me' and 'those who affect to be thought to know everything...often remain long ignorant of many things others could and would instruct them in, if they appeared less conceited'. In him, we have a classic example of the possibility to change. He was a person who realised his errors of early life and affected to change by strict adherence to behaviours consistent with his values, which whilst dogmatic in itself is surely dogmatism of a decent kind.

Most of us find it easy to apply this to others, but not to ourselves. We know this from Solomon who was bestowed with the biblical gift of wisdom.

Baked Bread

A baker didn't much like having a beggar rattling coins outside his bakery. He came to Solomon: "oh wise one, is it fair for me to ask this beggar for money. She is surely taking advantage of the intoxicating aroma of my fresh bread?"

Solomon replied "If you have heard the rattling of her coins, then my friend, you have already received fair payment".

Evidence suggests that even Solomon was not quite so good at applying such wisdom to his own affairs.

Igor Grossman, Harvard psychologist, points again to our bias blind spot; it is particularly evident when we feel threatened and engage in 'hot' emotional processing. The next traffic accident you are involved in may leave you in a state in which you don't necessarily see all things clearly. As an alternative to the Taleb approach of simply avoiding eye contact, Grossman suggests addressing the asymmetry, with a form of 'self-distancing'. Imagine watching yourself from various perspectives, at home, on a TV screen, as a wiser future self, or in the third party. Taking a range of viewpoints has been shown to be an effective way of avoiding the interference from 'hot emotions'.

2. Challenge yourself

Thomas Aquinas, 13th Century philosopher deliberately argued against his own hypotheses, doing his best to make these objections as forceful and strong as possible arguing back with equal force until he reached some kind of equilibrium. (A similar method employed famously by Boris Johnson, former UK Prime Minister, although his motives for doing so may not be so pure!)

Angela Merkel, former German Chancellor and for a long time arguably the most powerful woman in the world, is famed for her 'analytical detachment', with the word 'merkeln' now understood in Germany to mean 'to take a patient, deliberative stance', although it is often used with a hint of a suggestion of indecisiveness. The term may have a rye sub-meaning but the success of this approach is surely beyond question.

Some suggest that you do well to imagine you are talking to a 12 year old; Richard Feynman's famous method for ensuring that **you** understand the topic at least.

3. Take advice from experts

The search for those illusive WMD in Iraq back in 2002 triggered the formation of a new US department, the Intelligence Advanced Research Projects Activity. There followed a four-year tournament to find the best minds to address similar future challenges. Philip Tetlock's 'Good Judgement Project' sought the 'super-forecasters', those elite people amongst us who have superior skills in forecasting future world events. The wide range of applicants was rapidly filtered. Perhaps surprisingly those who proved most adept were not the geniuses, in terms of IQ at least, but they were found to have common psychological traits, including 'open-minded thinking' and 'acceptance of uncertainty'. These 'super-forecasters' were not lucky guessers who stayed in the race, they showed precision of thought in terms of analytical reasoning and drew more on wider research from different cultures and other areas not specifically related to the issue being tested. And, although their predictions were more precise in terms of level of confidence, they showed more uncertainty in their language.

Grossman's findings are of course consistent with Dunning Kruger's; that confidence and competence are almost negatively correlated. The good news though is that his research has shown that those who did not forecast as well perhaps due to their over-confidence were still able to improve these skills with training. Igor Grossman advises that, to counter our ignorance, we should conduct ourselves with intellectual humility and open mindedness 'such that we can change our minds if better information arrives'. It is surely wise to look for better information, better ways of doing things, better ways of thinking.

To think is easy, to act is hard...but the hardest thing in the world is to act in accordance with our thinking

Johann Wolfgang von Goethe

When we do act in accordance with our thinking, and feeling, we achieve harmony. With self-awareness, and continued effort, we can keep improving our thinking and we can keep improving the way we act. There is hope for us yet...

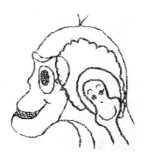

REFLECTION TIME

Biased Beyond Belief		
Mens Rea	Actus Rhesus	Guilty? ☑
1. Are you aware of the signal to noise ratio when making decisions?	Have you asked yourself what decision you would make tomorrow, next year, in many different environments?	☐
2. Can is not the same as do. Do you always exercise humility?	Can you avoid 'Hot Emotions'? Have you tried self-distancing?	☐
Be open minded – remember – YOU ARE THE GORILLA!		

PART 2

MENS REA

We can take steps to improve
– first we must understand…

This is what it feels like to
be us...

Chapter 1:
Meaning, Purpose and Well-Being

Meaning and purpose differ essentially in their position on our timelines. Meaning relates to our present and past, whereas purpose may extend way into the future, perhaps into Martin Luther King Junior's 'Promised Land'. Life has meaning if it takes us in the direction of our purpose. Our well-being depends on and is proportional to our sense of purpose.

In this section we will look in more detail at our purpose, our motivations, our hopes and fears and conclude with some ways that they might be 'met in thee tonight'.

His was a pointless and ugly purpose...not the sort to enhance a life, put a spring in a person's step, make birds sing and flowers bloom...

Douglas Adams

When Douglas Adams used his Vogon captain to explore our lives, he heaped it on -'it was not his purpose to worry about x or y - he had people for that...and so did they'[1].

We would do anything to ensure that our purpose is not pointless and ugly. The pursuit of something opposite is the meaning of life, isn't it?

Beyond pointlessness

In McKinsey's *Beyond Performance: How great Organisations Build Ultimate Competitive Advantage*, we are provided with a toolkit of measures that can be taken to give you more meaning, and help to drive that inner-you, the one who talks to you when no-one else is around, the one you dance and sing to. As Daniel Pink highlighted in his book *Drive*, the key to sustained engagement is intrinsic motivation. The McKinsey organisation understands that to allow us to find our intrinsic motivation the only really effective, self-propelling force, requires focus on engaging with a story. And not just any story but a story we care about. And what better than the story of our lives?

Susie Cranston and Scott Keller at McKinsey tell us that our engagement requires one or more of five basic stories, reflecting how we impact on our company, on our society, on our customer, on our working team and on ourselves.

Lady Kitty Chisholm emphasises the importance of intrinsic motivation, as she relates one of the innumerable experiments conducted on rats. On this occasion they are presented three scenarios; they are either locked in a room, given freedom to roam and a running wheel or they are forced to run on the same wheel for a fixed number of hours a day.

Only those rodents given the freedom to roam were found to have grown grew new brain cells. The new growth related to running on the wheel happened **because the mice had**

choice[2]. They ran because they wanted it. And this is how we are as humans. We don't change because others want us to, we change when we want it ourselves.

And what is more, we have a basic need to feel in control, as amply demonstrated by yet another of the myriad enlightening experiments by Daniel Kahneman*.

---

*Control and Endowment

Kahneman assessed the perceived value of lottery tickets[3], with half the subjects being given random numbers, and half allowed to choose their own.

When offering to buy the tickets back before the lottery, those who were allowed to choose their own numbers valued them five times as highly as those allocated random numbers!

Both groups required more than face value for re-sale.

Recognising our human foibles, Dr Steve Peters suggests we write a list of all the things we would like to be[4]. Would you like to be calm (not anxious), positive (not negative), happy (not gloomy)...?

Why not have a go...? Do it, now...

The list you have made describes who you REALLY are. In Peters' terminology, if you do not behave this way it is simply because you have not learned to master your gremlins, or your 'chimp' (your Old Mammalian Brain) YET. Peters provides a structured approach to realising your dreams but be sure to dream big. Our dreams should excite us, so that if we miss by a bit, we still achieve a lot. And we may well miss by a bit, as we can never control all things. Let's recognise that, up front so we don't get disheartened on our obstacle-rich journeys.

The Inner Theatre

Manfred Kets DeVries as The Leader on the Couch provides a psychoanalytical account of leadership failures in what he calls the 'Inner Theatre approach'. This inner theatre is the stage on which the major themes of our lives are played out, where we find what motivates us; what we feel most passionate about. If we don't know the answer yet, we are unlikely to be truly effective. It is our 'Motivational Needs System' (MNS), our unique inner theatre that provides the rational forces* behind our sometimes irrational behaviours.

> ***Essential Forces**
>
> De Vries introduces three essential forces:
>
> - Innate
> - parentally guided', or
> - needing to recreate positive emotional states of young childhood.

These forces, alongside our environmental influences and our needs for affiliation and exploration, shape our unique identities. They give us our story; our life scripts, our templates for interpreting our version of reality and they guide our interactions with others. We have a genetic predisposition to certain behavioural patterns, but we develop through a nature-nurture interaction and we can change with effort and awareness. Our brains may have a certain shape but we constantly remould and rewire throughout our lives.

Organisations spend small (and large) fortunes devising motivational tools, some drawing on the McKinsey wisdom, most focussing on sticks and carrots. Many claim to pursue a McKinsey type model but their actions suggest they favour sticks and carrots. In challenging times too many leaders tend towards chewing the ends off the carrots and generously doling out the sticks!

Organisations, having committed large sums to motivating their staff, spend similarly dubious sums trying to influence our preferences; anything to lure us towards their products. But this is no simple matter knowing how DAFT we are! Our preferences and our actions are not always totally rational, or indeed, all that predictable.

The famous Pepsi challenge, deconstructed by Martin Gladwell in *Blink*, highlighted an issue with our understanding of why we do

Back-firing

Our advertisers have not always got it right. When Dr Gemma Calvert, Chair in Applied neuro-imaging, University of Warwick, completed her FMRI study of smokers, she found that cigarette warning labels activate the nucleus accumbens, meaning it actually excited the craving (see dopamine effect of chapter 1). Yes, the warning labels actively encourage smokers to light up.

what we do. People on blind taste test prefer Pepsi (a short burst of greater sweetness), yet we buy coke. Coca Cola spent millions responding to the taste test by redesigning, (and then promptly dropping) 'new coke'. They failed to understand why we buy.

In 2003 Dr Read Montague, director of the human neuro-imaging lab at Baylor College of Medicine, Houston, used FMRi to examine brain activity before and after drinking Coke and Pepsi, (scientists love pitting these two against each other) and found that the activated regions indicated a 'mute tug of war between

Spend wisely

It used to be said that 'half of all advertising budgets are wasted; the trick is knowing which half', but with big data and social media and imaging technologies, the slogan may be running towards the end of its course as advertisers can almost see what makes each individual tick, and target their advertising accordingly.

rational and emotional thinking, preferring the taste of Pepsi, but nevertheless choosing coke'. Dr Montague concluded that the emotions rose up 'like mutinous soldiers' and forced selection of coke, against our better judgement. When McClure et al published the findings the following year, they suggested that the hippocampus (memory storage area) played a significant part in the decision-making process and that it was as if there were two interacting brain systems, one for taste and one, more powerful, for cultural influence with positive (and negative) associations like logo and bottle shape*.

> ***Bottle**
>
> Coke's iconic bottle was designed so the brand identity was recognizable even when the bottle was smashed to pieces.

Of course, we instinctively know about brand value and association with our preferred stories, but often doubt our own willingness to be influenced in this way. Ever since the pioneer film makers, the Lumiere brothers, directed our attention towards Lever's sunlight soap on screen, we have seen this in action, from extravagant watches, to luxury cars, and somewhat more affordably, Spielberg's strategic deployment of Reese's pieces to lure out ET, that lovable Extra Terrestrial (and to lure out Reese lovers - who tripled their purchases within a couple of months of the film's release).

The story of our lives, like those of Spielberg's Elliot, really ought to address the hopes and fears of all our years…

HOPE – Optimism and positivity

Mice exposed to hopeless conditions give up and die more readily than those with even a glimmer of hope. Even a small amount of illumination can reverse their sense of hopelessness. A light at the end of the tunnel keeps them hanging on in the cruel world of the University laboratory[4].

We mostly hope for the best. There seems little point doing otherwise.

Benefits of Optimism

A Harvard health study suggests a close link between optimism and physical health, as it enhances psychological resilience and reduces mortality risk. Eric Kim, research fellow in the Department of Social and Behavioral Sciences and co-lead author of the study, observes that most health efforts tend to focus on reducing risk factors for diseases, but seldom address this optimism, even though optimism has been shown to be associated with healthier behaviours and healthier ways of coping with life challenges. Kim's study suggests that higher optimism directly impacts our biological systems.

The study analysed data from 2004 to 2012 from 70,000 women enrolled in the Nurses' Health Study, a long-running study tracking women's health via surveys every two years. They looked at participants' levels of optimism and other factors that might play a role in how optimism may affect mortality risk, such as race, high blood pressure, diet, and physical activity.

The most optimistic women (the top quartile) had a nearly **30 percent lower risk of dying** from any of the diseases analysed in the study compared with the least optimistic (the bottom quartile). The most optimistic women had a 16 percent lower risk of dying from cancer; 38 percent lower risk of dying from heart disease; 39 percent lower risk of dying from stroke; 38 percent lower risk of dying from respiratory disease; and 52 percent lower risk of dying from infection.

While other studies have linked optimism with reduced risk of early death from cardiovascular problems, this was the first to find a link between optimism and reduced risk from other major causes. Postdoctoral research fellow Kaitlin Hagan, co-lead author of the study, advocates low-cost **'optimism enhancement programmes'**; for example, we can think about and write down the best possible outcomes for various areas of our lives.

In another study, the same applied to married couples who came down with cold symptoms, correlating to their levels of marital strife! Optimism played a significant part here too and it was seen that 6 years after their first heart attack, of 122 victims studied, 21 of the 25 most pessimistic died, compared to just 6 of the 25 most optimistic. In fact, **mental outlook provided a better predictor of survival than any medical risk factor**[6].

But, and there is always a but, the neuroscientist Tali Sharot from the University College of London explains that our optimistic bias can lead us to overestimate our likelihood of having positive experiences and underestimate our chances of experiencing negative ones. We may overestimate our longevity and our professional success and underestimate the chances our relationships will fail or that we will fall ill.

Evidence abounds that countries whose leaders fail to plan and rely on heavy doses of blind optimism fare worse in a crisis. Hope may make you smile in the very short term, but will not make sufficiently detailed plans, will not protect at times of crisis, will not take the right evasive actions and administer the right drugs at the right time. Forward planning is still the key to success in life.

Warning about Optimism

When you open the door to your human spirit, this doesn't mean 'nothing bad will ever happen to me'.

If you take your optimism too far not only will you underestimate the time and effort you need, you will sign up to unrealistic deadlines, and fail to take necessary precautions. You will dodge medical tests, maybe even avoid seat-belts and a safety helmet, perhaps even stop looking before you cross the road.

Steve Job's reality distortion field was an outlying example of the downside of positive (or strength) psychology, in which we promote our optimism by focusing on our strengths. When we do this, we too can get a distorted sense of our own invulnerability. The Gallup Clifton Strengthfinder7 approach, which is the essence of positive psychology, is admirable in many ways, but we should take some caution as excessive focus on strengths can lead to over-reliance and abuse at the expense of our whole being. It can promote excessive faith in chance and a consequent lack of belief in our ability to influence our outcomes (our mindset). If we 'believe our own hype', we can induce a sense of victimhood when our luck turns.

Pendleton and Furnham show that, whilst most strength psychologists imply a linear positive relationship between strength use and performance, the actual reality is a U-Shaped curve[7] as overuse can result in 'derailment'; if we are too optimistic, we can be blind-sided by, or at least insufficiently vigilant to real problems lying ahead. This is not a problem for us, of course, but surely we have all met successful leaders who have come unstuck, showing a belligerent refusal to accept reality when it is less than ideal, providing our own experience of the downside element of the Stockdale paradox (see box below*).

Beware of these leaders as they will not take the appropriate steps to improve the situation. Sadly, at some point, we do tend to see the worst side of their characters, where blame and bullying come to the fore as they deny reality and persist with their increasingly untenable delusions (*see Some Other Substantial Reasons*).

So, perhaps it's ok to hope for the best, as long as we plan for the worst...?

When you plan for the worst, what are you doing inside? We know that we are primed like an old pump, consciously and unconsciously; our Reticular Activation System filters the information we pay heed to – they are on the look-out for dangers, for downsides, for worst case scenarios – let's pump that pessimist with a steady flow of such images and ideas!

As we suffer this bombardment of negativity, knowing our inherent hatred of losses and our fear of failure, we stoke our fire of pessimism, and as we seek to quell the flames we will not be in the frame of mind to seize opportunities as they arise. What is more, we will not feel warm and fuzzy inside. Occasionally as a student I played the odd game of Bridge. I was so focussed on getting rid of my losing cards, so I could have a hand of winners, that I often lost most if not all of my potential winners. I would lay down the 'losers' early and cement their losing status. Not only was this 'suicidal' but my focus on the losers reduced my focus and memory of the other cards, all in all making me a pretty lousy Bridge player. Focussing on our losers is seldom an effective way to win. That is not to say that winning is essential, but that if you want to win, it is a good idea to frame your game accordingly.

So, hope for the best and plan for the best?

We know that high performers spend a large portion of their training time analysing and improving their weaker areas, what some call 'deliberate practice'. They create improvement plans, which they follow religiously and refine continually. They also know that there is a time to perform and a time to reform. They do not try to fix the leaking roof whilst in the rain.

Martin Seligman, the most famous name in positive psychology, has shown in numerous studies an overall better performance from optimists. They see failures as learning opportunities, things that go wrong provide a rich seam of opportunities for improvement. They do not wallow in the thick mud of mishaps and rejections. The long list of incredibly successful authors with hundreds of rejections bears testament to that. 'No's' can be a source of motivation to persevere. Optimism aligns with self-belief – you are optimistic because you can envision your success, because you believe in yourself. Self-belief means maintaining a sense of personal control, an essential ingredient of well-being.

Optimists see the glass as half full; we should also consider the angle of the glass...if the glass stands tall, if it has the optimal attitude, it has the greatest capacity - many optimists overcome barriers by simply looking beyond them. They say that 'if you don't see barriers they are not really there'.

Of course, there needs to be an anchoring in facts; deluding oneself with naïve optimism may see repeated failures as a personal judgment, which ultimately can be destructive. There are also times when we cling to hope, and it can become our enemy. It can prevent 'closure', the psychological state of resolution of an emotional trauma, or worse.

---

*Stockdale Paradox

In his seminal leadership study, related in his book Good to Great, Jim Collins examines our 'hardiness', with naturally the best leaders demonstrating the highest 'hardiness' quotient. In what he terms the Stockdale paradox, Admiral Jim Stockdale, a 3 star officer who survived 8 years imprisonment in Vietnam during which time he was tortured no less than 20 times, explains that the optimists, as he describes them, were the ones who didn't make it – they believed in an unrealistic conclusion (for example; they would be home by Christmas, Easter, the next Christmas...) and eventually they yielded, and gave up hope altogether. Admiral Stockdale advises us not to confuse faith that we'll prevail in the end with the discipline to confront the most brutal facts of our reality, which thankfully are not likely to ever be as grim as his experience.

On balance then, it seems wise to...

Hope for the best, plan for the best, AND, whilst retaining our positivity, ensure we embrace our reality and have contingency and improvement plans.

There are still so many reasons that a considered level of optimism is good for our health. Not least because as optimistic patients we tend naturally to do things that make us healthier. We follow our doctor's advice, and we generally take more care of ourselves. What is more, when we expect the future to provide us good things, our stress and anxiety levels reduce...

When Leo Varadkar, the Irish PM, expressed his view of the likelihood of a deal (on Brexit), he stated that he was 'on the optimistic side of a 50:50 chance of a deal'. Clearly his glass was half full, and whilst not indulging in excessive optimism, it tilted in the right direction and he did at least choose the biggest half!

Optimistic people tend to have higher academic achievements and more often accomplish their goals. Your optimism wards off discouragement at the first hint of bad news. Studies show that optimists work more hours, persevere more, and end up earning more money.

Why not give it a try...what is the best possible outcome for your marriage, a trying friendship, your career, or whatever comes to mind that you may be concerned about right now...?

And as Helen Keller put it...

'No pessimist has ever discovered the secret of the stars, nor have they sailed through unknown waters, nor have they opened a door to the human spirit.'

FEAR – Reasons (not) to be fearful

Don't be too timid and squeamish about your actions. All life is an experiment. The more experiments you make, the better

Ralph Waldo Emerson

Firstly, please note that fear level and risk level are far from the same. Our emotions intervene meaning our fear does not always accurately reflect the underlying reality. In fact, our phobias are mostly irrational, even when they do may make evolutionary sense. Spiders are mostly safe and harmless, but has it always been so? We are programmed to be afraid; our self-preservation demanded it, and we can see fear of the unknown in the eyes of our children all the time, as they look to us, to our facial expressions, for cues as to the validity of those fears.

Alongside the genetic irrational fears and phobias, as children, and indeed as adults, our fears are as plastic as our brains, morphing as we travel along our journey through life, reinforced or dampened by associative and social learning. We can condition chimps to fear snakes. Thankfully though, there does seem to need to be some inherent potential risk - no-one has yet managed to train them to fear flowers.

Fear means stress

Experiencing the butterfly effect is a natural consequence of small worries or excitements, like standing up to give a presentation. Of course, the gut – brain link has been well documented with some referring to the Gastro-Intestinal tract as the 'second brain'. Fear signals manifesting as a fluttering sensation are associated with the fight or flight response. The body tweaks itself in many ways, dependent on the level of fear. We experience changes in our microbiota and a redirection of blood from our stomach muscles to fill other parts, like our leg muscles, ready for an urgent response (escaping a hungry lion - now more likely meaning running away to hide in the loos).

That little delicate almond in the brain is also like a butterfly, with the reward system on

> **Easy for you to say**
>
> The early findings of the psychologist Robert Ader that the immune system is intimately connected with the central nervous system, opened the way for the field of study psychoneuroimmunology, better known as PNI, from which we now know that vital chemical messengers in the immune system correlate with those that regulate emotion in our brains.

one wing and the threat system on the other. If we can balance these two, our amygdala will stop us flapping. We gain a sense of balance and feel like we can fly. When we are emotionally in control, we have the best chance to soar high, as high as we want.

A word on the immune system, or the 'body's brain', as it is described by neuroscientist Francisco Varela at Paris Ecole Polytechnique. Our immune cells travel the length and breadth of our body, within our blood stream, performing security walks, checking for intruders and attacking them accordingly. If they make a mistake and there is 'friendly fire', we may see an immune disease, like lupus or innumerable allergies.

> **Good to talk**
>
> David Felton observed how emotions effect our autonomic nervous system, our body's internal regulator, and with Susan Felton they have identified the meeting points where the autonomic nervous system talks directly to the cells of the immune system - the lymphocytes and macrophages. It is now known that neurotransmitters pass signals similar to the synapses in our brains.

The hormones released, notably under stress, have a direct impact on our immune cells. Hormones suggest 'clear and present danger' and they take over, hindering the immune cell activity, like a commando squad standing the security guards down whilst they deal with an imminent terrorist threat.

Some of us are more able to counter the potential triggers. As an example,

> **Stress colds**
>
> Sheldon Cohen, psychologist at Carnegie Mellon University worked with specialists at Sheffield on the impact of colds and stress, identifying that when under stress, due to our weakened immune system, the likelihood that we catch a cold increases by 20% (from 27% for non-stressed up to 47% of stressed people in their study, when exposed to the cold virus).
>
> The same applied to married couples who came down with cold symptoms, correlating to their levels of marital strife. (see benefits of optimism),

where one person feels totally unsettled by the sight of a sinister human-like machine, another can totally disregard this 'uncanny valley effect'. Henry may be nothing more than your friendly dust-buster, but his shifty eyes put me totally on edge. Of course, we are all different, and our vulnerability to stress varies accordingly.

And few of us are as cool under pressure as Captain Sullenburg, who landed his jet on the Hudson ensuring the survival of all 155 people on board or as unphased as the legendary astronaut, Leroy Gordon Cooper Jr, Gordo, who when faced with making an emergency landing in his capsule due to electrical failure, handled that 'with the nonchalance of a commercial airline pilot'[8].

The *'diathesis-stress model'* in psychology maps our predispositions to our environment, identifying personal resilience thresholds. It is sometimes used to predict or explain psychological disorders. Most of us manage to steer clear of the thresholds, but we do still have egotistical brains. We still fear humiliation, and we still seek approval of others. We still worry about all situations where we might get it wrong in front of others, with varying levels of performance anxiety. We are all paranoid. As Douglas Adams noted, that is perfectly normal. And as we have already established, a little paranoia can indeed be a good thing. Some amongst us fear queuing up to pay for shopping (in case we can't work out the change quick enough), some of us shudder of the prospect of talking in public, some of us don't notice that drip, drip, drip of the leaky shower, because we lack the confidence in our ability to fix the plumbing. We all live with a constant tussle between facing our fears and avoidant behaviours.

Most of our fears and worries fizzle out, with relatively minor impact but, if we do start to respond to the feelings of fear, our physiological changes are re-encoded and sent back up to our brains, reconfirming our fear. After a significant fear has 'ended' (you gave your presentation) – the flight or fight incident over, our sympathetic nervous system steps aside, handing over to the parasympathetic nervous system to tidy up after it. Unless we are Gordo, our body may take as much as an hour to calm down, during which time the surfeit of hormones starts to impact our well-being.

The Axis of Evil

In times of stress, the **HPA axis** is activated[9]. This 'axis of evil' leads to the production of cortisol. Cortisol helps deal with the urgent action, but in excess, or when it persists, it can cause nervous tension reducing our sense of control.

*In 1967, Thomas Homes and Richard Rahe introduced their stress scale, attributing 'scores' to different stressors, which they termed 'Life Change Units', or LCU's. Stressors affect your feeling of control, (actual control is not necessarily affected), and the test is regularly used today to assess overall stress levels (the tests provide an overall annual score).

You can also check the LCU's for your biggest stressor(s), for example; you get 47 LCU's for being sacked, 65 for marital separation or 63 for going to prison…

---

*Based on such assessments, our well-being is unsurprisingly inversely correlated with our level of stress.

Stressed thinking

When under stress, we are emotionally upset, we do not remember, learn or make decisions clearly. Stress can make us daft.

*Winston Churchill suffered with the black dog of depression, yet few would argue about his mental strength.

---

*Never, never, never

Never confuse Mental Health with Mental strength.

As Amy Morin points out in her book *13 things mentally strong people don't do*, physically strong people can have physical ailments, and it's perfectly possible for mentally strong people to have mental health issues, like anxiety.

Mental health issues do not define our mental strength.

With our inability to process negatives and the particular resonance of the number 13, clearly Amy Morin knew what she was doing when she presented us with her 13 things not to do!

Of course, with the additional hormones, and noradrenaline priming our system, the more stress we are under the more frightened, insecure and uncertain we feel and the more irrationally we tend to behave. Most of us give scant credence to most of our superstitions like lucky pennies and broken mirrors. But run of the mill superstitions and conspiracy theories gain more attention from us when we are stressed. In short, when stressed, our thinking is even more irrational than normal.

This emotional thinking is the same reason there is no row 13 on many airlines (eg Air France), and although car crashes do increase on this day, it is our stress response that makes this so. In China and much of Asia the number 8 is celebrated and they shy away from the number 4 (which sounds a

Emotional Thinking

Dr Bruce Hood, professor of experimental psychology at Bristol University demonstrates that people become stressed when they don't feel in control. He asks a room full of scientists to volunteer to wear a sweater he holds up before them, offering £10 to anyone who will try it on. Most are willing, until he announces that the sweater used to belong to Fred West, the serial killer. Dr Hood notes how the others edge away from the few who do elect to wear it, as if 'evil has become physically manifest inside the clothing'. Of course, we then learn that the sweater had not been worn by Fred West at all and, thankfully, those brave souls are safe to approach again!

bit like death in Mandarin, *'shi'*). Heart attacks show statistically significant increase on 4th of the month, probably out of a slight increase in stress. Nestle aren't complaining about irrational behaviour though as kit kat's success in Japan is surely partly because it sounds like Kitto-Katsu, which means 'win without fail'.

I don't remember being particularly stressed, on that Friday 13th, when as a teenager I ploughed my bike into the back of a car. My stress levels had certainly increased by the time I hit the bonnet! A memory was given greater prominence in my hippocampus due to my amygdala emphasising the emotional impact of the event; no bones were broken but the fruits of an entire year of early morning paper rounds were concertina'd and I learned a vital life lesson – in addition to not fixing your roof when it's raining, never attempt to adjust your spokes whilst your wheels are in motion (see FLOW, section 4).

Of course, this was relatively trivial, but at a certain point our brain's system for preventing future trauma by etching it on the mind in this way can be so severe that it perpetuates the trauma, as is the case with unfortunate sufferers of Post Traumatic Stress Disorder (PTSD).

Hair Triggers

In the case of PTSD, memories seem to be emblazoned in the emotional circuitry by an over-aroused amygdala. The hair trigger phenomenon means the release of large quantities of adrenaline and noradrenaline. The same profound response is later based on a low-level trigger with the slightest association to the original cause of the deeply felt trauma.

PTSD can have other severe effects with endorphins designed to reduce pain, also impacting the sense of pleasure, and a notable shrinkage of the hippocampus impacting ability to deal resiliently with future memories and unrelated emotional events.

Emotional Extremes

In some cases, an excessive fear response sends a signal to the brain, which seeks to justify this response. In extreme cases, if we do not have some kind of circuit breaker, this can lead to a self-fulfilling spiral, which can be very serious, even if the initial fear response was unjustified. Before long, we may need someone to pass us a paper bag! (to breathe into, to regularise our oxygen/carbon dioxide levels*).

> ***Don't Panic!**
>
> If you are having a panic attack, don't panic! Panic attacks arise when rapid breathing encourages oxygen to flood the bloodstream in preparation for urgent action. Our fright or fight signal sends a spiralling message of impending doom which requires a rebalancing of blood oxygen and carbon dioxide levels.
>
> Easy enough to spot, after your blood oxygen levels have regularised.

In a rather less immediate way, the impact if our defence systems are always 'on', is rather more damaging. A sustained stressful state may trigger the use of external aids, like say, alcohol. These can diffuse short term tensions but regular use for persisting stress symptoms can promote a 'stress cycle' with escalating severity and challenges, and ultimately anomalous dopamine system activity. At the extreme this can cause psychosis and hallucinations. Of course, it is a good idea to find ways to dismount the stress cycle, before we put our physical and mental well-being in jeopardy.

We should remember that when a rat is granted possession of a lever so it can control the electric shocks for itself, it suffers less from the same shocks and recovers more quickly, and without lasting signs of the stress. It is a lack of sense of control, a sense of helplessness, which seems to be the biggest cause of vulnerability. If we believe we can't change things, we lose hope and stop trying. Belief that we can change our situation for the better always helps. As so many Holocaust survivors discovered, there are always opportunities to change our situation and always ways to tackle our limiting beliefs. That is optimism and a reason to be cheerful...

Reasons to be cheerful – Happiness

Apart from Cheddar Cheese and Pickle and saying 'Okey Dokey', (and anything else from the list provided by Ian Dury and The Blockheads[10]), there are many scientific reasons that being cheerful is a good idea. Like Reese's pieces, we can find little nuggets of happiness everywhere.

> **Note on cheerfulness**
>
> • Cheerfulness is a perpetual lubrication of the mind.
>
> • Over lubrication may cause trouble, under lubrication may cause a breakdown.*
>
> *Shite's Miscellany, by Stephen Blake and Andrew John

The media dubbed happiest man in the world, Buddhist monk Matthieu Ricard says that achieving durable happiness is a skill, and as such it requires sustained effort in training the mind and developing a set of qualities such as inner peace, mindfulness and altruistic love. It goes way beyond merely being unflappable, although that certainly helps.

> **Note on mindfulness**
>
> Susan Smalley and Diana Winston tell us, in *Fully Present: The Science, Art and Practice of Mindfulness*, that 'Learning to live mindfully does not mean living in a perfect world, but rather living a full and contented life in a world in which both joys and challenges are a given'.

Gretchen Rubin, writer on the Happiness Project (see her website[11]) says that 'you're not happy unless you think you are happy', with Ken Robinson concluding; 'you are happy if you think you are.'

So, you want to be happy? You want to know the meaning of your life? What are you waiting for? Just think you are - that's it; that's the answer. That's your number 42[12]!

Found this out a bit late? Take heart; it's never too late. Remember, you'll be fifty anyhow? Could read 60 or 70 or 80 or *insert number denoting your definition of old*. It is never too late to take the plunge, to follow your dreams, to live your best life. All it takes is a little courage and imagination. As Albert Einstein put it 'Imagination is everything – it is the preview of life's coming attractions'.

Late starter?

It could be you - Ken Robinson introduces Othmar Amman, the celebrated architect who won major awards and contributed to some elaborate structures including the Delaware Memorial and the Walt Whitman Bridge. He didn't start his architectural career until after his 60th Birthday and created all his masterpieces in the 26 years after that.

If you find yourself, as I often do, saying 'I am getting old too fast', just remember that getting old doesn't seem that appealing...until you think of the alternative! If nothing else, being happy and being optimistic will help you live longer. Emily and Laurence Alison, in their insightful book *Rapport* relate research into positive emotions by Barbara Frederickson at the Positive Emotions and Psychology Lab (PEPLab), who states that 'happy people tend to be healthier, more physically active, more productive, more successful and even more generous.' Of course, she might be biased.

You don't think you are that kind of person? We may not be responsible for the nature of what Dr Roberts calls our 'chimp', but we are responsible for managing it. It really is our attitude, not our aptitude that will determine our altitude.

Attitude, in geometrical terms, is the angle of inclination; if we are so inclined, we can change our attitude.

Improvement Actions:

As Maya Angelou says, caged birds sing because they can be freed. As can we. Let's take a look at some actions we might take...

1. Take Note

Our physiology gives us disease as a form of feedback. How kind! Our basic programmes, like our immune system, promote self-healing. Stress is a great thing, within certain parameters. It is a performance enhancer, a spur to action. Too little stress and we risk fizzling out - If we stay in our comfort zone, the zone shrinks over time, and what was once comfortable becomes suffocating. If we push ourselves too far, too quickly, if we take on too much stress, then our performance drops, and at the extremes the elastic may snap.

If we feel we need to reduce our stress, it is fair to assume we are getting the right signals. So, we need to heed the message, and proceed, with a plan. Always start from where you are! With a plan we circumvent Dr Roberts chimp – our emotional autopilot[13].

Why don't they treat me the way I want to be treated? Why do I end up doing what they want, rather than what I want? A lack of sense of control can make us feel angry and stressed; we can feel trapped in a wheel of despair, or in an endless maze, with no way out and the light at the end of the tunnel merely illuminating our sense of hopelessness. We need a plan.

Carl Jung said 'What you resist, persists'. Holding resentments allows others to impact your well-being with no cost to them. Resentment is like drinking poison and then hoping it will kill your enemies. So said Nelson Mandela; we resist others rather than taking control of our self. People-pleasers tend to do this and can become resentful and bitter. Many relationships falter because of it; 'I do so much for you, but you don't do anything for me'. Bronnie Ware found that one of the most notable deathbed regrets is attempting to please others rather than being true to ourselves. If someone has offended us, we are well served to remember that forgiveness reduces stress, which reduces blood pressure and heart rate, increases our tolerance to pain and can help us live longer.

2. Take Control

When we have a plan, we gain a sense of control. We choose to be like the lever-controlling rats, rather than the helpless victim rats. It is not helpful to empower others to have power over us, and having our own plan helps to ensure we act in our own best interests. We will not act in our own best interests if we feel the victim of others, or if we feel beholden to them for self-approval. A sense of victimhood may lead us to do things we regret. When we regain our sense of power, we reduce our risk of mental health issues, like depression or anxiety.

Maya Angelou said that 'you may not control all the events that happen to you, but you can decide not to be reduced by them.' It is important to distinguish between controlling all events and retaining a sense of control. The super-worriers amongst us tend to be those who try to control everything. It is the innocent desire to reduce anxiety by fixing everything, what Amy Morin calls the 'superhero complex'[14], which can create problems as we never feel we achieve enough. If we search hard enough, we can always find opportunity for failure. When we do this, we adversely impact our relationships as we unconsciously tell those around us that we don't trust them; the classic micro-manager problem – leave it to me, because I can't rely on you to do it right.

You'll probably know someone who suffers from what Dr Steve Peter's terms 'Mushroom syndrome'...unless it's you? If you feel a compelling need to worry about something all the time, you may have picked up the unhelpful and destructive habit of finding a new problem to worry about, a new mushroom growing, wherever a space is made for one. As this is a learned habit, we can take steps to follow a different, less stressful course. In the same way that our fears fizzle out, most worries never amount to anything and **most issues get resolved whether we worry or not**.

3. Take Care

If we can capture the spirit of the serenity prayer, and in the words of Depeche Mode's Martin Gore, 'Get the balance right[15], then many stresses will not find their way into our heads at all. When we have the right balance, we recognise how our behaviours can affect our chances of success as well as recognising the part external factors play. This 'bi-locus of control' is the antidote to a complete internal or external locus of control. It is here that we find the serenity to accept the things we can't, the courage to change the things we can, and the wisdom to know the difference.

Only when we become aware of our tendencies, will we take what Dean Burnett, the neuroscientist calls 'the high road'[16]. This can control or at least subdue our unwelcome excesses of emotion and is what some refer to as 'pressing the pause button'*.

*Taking the High Road

Instead of responding immediately to the sensory signal from the thalamus to the amygdala (the 'low road' is much faster), we allow the sensory cortex time to intervene and moderate our responses.

Our learned fears are often resolved over time due to natural immersion; we encounter different versions of our pet fear regularly enough to know that there's no need to fear it. (Clearly PTSD etches the memory so deep that normal learning is ineffective). Immersion therapy (IT) is a controlled version of the natural phenomenon. With techniques like IT we choose to take the high road, teaching our neocortex to inhibit our amygdala, stopping the amygdala providing that unfavourable 'hair-trigger' response. We manage to climb down from the chair and face the Siberian Hamster head on.

Our moods swing of course throughout a typical day, and we can choose to let those moods take control of our actions, or we can actively manage them. Recall Robert Thayer's four basic moods; calm-energy, calm-tiredness, tense-energy and tense-tiredness. Moods which are calm are intrinsically avoiding stress. We can be aware and use them to plan our daily actions. In the same way a 'morning lark' would plan their most challenging tasks in the morning or vice versa for the 'night owl'. When we are in 'tense-energy' mood, we are wired and buzzing for action – this can be an advantageous state when we want to deliver a focused activity, perhaps when we are in 'Flow' (see 'Achievement'). Tense-tiredness however should be eliminated as it is never helpful.

If you think you might be tense-tired, can you do some autopilot tasks, focusing on tasks you can control, or do some light exercise to lower cortisol? If your mood doesn't change fairly quickly, if you still feel anxious or irritable, if pessimistic thoughts persist... then it might help to seek another way to relax – perhaps you need a nap? (see 'Sleep').

4. Take Action

Primal scream therapy became popular for a while and the sense of release may be tempting, as we get in touch with our feelings, and disregard others sensibilities, but venting has been shown not to work. It may simply be because we are still focusing on the problem and not on the solution. It is not helpful to focus on how you feel - better to move on quickly to what you can do differently. When we have a plan, we can focus on the solution.

Embracing change, which Amy Morin points out makes us mentally stronger, does require some deliberate actions. One approach suggests five stages – precontemplation, contemplation, preparation, action and maintenance. The maintenance stage is crucial for sustainment.

Many of our stressors link to our self-image. Our brains are obsessed with impression management; trying to make us look good is our brain's default mode. But where there is dissonance; where our thinking and acting don't match up, we feel stressed. Mindfulness and meditation work because with heightened self-awareness we can find harmony. If we can label our stressors, like all our emotions, this can help us to manage them.

Choosing meditation/mindfulness

Dan Harris, the news anchor describes in his autobiography 10% Happier how he suddenly started suffering panic attacks and anxiety whilst reading the news.

He decided to take action; Meditation. He believes this improved his mood by 10%, 'getting to know yourself is as important to your well-being as getting to know others is to those relationships'.

Mindfulness is now scientifically proven to strengthen connections between the amygdala and the PFC.

Matthew D Lieberman, a UCLA psychologist, found that even labelling a photo of a face takes away some of the judgmental emotion. When you say 'he is an angry person' it can defuse the tension of our encounter[17]. By taking action to reduce the amygdala response, you help yourself to choose to take the high road.

5. Take Two

The high road includes the tried and tested technique for self-management; cognitive reappraisal, more commonly known as reframing. We know from the previous section the impact of framing on our judgements, we can use this to 'fool ourselves' into changing our responses. It is perhaps the single easiest way of changing your life.

If you can decide what you want to change, then start re-framing today. Do you think 'people are always trying to upset you', then start a list of times when people have tried to please you. If you think 'I am afraid of presenting', then write down how others will benefit from what you have to say. Practice saying, 'sometimes people try to please me, and I have some important things to share that people want to hear about'. In short, exchange self-pity for gratitude, focus on what you can give to others rather than what you'll get from them.

Be wary of your biases. The availability bias means that we

> **Follow the Piper**
>
> This is what Katie Piper, the model turned author and presenter did when, after her brutal life changing acid-attack, she quelled her suicidal thoughts, picked herself up and re-framed her life to be an inspirational spokesperson for framing away self-pity.

easily inflate our worries with our tendency to overestimate risks based on small amounts of specific evidence. If we see news coverage of fighting in a city, we assume that city is unsafe. We have little ability to judge the risk to us and one small incident in a city of a million people can assume almost the same weight in our minds as one in a village of 1000.

In the same way that we'd rather buy food that was 90% fat free than 10% fat, we feel better when we present our life with a positive frame, and whilst not to the extent of delusion, we do promote better outcomes.

As Meister Eckhart, the German theologian put it in the Thirteenth Century, 'if the only prayer you said was 'thank you', that would be enough'*.

> ***Be grateful**
>
> People who feel gratitude don't get sick as often, they take better care of their health, sleep longer, have lower blood pressure and generally better immune systems. What is more, they experience more happiness, joy and pleasure, and have a richer social life, showing more kindness and compassion to others.
>
> So says a study in the Journal of Personal and Social Psychology. Another survey shows gratitude improving happiness by 25%.

In a similar vein, it is not helpful to dwell in the past, replaying, re-living or regretting. When we focus on the 'should haves, would haves, and could haves' we are focusing on the problem, not the solution. There is no plan, there is no 'will do'. What is more, our memories will be distorted by our focus; we will tend to overstate the 'good old days', and dwell on the worst of the present and a pessimistic future, encouraging more stress and less time to work out how to get off the hamster wheel. Such irrational thoughts about past failures can deter future effort. It is perfectly possible and very effective to show yourself the same compassion you would show others. Things can get better, we can see the opportunities, we can get better...if we try.

6. Take a Reality Check

Trying doesn't mean trying to please everyone. Clearly, that is not possible, yet many of us waste time and energy in this hapless pursuit. As Amy Morin says 'the decision not to be a people-pleaser* leads to greater

> ***People Pleaser paradox**
> When we focus on trying to please everyone, we fail to please ourselves. When we fail to please ourselves, we fail to please others.

self-confidence, improved will-power, and more time and energy to focus on your goals, leaving you feeling less stress, likely to enjoy improved relationships and soon you find yourself in a spiral of self-improvement'.

We are still allowed to please some people though! Strong relationships are fundamental to our well-being. The quality of our connections and relationships are a significant factor in our longevity. When Milton Hershey chose not to resent his colleague for leaving the Hershey company to start his own candy manufacturer in direct competition, his friendship with Harry Reese became stronger[18]. They remained lifelong friends with mutually beneficial supplier relationships until the two companies merged after their deaths and long before Stephen Spielberg gave their brand its Extra-Terrestrial boost.

We stated that positive affirmations and optimism are important, but not to the level of delusion. It was valuable to Mohammed Ali to say 'I am the greatest', in the context of boxing. It would not help me or you! It will not promote change unless we change our core beliefs – can you really say, 'I believe!'?

Ali oozed confidence. But when we choose to be confident based on our ability to achieve, we open ourselves up to knock-backs. When we choose it based on doing our best to achieve, putting in our best effort, **trying**, then we can be confident even when things go wrong. We position ourselves to deal with the consequences.

Dr Peters' gremlins
As Peters says, 'belief that we are meant to be perfect is a powerful gremlin explaining why some people are afraid to fail, therefore afraid to try'.

The Sapir Whorf Hypothesis tell us that the words we tell ourselves shape our outcomes. When Yoda says 'do or do not, there is no try', he doesn't really mean that; he is just shaping the outcome. He really means, 'Have a plan that you can believe in and then move Heaven and Earth to deliver it, or don't, there is no third way'. Now, where can I find the number for George Lucas so I can explain his error!

7. Take Stock

It is perhaps surprising how many people suffer anxiety due to the impostor syndrome, the corollary of the Dunning Kruger effect, in which confidence is apparently deprived from the competent and dosed out liberally to the incompetent. Estimates suggest 70% of us have felt a withering blast of unworthiness at some point in our careers. Often, we link our self-worth with a high achievement emphasis at home. Dr Pauline Rose Clance, Atlanta clinical psychologist and co-developer of the 'impostor phenomenon theory', has also demonstrated a strong minority effect, for example; 93% of female African American College students suffer from it[19]. The stoic tendency to show a stiff upper lip can cause internal build-up of stress. The pressure cooker needs release and Dr Clance advocates dealing with it by embracing it, taking stock, not comparing too much with others, getting other opinions, staying challenged, talking about it, shifting the focus by mentoring others and above all, being grateful and celebrating your success.

In this Formula One race through life, Burnett offers an unusual antidote; reading out loud. Manic patients regularly complain of a 'racing mind', and aren't we all under pressure to do more and to do it quicker? By slowing ourselves down, by thinking at the writer's pace, we enhance our appreciation of the text, of our lives. He reminds us that the idea of reading quietly to yourself was not even a thing before the time of St Augustine of Hippo (whose silent reading was regarded with awe, admittedly at a time when most people couldn't read at all).

8. Take the Right Medicine

There are now of course various medical interventions, like Trans-cranial Direct Current Stimulation, which provides supposedly harmless electrical boosts, and shows some enhancement of memory and language.

Before we master the DNA changes, the cutting and splicing, there are also ever-improving drugs (e.g nootropics) designed to enhance mental function, rather like those taken by Daniel Keyes' Algernon, the simple bakery-assistant-turned-genius, which are coming soon...

In the meantime, try the 'cuddle hormone'. Oxytocin is released upon physical contact and the body releases endorphins which induce a sense of well-being as well as reducing pain and managing the stress hormone, cortisol. Even a handshake produces a small dose, conveying as it does a message of safety (unless of course either party is trying to get the upper hand with some handshake power play or conversely showing subordination or the contempt of a sopping fish).

The impact of the hug and the detrimental effect of its decline post-pandemic left an oxytocin deficiency requiring replenishment. The leakage of social capital should not be underestimated, as Kyrie and Brielle will testify.

Kyrie and Brielle

Kyrie and Brielle Jackson were born on 17 October 1995 at the Massachusetts Memorial Hospital in Worcester, Massachusetts, weighing just two pounds. Kyrie fared well but Brielle struggled desperately until neonatal nurse, Gayle Kasparian, recalling a European technique, broke protocol and put Brielle in the incubator with her sister Kyrie. When Kyrie and Brielle snuggled, Brielle perked up almost instantly, with dramatic increase in blood-oxygen saturation levels and easy breathing. Her frantic crying stopped, and her blue skin returned to a normal baby pink. Both fared well and were soon well enough to go home and read about their miracle start in countless articles to swamp the internet over the coming years.

Kangaroo care is a recognised and often effective method of treating babies who don't respond well to incubator conditions, whereby prolonged skin-to-skin contact, usually with their mother, is used in many labour and delivery units these days.

And, 20 years on...August 2020.

Kyrie and Brielle- Credit: LifeNews

Our main relationships are our strong ties, but the importance of our weak ties, our day-to-day loose connections should not be underestimated; a small effort to build on these weak-tie type interactions, small talk in shops or playgrounds, can pay rich dividends. Gillian Sandstrom and Elizabeth Dunn at the Universities of Essex and British Columbia calculate an improvement in the measure of happiness of a massive 17%[20].

Other studies have confirmed that a good balanced ratio of strong and weak ties can impact productivity and creativeness, providing benefit in much the same way for the individual as diversity does in the workplace, as a wide range of connections bring wildly different and equally precious perspectives.

9. Take Mind and Body as One

'You are the head' said one Goggleboxer to his wife[21]. He was referring to the planned 'world's first head transplant' by Professor Canavero (Also known as Dr Frankenstein).

The idea that you are the head doesn't hold much sway anymore as the inter-relation between head and body is er…self-evident. Whilst the head, the brain specifically, may be the source of our thinking, planning and decision making, other parts of the body compete, notably the gut (and for men, at least according to the author Martin Amis, a certain other male organ!).

Of course, we now know that the body informs the brain as much as the opposite – when we smile, we tell our brain we are happy, we produce the neurochemicals to make it so in a self-fulfilling spiral. We know Kahneman's pencil smile, the Botox effect (or 'facial feedback hypothesis') tells the same story. With a generous Botox boost, your smile 'freezes'. The frozen smile sends signals of happiness back to the brain. Darwin believed each emotion carries a distinct facial expression; we now know that it's not a one-way street.

Of course, it is not just in our smile. When Oscar wasn't allowed a banana yesterday, when he expected it, he started crying; at first gently and then building up to a crescendo in which, after several ear-splitting minutes, he had surely forgotten why he was crying, but it would be hard to deny that he was now genuinely and deeply upset about his life circumstances nevertheless.

It is the essence of Amy Cuddy's power pose, her core message about presence. We are the way we act. Taleb reflects on his observations of successful traders, 'One can notice in the posture who is profitable. He is walking upright, in a dominant style, and talking rather more than the less profitable one'.

Of course, we suspect that the outcome triggers this behaviour, but the brain finds it contagious.

Body Awareness

The insula or insular cortex is the part of the brain with primary responsibility for body awareness. It does this unconsciously of course.

Our central nervous system links to our peripheral or somatic nervous system, which consists of our autonomic nervous system, our sympathetic nervous system, which deals with urgent matters like flight or fight, and our parasympathetic nervous system which rather more gently monitors and tweaks dealing with the more gradual processes, like digestion. Together they manage the function of our entire system from the top of our head to the soles of our feet.

If you doubt the interconnections, think of phantom pregnancies, phantom limbs and even phantom table-hands (see box).

Taleb anecdotally supports what scientists like Charles Darwin and Desmond Morris have demonstrated. These traders may be able to hide their facial expressions but the body leaks freely; 'their gesture and gait reveals all'. What is more, people know how a confidant person acts and treat them differently too, which can have a self-perpetuating effect.

99% of who you are is invisible and untouchable

R Buckminster Fuller, architect and author

Table Hands – just a bit of fun

Try this Vilyanur Ramachandaran experiment with your partner or a close friend.

Place one hand, palm down on your knee under the table and get your partner to tap or stroke it and at the same time to do the same to the table directly above the hand. Keep doing it for a few minutes, focussing on the table. They might now bang the table with a hard object.

Did your hand meld into the table....and then did you feel your skin crawl when they banged the table? Did hitting the table even 'hurt'?

Vilayanur Ramachandran, a leading neuroscientist and specialist in this area, investigated this phenomenon measuring skin conductance. He explains that, provided the taps or strokes are synchronised, your brain assimilates the table into your body image. And it can do it in a matter of minutes as our body imaging process is very malleable.

Similarly, we can adopt fake hands and even persuade ourselves that fake fingers are ours when they are very far out of arms reach![22]

Given the indisputable interconnectedness of body and mind, it makes sense that we have a holistic approach to life, as if the brain and body are in symbiosis.

Maintaining a healthy body requires attention to the big three, the holy trinity if you will - Exercise, Nutrition and Sleep. A healthy mind demands the same. Our mental well-being demands a combination of our mental health and mental strength. When we **choose** to focus on our mental strength; when we address our limiting beliefs and behaviours we positively impact our mental health and we position ourselves to meet our greatest hopes and conquer our greatest fears. We set ourselves on our path to happiness.

And sorry, Dr Frankenstein! The head transplant surgery, planned back in 2018 had to be cancelled because the willing volunteer, Valery Spiridnov, the 33 year old sufferer of spinal muscular atrophy, fell in love and changed his mind about having a new body. He is alive and well and currently studying the computer analysis of emotions at the University of Florida[23].

He does not feel the 'Florida effect', nor does his wife or young son. Surely his story shows how we can choose to reframe our lives, and in doing so we can enhance our meaning and our well-being.

REFLECTION TIME

Meaning and Well-Being		
Mens Rea	Actus Rhesus	Guilty? ☑
1. You can choose your frame of mind	Do you choose positivity, choose optimism, choose life*?	☐
*you're addicted so be addicted; just be addicted to something else - Train spotting 2		
2. You can take control. You can make Happiness happen.	Have you found meaning? - it's on your path to well-being...	☐
Well-being means Body and Mind are one – Meaning requires Exercise, Nutrition, Sleep....		

Look after your body and it will
help you look after your mind...

Chapter 2:
Exercise

So, you have meaning and you have your mental well-being in mind. How do you keep it there?

Our mind will ensure we take the actions to sustain our body, and our body rewards it by sustaining the mind. Look after your body because that is where the rubber meets the road.

Exercise is the first of the Holy Trinity, the father of our well-being. It is not about being an Olympic athlete, a superman or wonder woman. It is about the rather less exciting but equally important creation of habits to keep our bodies and minds together.

This is not really an exercise book, or even a book about exercise. What is more, there are plenty of fitness experts who can give you a fitness programme tailored to your individual needs. I am not able to do that. I can however provide hints that show you why exercise is important to your well-being, and to encourage you to start thinking about the kind of actions you might take.

> **Sitting on a timebomb**
>
> If you have a sedentary lifestyle, you are literally doing this.
>
> Sitting for just 1-2 hours a day increases our risk of early death. Muscles that help regulate blood sugar levels have to be active to do so.
>
> Keith Diaz at Columbia University: 'every 30 minutes sitting replaced by light physical activity reduces risk of early death by 14-17%, with vigorous exercise increasing that to 36%[1].

Oiling the chain

Regular exercise releases serotonin, dopamine, noradrenaline, all of which we know are great for mental health, reducing risk of depression at least as effectively as anti-depressants. Aerobic activity cuts dementia risk by 50% and we benefit from an increase in the blood volume in our dentate gyrus, a part of the brain that helps our hippocampus store memories. The levels of the molecule 'brain derived neurotrophic factor', or BDNF, which helps the brain produce neurons and enhances neuronal connections, has been shown to increase significantly after a variety of aerobic or High Intensity interval Training exercises. It also has an anti-inflammatory effect, and we now know inflammation can lead to anxiety and depression.

Exercising outdoors bestows even more benefit, as being close to nature is proven to improve our mood and markedly reduce levels of depression and anxiety[2]. Well-being appears to be enhanced by seeing pictures of 'nature', although the effects are not fully understood, some soothing, woodland screensavers, and outdoor soundscapes may even be beneficial if confined indoors for long periods.

DNA

Genes are the instructions for building proteins. Some sections of our DNA contain what are known as 'gene enhancers' which regulate which genes are active in which tissue.

Some sections of our DNA are known risk areas for development of diseases.

The Copenhagen epigenetics* study[3] subjected healthy young men to a six-week endurance exercise programme, with a before and after thigh muscle biopsy. After the exercise regime, the structure of the skeletal muscle had been altered. Specifically, exercise had 're-wired' the gene enhancers in those regions of DNA that are known risk areas.

The science is in its infancy, yet these kinds of studies are starting to provide explanation for the well-known effects of exercise on our physical well-being.

> ***Epigenetics**
>
> how your actions and environment change the way your genes work
>
> University of Copenhagen research study shows evidence of 'a functional link between epigenetic rewiring of enhancers to control their activity after exercise training and the modulation of disease risk in humans'.

Getting a Grip

In just 35 years, our physical strength has declined, specifically our grip strength, by 20%, (according to a survey by Elizabeth Fain, occupational therapist using the standard hand-held dynamometer). Our societies have drifted dramatically away from the physical, with safety concerns preventing children walking to school, on-line entertainment dominating youth past-times, the automation of heavy physical tasks and a tendency towards smart phone and device use in all age groups.

Grip strength is a strong indicator of physical health, as demonstrated by a study in the Lancet in 2015, in which 140,000 people were tracked across 17 countries over four years[5]. Grip strength, which

> **Older but Weaker?**
>
> Daniel Lieberman, Harvard University paleoanthropologist, observes the apparent conflict between declining strength and fitness in the modern world and our increasing lifespans. Modern medicine and associated treatments may keep us alive longer but we are also weaker for longer[4].

has been progressively declining over millions of years as we make the shift away from our arboreal ancestors, was shown to be a strong predictor of cardiovascular and other causes of mortality, even more so than blood pressure. Grip strength is routinely used as a measure of aging, with low grip strength even associated with declines in cognitive performance.

Moving onwards and upwards

Moving your body in different ways can impact on the way your mind works. Different speeds of running or walking have different mental effects. At low pace, we free the mind to be more creative, by reducing pre-frontal activity, which is the more rational kind. At high pace, we impact more severely the blood flow which seems to generate grey matter, particularly in the hippocampus, the seat of memory.

Slave to the Rhythm?

Babies show natural rhythm and the better their rhythm, the more they smile.

Toddlers are more likely to help an adult after being bounced in time with the music. It seems that **synchronising is sympathising**.

In adults too, predicting a musical pattern gives a dopamine fix – we feel good. If we move to the beat, we get a second fix. And maybe even a sense that we control the music[6].

With movement, we increase our strength. Strength by middle age correlates with grey matter and memory and perhaps as a result it is also equated with lower cognitive decline, higher self-esteem and general well-being. If we feel strong, with better coordination and balance, we feel better able to tackle life's challenges.

Stretching the point

At the end of a long period of inactivity, it feels great to have a really good stretch. This 'pandiculation' is nature's way of waking up those muscles. This is exercise. We can wait for the reflex yawn and stretch, or we can actively manage our muscle movements. Our muscle movement determines our flexibility. Our flexibility has a substantial impact on our physical fitness. We can increase our muscle movement with practice.

When we are under stress, we tighten up. Stretching can lengthen muscle and connective tissue, restoring mobility in underused joints. Of course, stretching should be gradual and flexibility cannot be rushed. What is more, it does not appear that extremes of suppleness bestow any particular health benefits, even if they might be quite impressive at parties.

Slouching or scrunching is associated with negative feelings. Psychologists know that an upright, stretched posture leads to reduced stress[7]. It is possible that the neural pathway linking the brain and the adrenal glands may help to control the adrenaline rush and the adrenal medulla is affected by the muscles that support a strong upright posture.

At a stretch

The American College of Sports Medicine recommend that we '**stretch all major muscle groups at least two or three times a week, holding the stretch for anywhere from 10 seconds to 1 minute**'. A study of 1354 Japanese Men aged 35 to 59 showed that the least flexible showed higher levels of atherosclerosis – a risk factor for cardiovascular diseases. Caroline Williams, in Move shows this as one of the many studies that suggest keeping joints well-oiled is beneficial, perhaps due to a boost to natural levels of secretion of anti-inflammatory molecules.

Improvement Actions

Thy these three simple steps you can take to improve physical fitness.

1. Do some (exercise)

Don't dig out your brain trainers, dig out your running or your walking shoes. As Nike slogan says, just do it – I would add though, no fancy footwear required - you could always do it barefoot!

I'm not suggesting we forget exercise for the mind; intellectual stimulation, challenge, purpose, achievement, fun and laughter are vital, but we do now know that those 'brain trainers' which surged in popularity around the millennium only improve your ability to perform those specific tasks with minimal impact on cognitive range. They don't make us any cleverer.

Unlike a good walk; a twenty-minute daily walk. As well as reducing stroke risk by 57%, regular exercisers have better cognitive test scores, better long-term memory, better reasoning, improved attention, better problem solving and more abstract thinking ability[8]. There are no drugs that can rival its effect on our overall health and well-being, with the benefits most profound in those who have experienced the most stressful life events. Many doctors now prescribe 'exercise pills'.

> **Skiing reduces anxiety**
>
> Those who took part in the world's largest long-distance cross-country ski race had a significantly lower risk of developing anxiety than non-skiers.
>
> A physically active lifestyle leads to 60% lower risk of developing anxiety disorders[9].
>
> Based on a survey of nearly 400,000 Swedish people monitored between 1989 -2010.

2. Ask yourself - Are you sitting on a timebomb or a goldmine?

If you spend large tracts of time inactive, then your body and mind will thank you for taking the time to consider some compensatory movement. If you create a routine pattern of exercise, you will be defusing the timebomb. If you really focus, you can turn your body into a goldmine, reaping spiralling benefits to body and mind as if you were some kind of perpetual-motion machine.

*Keep writing those jokes,
every day – don't break the chain*
Jerry Seinfeld

The scale of impact is dramatic and confirmatory evidence so prevalent as to be more certain than the 1969 Moon landing. Exercise is clearly an essential part of a well-being programme. Most advisers suggest that those who are office-bound or sedentary mix it up during the day, and perhaps start and finish with some exercise. A well-oiled chain will run smoothly. It is said that whereas it may take up to 6 months effort to reach your desired fitness, you can lose all that benefit in just 6 weeks. So, don't beat yourself up if you miss, but do your best to get back to a routine. The odd day without oil should not break the chain All your good work will not be flushed away, unless you use it as an excuse to sit for too long…

And if you must sit, why not try sitting on your haunches? Squatting keeps hips, calves and ankles mobile and, as

Squat your way to fitness

Most of us have lost this ability. Don't think it looks cool enough? Well, you are missing out! With practice you can comfortably sit anywhere, with no equipment required. Dr Bahram Jam, a physical therapist says that eschewing the squatting position has created numerous health problems.

What is more, every joint in our body has synovial fluid to provide nutrition to the cartilage. Joints, like hips and knees need to go past 90 degrees to get the full movement and compression required. In line with our human policy of 'use it or lose it', the body says 'I'm not being used', the joint degenerates and the synovial fluid stops being produced.

well as suppleness and flexibility, it is a form of low-level muscle activity (exercise) still used by traditional 'Hunter-gatherer' type tribes (like the Tanzanian Hadza)[10]. It remains popular across Asia. Squatting has been linked to many health benefits, including improved posture, reduction of spinal problems, cardiovascular health and even mental well-being. A less sedentary lifestyle is associated with lower levels of depression although it is not clear if this identifies cause and effect.

It is also worth noting that The British Heart Foundation state that poor health effects from too much sitting are separate from whether you are physically active or not, so even if you don't exercise, it is beneficial to avoid excessive sitting[11]. Generally, our minds work better when we sit less...

3. Find a pattern that suits you

It is not helpful to focus on the trend of physical decline, as overall patterns do not define our status as individuals. There are of course a million books guiding you to the appropriate exercise regime to enable you to achieve your desired fitness and your body image. This isn't one of them, although using an understanding of growth mindset, you will now believe in your ability to change. Mr Puniverse will never achieve the stature of Atlas, the Greek Titan, but Dwayne Johnson, The Rock, had to work on achieving his physical fitness and physique and we can all move our own dials, with the discipline of habit.

> **It must be love**
>
> And don't we owe it to our small but so faithful friend?
>
> Small enough that it could fit neatly into the palm of a hand...
>
> Faithful enough to battle on despite all the strain we put it under.
>
> Our miraculous little pump beats every second without a rest, and continues to do so, we hope, for as many as 3 billion cycles...

On a cold winter's night after a tough day, you might not really fancy it. This is where habit, your over-riding plan, kicks in. And, if you really don't know whether you can face a run through the dark, cold misty night, put on your running shoes and they will tell you. And above all, your mind, and your heart will thank you!

And a note of caution. Don't expect exercise alone to keep you in your desired shape. Your metabolism will adjust to your exercise pattern.

And in any case, when you burn more calories, your body seeks more intake...

Don't forget that Calories Count

Intake of calories is significant and notoriously difficult to count. We have a great tendency to forget. According to Herman Pontzner in Burn, based on research in thousands of cases, women tend to underestimate their daily intake by 15% and men by 50%[12]!

As a final point, remember it was Marcel Proust who preached that we should 'live according to our soul' (the Indian concept of Dharma). In other words, he said, at length, that we should follow our dreams to achieve fulfilment. His father, Dr Adrien Proust, was a more practical man, a renowned medic and author. His work is believed to have had a major positive impact on physical well-being, particularly tackling the ravages of the cholera epidemic of the time. His book Elements of Hygiene provides some useful exercises for wellness too...

Swinging your arms

Jumping off a wall

This prescient book was published in 1888[13]. He proposes a number of regular exercises specifically aimed at teenage girls in order to produce a 'vigorous new generation of French citizens'.

If those are a little too strenuous, this one may also be effective:

Balancing on one leg

Perhaps the perfect accompaniment to Marcel Proust's medicine for the soul!

REFLECTION TIME

Exercise		
Mens Rea	Actus Rhesus	Guilty? ☑
1. Mind and body work together...or not at all.	Are you keeping the cogs well-oiled...so your chain doesn't seize up?	☐
2. It is not great to take everything sitting down	What exercise are you doing today?	☐
Good nutrition, and healthy sleep patterns will complete your Holy Trinity...		

The not-so surprising impact of what we eat on our body and mind...

Chapter 3:
Nutrition

Let food be your medicine
Hippocrates

If exercise is the father, nutrition is the son. We are what we eat. We like to complicate this but really there is no mystery; we are the carbon-based product of biological mathematics. The trouble is, as we have already established, we are not very good at maths and whilst the theory is simple, practise, as always, must play catch up.

According to the World Health Organisation over 4 million people die each year as a result of being overweight or obese[1]. Overall obesity has tripled since 1975, in a period in which the world population has almost doubled[2], surely questioning those Malthusian doom-mongers as scarcer resources are shared among burgeoning communities. Of course, there are huge disparities which should not be ignored but for the purpose of this book, let's assume we do have choice about what we put into our bodies.

Size isn't everything

But it is quite important to the formula for determining our weight gains or losses.

Where S=Size now, I= Food intake, Z= previous siZe and E=Exercise.

The formula 'S = I+Z-E', is well known to us all, but we tend to forget.

Of course, for this equation to be valid, Exercise here means a complex mixture of the obvious physical movements discussed in the prior section, alongside metabolism and digestive processes. And equally importantly, SIZE isn't everything, as Granny will tell you.

Everything in moderation, and a little bit of what you fancy never did anyone any harm

Granny Kath

Granny's wisdom would have us breakfast like a king, lunch like a princess and dine like a pauper, because the way we process our food intake varies significantly dependent on our circadian rhythms (body changes throughout the day). I concede that my simplified SIZE formula ignores such complexities. Several studies show an association between late night eating and diabetes or obesity. It appears that melatonin, which builds up in preparation for sleep, may also interfere with our ability to process glucose.

The Nutritionists' model

Kate Moss once noted that 'nothing tastes as good as skinny feels'. She was not 'the nutritionists' model'. That model predates her. It was brought up to date in the early 20th Century by Bernard MacFadden, who Ben Goldacre explains, 'aimed to reflect contemporary moral values'[3]. MacFadden became the greatest health guru of his time selling granola bars and a range of health and beauty products. He focused on 'beautification through nutrition' reflecting his (now non-pc) view of the importance of appearance. (Kate, take note!)

> **Size really isn't everything!**
>
> McFadden didn't stop there – he also invented a 'peniscope' – yes, a suction device for enlargement (with a broadly similar design still available today, apparently!)
>
> Perhaps for similar reasons, he changed his name to Bernarr, reflecting his desire to appear 'more like a lion'!

Nutrition science developed such a bad name over more than a century with snake oils, Gillian McKeith's horny goat weed complexes, colonic irrigation treatments and most of the Gwyneth Paltrow range, that today it is still fighting to get the credibility it deserves when there can be little doubt that it is a fundamental element of a sensible formula for good health.

Five appetites, one belly

When animals have an unrestricted choice of foods, they manage to achieve a balance of nutrients, of carbohydrates, fats and proteins. It is when they are deprived of one that they over-eat the other, as they chase the missing ingredient unhelpfully.

In effect, they have dual appetites and need to satisfy them both. We humans show the same tendencies, with multiple appetites rather than just one big one.

The dual appetites in animals guided related research on humans. We now know that we have five appetites; protein, carbohydrates, fat, sodium and calcium. A prime example of a study testing this involved a group of unfortunate subjects who were afflicted with a four-day Swiss chalet retreat, where food intake was

> **Eating like Animals**
>
> According to David Raubenheimer and Stephen Simpson, in their book Eat Like the Animals, anthropologists have discovered that the wild Cape baboons manage a balanced diet without sophisticated programmes. They take in four times as many of their daily calories from carbohydrates and fats as they do from proteins.
>
> The two research scientists, who also examined and tested varying locust diets, identified the two distinct appetites, one for proteins, one for carbohydrates. When deprived of one, they over-ate the other to satiate that appetite, hence over-eating overall. When they were fed a high protein diet, they actually ate too few carbohydrates. In this case, it shows that when juggling two appetites, protein gets first dibs.

controlled and monitored. When the diet was low in protein, the subjects ate 35% more calories. When the diet was high protein, they ate 38% fewer calories[3]. This makes sense from an evolutionary point of view as it is most effective for us to be able to focus on the key ones, and to those in short supply, like sodium.

Reducing protein in our food (as we did in the period of 40 years 1961-2000) saw US calorie intake up 13%[4]. When protein starved, our appetite is not satiated and we seek out alternative sources. Hence the significant increase in ultra-processed foods like savoury snacks and much junk food, sometimes called protein decoys (especially those with the taste of umami – the principal flavour of protein). In very recent times, protein-rich foods have become a nutrition conscious person's friend; they are wittingly or unwittingly satisfying a dominant appetite and in doing so they tend to reduce overall calorie intake.

Fibre in our diet reduces our appetite too, and it is unsurprisingly hard to find in the ultra-processed foods we grasp for when we are in a hurry, like pizzas and cakes, crisps and biscuits.

Complete proteins

Protein comprises 20 amino acids. 11 of these are produced by the human body.

Proteins like meat, fish, eggs and soya, which contain the other nine; the 'essential amino acids' the body cannot synthesise, help to create our core neurotransmitters like noradrenaline, and help to keep to us motivated to meet our other challenges, like following the complimentary exercise regimes we have just set for ourselves...

Is 5 or 7 the magic number?

From our memory studies, we know that both numbers (5 and 7) fit neatly in our working memory range, which is probably why these numbers have been adopted for our daily fruit and vegetable intake recommendations – The World Health Organisation suggest 400g of fruit and vegetables a day; 5-a-day, based on 80g portions. WHO states that...

"There is epidemiological evidence of an increased risk of cancer with low intake of certain fruit and vegetables and their contributions to micronutrients as well as to dietary fibre"[5]

Tell me what you eat and I will tell you what you are

Anthelme Brillat-Savarin, Lawyer and Politician

Hunger – it's all in the mind

Of course, it's not all in the mind, but hunger's role and its impact on our emotions and decisions is greater than we might think. Those Israeli judges (see Rough Justice Section 5.5) amply demonstrated how someone else's hunger can affect your life. Having your parole hearing at the wrong part of the judges' schedule almost certainly left some people unjustly languishing in jail...

Have you ever wondered, what is the worst decision your hunger could help you make?

When our energy levels are low, our patience suffers. When our patience is low, reasonable behaviour becomes more challenging; all bets are off. This is why, if you have been slaving away all day, and just haven't had time to eat, nutrition experts say 'don't starve yourself. Don't cut off your nose to spite your face; eat whatever is available. If all that is available is a sugary, cream donut... 'eat that fxxxing donut!', they say.

Apart from our emotional reaction, a blood sugar dip will induce hunger and tempt us towards higher overall calorie consumption. When our stomach has been empty for about two hours, it begins contracting, sweeping any remaining food into the intestines. We feel a 'rumbling'. The sound of our digestion or 'borborygmus' is usually good enough indication that it is time to start considering a top up...

In the new field of research called psychobiotics, Professor

> **Too much grazing? – Too much grehlin**
>
> The cells in the stomach and intestine produce two hormones to control our appetite; leptin makes you feel full and grehlin makes you feel hungry.

Tanya Byron explains, 'food that we know is associated with good gut health might also show significant benefits for our mental health.' We now know that the vagus nerve links our brain to our gut. As with the immune system, this link appears to work both ways. Professor Philip Burnet, of Oxford University, works on psychiatric disorders and mood management. In his experiments addressing the effect on neurotransmitter systems of gut bacteria, he saw participants who took probiotic supplements recording a 50% improvement in mood. This compared to a significant but more modest 20% improvement for his placebo group[6].

And then, when we feel hungry, the heightened grehlin level makes us reach out for those quick fixes, the kinds of food associated with obesity. Lack of sleep has a similar effect- it seems to promote grehlin production. Grehlin reduces our control of the supervisory regions of our prefrontal cortex. These are the regions that help manage our impulse control (our will power). This probably explains why we veer towards junk food, sugars and complex carbohydrates, cakes, pizza, fries... after a hard day 'at the office'.

Repeated denial of food*, on the other hand, can result in the body shedding both muscle and fat with levels of vital nutrients like phosphorous and magnesium also depleted. When low on sugar, cortisol and epinephrine are released to attempt to normalise our blood sugar levels. We already know the effect of these hormones coursing our bodies; they make us feel tense, stressed, irritable and hence, 'hangry'. Neuropeptide Y plays a role too, sending us that hungry feeling, to accompany the rumbling. This hormone is also linked to aggression, and perhaps contributes to our need for 'hanger management'.

All in the mind, and the gut

*Attempted denial can have a counter-intuitive effect too – just thinking we are either depriving or treating ourselves influences production of hormones in the gut which increase or suppress appetite.

Which is why eating so-called health-bars or the like can be counter-productive - reframing our food intake can be as effective as changing our diet.

Nibbling a bag of assorted veg is better for you than a bag of salted peanuts...If you can persuade your body that it is as satisfying, then all the better!

Abstaining from food can aid the healing process

Hippocrates

Is Hippocrates right?– His oath commits that he will do us no harm... First he says 'food should be our medicine, now he tells us to abstain...so which is it?!*

---

*Fasting

Hippocrates, the father of Western medicine, should make his mind up!

In the observance of religious rituals (eg Ramadan, Lent) and in a myriad diets (eg Ayurvedic medicine), we are required to fast, or to abstain from certain food groups for extended periods. Is this harmful to our health?

Many argue the benefits, suggesting that a reduction to your normal eating patterns gives your body time to focus on other important functions, including disease prevention, inflammation management and chronic conditions such as heart disease, multiple sclerosis and rheumatoid arthritis. Several studies suggest it can improve blood sugar control and reduce the risk of diabetes. One study showed that a nightly 'fast' of more than 13 hours could reduce the risk of recurrence in those diagnosed with early-stage breast cancer. And studies in animals suggest fasting may positively impact Parkinson's, Alzheimer's, general cognitive function, nerve cell generations and yes, even weight loss!

On the other hand, it may lead to an increase in the stress hormone, cortisol, which may lead to even more food cravings. It may encourage compensatory overeating and binge eating. It often results in dehydration as when you don't eat you also forget to drink. You will feel tired because your body is running on less energy than usual, and your sleep patterns may be disrupted. As the biochemistry that regulates our mood also regulates our appetite, the activity of neurotransmitters like dopamine and serotonin is affected and increases the risk of anxiety and depression. And, there is a good chance you will feel irritable when fasting.7

On the other hand, taking control of your diet brings with it a sense of control and with religious observance encourages higher thought, consideration beyond ourselves, and other reflective practices all of which are beneficial to our well-being.

The Daft Apeth concludes that it is a personal choice which requires a weighing up of pro's and con's for you as an individual, with any drastic action taken advisedly and preferably under medical supervision.

In any case, stay well-hydrated and concentrate on eating well when you do eat, bear in mind energy balance and the impact of putting yourself under unnecessary stress.

Perhaps Hippocrates was right after all.

Improvement Actions

With a little conscious effort, we can improve our nutrition, and in doing so we can improve our well-being...

1. Diet Management

Managing protein targets as part of a balanced diet seems sensible, with indicatively 15-20% of daily calorific intake ideally protein (approx. 4-5 grammes). Proteins are particularly important because the associated amino acids act as building blocks for neurotransmitters, like tryptophan, which is a precursor for serotonin and melatonin.

2. Personal plans

Of course, to really optimise our diets requires a plan, and as our response to food is so individual, our plan should be individual too, as one person's healthy tuna sandwich lunch is, at the extreme, another person's diabetes and obesity in waiting*.

> ***Wise men**
>
> A team at the Weizmann Institute of Science in Israel studying the effect of artificial sweeteners found that the impact was highly personalised in respect of glucose spikes (a known trigger for diabetes)[8].

Current reliance on our glycaemic index wrongly implies that we have a higher level of similarity than the Weizmann tests showed. Almost all food types affect each of us differently with some people having a healthier response to mass-produced white bread than to wholegrain sourdough.

Highly unique responses were seen in the first 800 volunteers in terms of glucose spikes and now big data tools and AI have linked 50,000 individuals' responses to their individual microbiome composition. Other similar tests have measured a fat class called triglycerides, which cause other chronic conditions as well as diabetes, like heart disease and metabolic problems[9]. These are sending the same new message – we all have unique optimal nutritional needs.

There are personal apps like Zoe[10] and the Personalized Nutrition Project[11], and it won't be long before we are able to reliably define our perfect diet, which will be great news for some as it may even mean that chocolate and ice cream are put back on the menu, even for some pre-diabetics! In the meantime, we will still have to make some subjective judgments.

3. Eat well

Nutritious food provides enough energy to fuel your brain when it needs it and then protects against unwelcome emotion swings.

Until we can get our app to tell us the exact diet for our personal needs then it seems wise to focus on maintaining a balanced diet with complete proteins, plenty of fibre, vegetables, fruit and nuts. Fruit and nuts being particularly good snacks, fruit for its fructose sugars, which give us immediate energy boosts, and nuts (and seeds) for the proteins and fats which sustain our energy levels and stabilise our blood sugars[12].

4. Takeaways

And if there is one take-away from this section, let it be that we should avoid excesses of over-processed foods prevalent in most takeaways, restricting your junk food intake to when your mind or body really needs 'a little bit of what you fancy'! It really is ok to have that fruit and nut enrobed in finest milk chocolate, occasionally (yum, my favourite!).

Don't forget Water

Total body water comprises approximately 45–75% of our body weight and is the main constituent of our muscle mass. Water transports nutrients, regulates body temperature, lubricates joints and internal organs, provides structure to cells and tissues, and can help preserve cardiovascular function. Water consumption may also facilitate weight management and a deficit can impact physical and cognitive performance[13]

Current recommendation is around 2 Litres a day for the average person – you are not average, so be governed by your senses!

And, whatever else you do, keep your energy levels up, stay well hydrated and continue to avoid the dietary advice of Gwyneth Paltrow (if indeed it is such) and Dr Gillian McKeith.

REFLECTION TIME

Nutrition		
Mens Rea	Actus Rhesus	Guilty? ☑
1. Good food creates good mood - Eat what you like, when you like…	Do you choose to like to eat food that nourishes you, at times that suit your circadian rhythms?	☐
2. Do you know your personalised dietary need? Your body and mind will tell you if it is right for you	Do you feel your energy levels remain stable? Do you feel good physically? What can you do to increase your stable energy levels?	☐

Nutrition		
Mens Rea	Actus Rhesus	Guilty? ☑
3. Treat yourself but don't spoil yourself - seldom pleasures bring the sweetest joy	Do you ask yourself – do I need the whole cream donut, or will one bite do? ASK NOT WHAT THE DONUT CAN DO FOR YOU...!	☐
Unsure whether to eat that next donut? Sleep on it - sleeping well helps us manage our diet better...		

The most neglected of the holy
trinity of physical well-being

Chapter 4:
Sleep

Sleep is the third pillar of the Holy Trinity, the spirit that brings it all together. Without it we die.

I'll sleep when I'm dead

Jon Bon Jovi

An estimated 1 in 5 adult drivers admit to having fallen asleep while driving in the last year. This 'drowsy driving' causes more than 100,000 crashes and 1,000 deaths each year[1].

Hibernating animals do it[2]. They routinely break out of hibernation, using up valuable energy resources, so that they can sleep. There are some

Lack of Sleep costs

When the oil tanker Exxon Valdez, ran aground on Bligh Reef, Alaska, spilling 11 million gallons of crude oil, contaminating over 1300 miles of coastline, it was being steered by third-in-command, whilst its Captain, Joseph Hazelwood took to his bunk. Over a quarter of a million birds were killed, as well as countless marine animals, including at least 22 killer whales, and the economic impact, amounting to $5bn, left devastated communities and broken families in its wake.

The unqualified third in command had slept for just 6 out of the past 48 hours.

birds who can sleep with half a brain still 'on'; those at the edge of a 'V' shaped formation do it, dolphins do it, humans cannot. We have two hemispheres but evolution hasn't deemed such adaptation to be beneficial. If we don't sleep, our organs start to eat themselves up from the inside. We can survive longer without food than without sleep.

Jon Bon Jovi should have said 'I'll sleep or I'm dead', or at least "I'll sleep when I'm dead tired", although admittedly neither sounds as cool. Yet sleep is something to cherish. Those who promote the machoism of 'burning the candle at both ends', figures like Donald Trump and Margaret Thatcher, who claimed to survive on 3-4 hours sleep a night, should probably be pitied. Sleep is not the enemy of productivity; it is its best friend!

> **Genetic exceptions**
>
> Two DNA mutations have been found, which when engineered in mice showed them sleeping 4 hours without any cognitive impairment or obvious health impediments[3]. It is not clear whether Trump possesses this particular mutation!

We work hard, exhaust ourselves meeting unfeasible deadlines and commonly neglect our recuperation, our rest time, our relaxation, and most importantly our sleep. The World Health Organisation defines lack of societal sleep as a 'global health epidemic' affecting one in two across most developed countries[5].

As a child, I used to dream that they (the world's experts) would

> **Just can't get enough?**
>
> It is estimated that in the US, 65% don't get enough sleep (7-9 hours), 39% in UK, 66% in Japan.[4]
>
> If we have just six hours sleep for six days, which is common, our performance degrades as much as if we miss sleep completely for a straight 24 hour period.[3]
>
> And what is more, our brain's cycle doesn't have a catch-up phase! And we cannot gain credits.

invent a machine that would enable me to study whilst asleep; perhaps piping audio lectures into my head, adding to what I do, or even saving me the bother of doing it at all, whilst awake. It turns out that it has already been invented and it's called our brain! Yes, it turns out that sleep is not time wasted; it is consolidation and thinking time for the sub-conscious. When we have a particularly knotty problem, and say 'we'll sleep on it', our brain literally works on that problem, whilst we are away in the land of nod.

Research using latest technology has proven that sleep is so much more than just 'not awake'. It is more than just time to re-charge the batteries. It is when our memories are transferred from short term storage in the hippocampus, to longer term storage areas. It is where waking thoughts are made sense of, filed, networked with other thoughts and ensuing ideas developed. It is where our physiological stability is maintained through management of our cardiovascular health and our body temperature regulation.

In short, if you are not getting enough, then you are not going to reach your potential, you are not going to be your best self.

It has its time and its place. For most adults this is in bed, for eight hours a night, timing dependent on circadian rhythms, and personal preferences. If we plan based on our moods, as described by Robert Thayer, to sleep when we are disposed to be 'calm-tired', we will optimise the benefit.

As with all animals, we have an internal clock, (governed by our *suprachiasmatic nucleus*), which dictates our daily cycle; our circadian rhythms (circa – about, dian – a day). Our personal preference lies somewhere on a scale, tending towards 'morning larks' at one end or 'night owls' at the other.

Downsides of sleep

It's not a good idea when you are at work (unless your work is as a research assistant at a Sleep Lab), when operating machinery, or when driving.

It could make you vulnerable to attack and in humans it cannot be done effectively with 'one eye open'.

> It's not great, at least unsupervised, if you are predisposed to sleepwalking into a busy road, or to a relative's family to commit multiple unconscious murders (as in the horrendously unfortunate case of Kenneth Parks).[6]
>
> Normally, when we are asleep, our waking signals, which continue to flood the central areas of our brain, are blocked by the thalamus, which acts like a switch, a sensory gate which is firmly shut so you don't physically act out your dreams. When we sleep-walk or talk, or murder, the switch has failed to operate properly!

The structure of our society favours the morning lark, as a night owl may be technically awake early in the morning, on the train, or the school bus, or driving to work, but their pre-frontal cortex remains in an 'off-line' state. A night owl prefers high level brain activity at night and is more vulnerable than a morning lark to sleep deprivation, unable to resist burning the midnight oil, while the morning lark may be happily tucked up at 10pm.

As with most things, the benefits balance out, however; the morning lark may win the sleep and resulting overall efficiency contest, the night owl is a better friend of Jon Bon Jovi, and way more fun at parties!

In the finite space in our cranium, within less than 2kg of brain matter, we want to optimise the power of this miraculous giant walnut, deleting unwanted data, efficiently storing the good stuff, and optimising the capacity to take on more.

Chemicals and rhythms in harmony

Alongside our circadian urges, an unconnected chemical system provides us with our sleep pressure signals. The chemical, adenosine builds up and so does our urge to sleep. We are at our best when our rhythms and chemicals work in harmony. These two separate waves then peak together, and our thinking brains make it happen.

Finding the sweet spot is a delicate balancing act and we now know that many of these optimising processes are carried out subconsciously whilst we sleep, and with two distinct phases reflecting the kind of processing the brain performs...

Not just what but when...

In the same way that our nutrition is determined not only by how much we eat but more importantly by what we eat and when, so the same of sleep. REM and NREM sleep happen in waves throughout the night, with a cycle of REM and NREM about every 90 minutes. NREM features more heavily in the early stage of sleep and REM is preponderant in the latter stages - for adults. The opposite is true in younger brains. In fact, we have shifting amounts of REM and NREM throughout our lives, dependent on age, with infants, teenagers, young and old adults having differing needs at different phases of the sleep process.

These two phases are termed REM and Non-REM (NREM) sleep; Rapid Eye Movement, and (imaginatively) Non-Rapid Eye Movement sleep are observable states although the activity performed during these phases of sleep needs the latest scanning technologies to interpret This understanding is still somewhat a work in progress.

It's all in the timing

A problem difficult at night is resolved in the morning after the committee of sleep has worked on it

John Steinbeck

As Matthew Walker, the asleep advocate, describes it, during REM sleep our emotions, motivations and memories are projected on our visual, auditory and kinaesthetic sensory cortices as if they were cinema screens, playing and re-playing the films of our lives, with our most current experiences predominating[7]. This mirrors the waking practice of visualisations which meditation practitioners advise as we consider our future path to enlightenment.

Whilst all mammals sleep, human REM sleep may be a significant contributor to the refinement of our animalistic emotions, as we now know that during this phase we increase our rationality, our emotional intelligence and our empathy, enabling us to function as effectively as we do as a society. We do still have some way to go, of course.

NREM sleep on the other hand is the time for storing and strengthening new facts and skills, reflecting on them, and pruning and deleting, prior to integration in the REM phases of sleep. NREM sleep is characterised by changing brainwave frequency, with four recognised stages, and the deepest sleep corresponding to our slowest brain waves.[8]

During deep NREM sleep, we prune and sculpt our memories preparing for the next spell of weaving of connections in REM sleep. The 90-minute cycle is like a football match, with all the goals towards the end, all the build-up play earlier on.

If you are a morning lark, yet don't manage to tuck in until midnight, you will have been missing out on vital NREM.

Twit twoo

If you are a night owl, but you have to get up for work or school, you might be particularly interested to think about the impact of having to wake up after 6 hours sleep - two hours too early every day.

You've been deprived of sleep, and mostly REM sleep and the associated integration benefits for longer than you can remember.

Imagine how much sharper, how much better your memory would be if you managed to get a regular 8 hours! (see 'napping' box for a potential solution to your sleep/party conundrum!).

Good sleep improves learning as Robert Stickgold at Harvard Medical School and Matthew Walker found; piano playing notably improved. Specifically, they found that what had been learned whilst awake was then embedded and rehearsed in sleep, unconsciously. The piano learner woke up able to play more accurately, more smoothly and without the awkward pauses where they had learnt the pieces in 'chunks'[9]. Sleep helped consolidate and smooth over the cracks.

It's Emotional

Extreme emotional swings whilst awake may earn you the psychiatric diagnosis, *'affectively labile'*. In our dreams these extremes are common-place. In REM, our brain's emotional regions are 30% more active than when we are awake. Conversely the areas associated with rational thought are reduced. The use of technology to study dreams remains in its infancy, although it has shown that whilst all the activities we visualise can't yet be explained (1-2% explainable), the emotions aroused in our dreams can be interpreted based on the real emotions of the subjects of the studies (35-55% explainable)[10].

Interpreting dreams

Pattern matching is now being deployed for analysis of our unconscious dreams, and as Matthew Walker describes, having mapped a brain's response pattern to enough images it is possible to match the brain patterns of a person in REM sleep.

A far cry from Freud's 'interpretation of dreams', we are well on the way to a genuine translation of our nocturnal meanderings. Admittedly we're not that accurate yet. We can see that a car features in a dream but not whether it is the gleaming red beast with the rampant stallion logo I aspire to own or the rather more mundane family saloon that I actually do!

A change in our brain's chemical mix also takes place, with reduced noradrenaline (associated with stress) during REM sleep. This is a major reason that sleep provides emotional healing.

Every night the REM pixies come out and caress our emotional centres, ensuring optimal emotional performance. Without sufficient sleep, our insecurities rise to the surface, we are more alert to dangers, more fearful. This can seriously affect our relationships. Normally we are remarkably good at reading people's facial expressions. When we are sleep deprived, we can't help noticing their sinister edge.

If we are meeting people for the first time this can have significant impact. As we have now encoded those feelings for use later, they will be hard to shrug off even after we have had our full night's sleep. Our unlucky job candidate will have an uphill battle, if indeed he got that far.

> **At the extreme**
>
> In the case of PTSD, it appears that the noradrenaline level may be so high as to prevent REM and hence prevent the 'sanding down of the edges' of severely traumatic emotions.
>
> (A drug, Prazosin which has been shown to reduce noradrenaline, also reduces the frequency of PTSD related episodes).

Impact of Sleep Deprivation

In order to sleep, to switch off, our thalamus is called to act. This happens when the hypothalamus (above the thalamus) releases the neurotransmitter, **Orexin**. The thalamus uses this Orexin to switch off the gate.

We can easily sabotage our sleep as is common in the elderly, those with mental health issues, those late-night blue screen users, and those with an overactive sympathetic nervous system. Excessive worry can switch on the fight or flight impulses - sending the heart-rate racing, increasing blood flow, producing cortisol and creating a vicious circle. With the emotional centre, the amygdala and hippocampus highly active, the thalamus does not get the signal, does not get the Orexin, and it does not switch off the gate.

Sleep deprivation tests can be both revealing and cruel. Some of the more extreme experimentation techniques have been outlawed in recent years as we have come to appreciate (or at least care more about) the deleterious effects of prolonged deprivation. We owe a debt of gratitude to the laboratory rats whose bodies have eaten themselves up from

Screen time impact

It is estimated that the effect of late-night iPad (or equivalent) use is a 90-minute lag in the rise of melatonin, which induces the desire for sleep, meaning you stay up later than you might otherwise have done, take longer to get to sleep and suffer sleep deprivation if you have to get up for school or work in the morning.

the inside due to enforced, extreme sleep deprivation.

With less than 4 hours sleep, your risk of a car crash increases 12x, due to slower reactions[11]. You will have four times as many 'microsleeps', which are sleeps of a few seconds, that you are not aware of, and the statistics confirm 'drowsy driving' is as dangerous as drunk driving.

In reasonably benign sleep-deprivation trials, students demonstrate vast mood swings, 'traversing enormous emotional distances, from punch-drunk giddy, to vicious negativity, rather like a person suffering from bi-polar disease'. Our emotional stability suffers. We all know that we are irascible, tense and irritable when we don't get enough sleep. It is also harder to experience positive emotions when suffering sleep deprivation.

This is a contributory factor for sufferers of depression - not having positive emotions is equivalent to emphasising the negatives. Brain scans have shown a 60% amplification in emotional reactivity in the amygdala. As Walker puts it, 'we suffer with too much gas pedal (amygdala) and not enough brake (pre-frontal cortex)'. What is more, the striatum, which sits just behind the amygdala, and is associated with impulsivity and reward shows hyperactivity suggesting a loss of control of our hedonistic tendencies. Conversely, our testosterone levels drop, and this can impact 'productivity' in all senses.

Sleep deprivation affects our genes too. Dr Derk-Jan Dijk, Head of Surrey Sleep Research Centre led a study which showed that no fewer than 711 genes had been affected after participants had just 6 hours sleep for one week. He found that the 'volume' had been turned up on many genes that were linked to cardiovascular disease and turned down on others linked to immune system optimisation. What is more, the chromosomes, the tight web of spiral strands of DNA, floating around in the nucleus of our cells showed fraying at the edges (like shoelaces without the aiglet), these capstone telomeres, which are an indicator of age, like a genetic version of the hand-grip test, reflected those of a much older person[12].

The Holy Trinity

Exercise, Nutrition and Sleep work together.

When we don't sleep our ability to exercise reduces too. Poor sleep has been shown to impinge on exercise intensity and duration the next day. If we maintain a regular regime of exercise, we keep our body fit and we improve the quality of our sleep. Our body naturally develops a self-sustaining cycle of well-being.

Nutrition affects our energy levels. Diets which deprive us of energy can hurt us in many ways. If we subject ourselves to severe caloric restriction, we reduce our ability to fall asleep.

As always, achieving a balance is most beneficial. Everything in moderation; Granny knows best.

Sleeping on a diet

Research has shown that eating 800 calories per day for a month makes it harder to fall asleep. It then reduces our NREM sleep.

High carbohydrate and low-fat diets increase REM sleep and reduce NREM sleep and vice versa.

Diet matters, and timing - which is why we should breakfast like kings or queens…

Actions for Improvement

As sleep is so important to our well-being, it is surely worth considering how we might make it work for us...

1. Think about Effectiveness

Avoid fatigue if you want to be your most effective. Tiredness explains a lot of our errors, emotional reactions, moods, silly decisions and even sillier mistakes!

Although she won't thank me for mentioning it, only yesterday, Jenny, my wife, bumped a brand-new Range Rover at the traffic lights at 0mph. She cost herself a small fortune and a respray to an innocent person's pride and joy whilst on her way home from an exhausting work shift. She was tired and therefore not focussed. If she now meets her plan to get her full 8 hours sleep a night and to be more rested for the next ten shifts, she will just about break even financially for the month!

Tiredness doesn't make good business sense. As Dr Peters says, 'when we get tired, the blood is sent to the 'chimp' who becomes the primary decision maker'. Whilst there are still work cultures and environments where longer hours are rewarded, most often long hours are actually a sign of reduced productivity.

I have been part of the culture. It is quite likely that you have too. I use to have to work longer to get enough done, to keep on top of my job. And thus starts a vicious cycle of longer hours, less rest, less sleep, reduced productivity, longer hours...etc... I have spent too long peddling this cycle. There are better ways. The rise of homeworking may help promote a more productive balance. It is nevertheless still estimated that the global economic cost of sleep deprivation skirts 2% of GDP, nearly as much as is spent globally on education.

As a leader, our sleep patterns do not just affect us, they affect our teams and our entire workforce.

Leadership

Leadership performance studies with leaders judged by their employees, and no knowledge of the sleep context, reported that reduced sleep predicted poor self-control and more abusive leadership behaviours. Employee engagement and productivity suffered as a result.

Even integrity is prone to take a nosedive. Dr Christopher Barns, Foster School of Business in Washington found that under-slept employees show less integrity. They are more likely to fake receipts and lie to get rewards, they take more credit for the good work of others, and show a greater propensity for blaming others for their own mistakes.[13]

Enlightened companies have recognised the value of sleep with the likes of Proctor and Gamble and Goldman Sachs providing 'sleep awareness courses', Nike and Google having 'sleep pods' and Aetna, the insurers offering their 50,000 employees bonuses for 'sustained good sleep'. In the words of their CEO, Mark Bertolini, 'you can't be prepared if you're half asleep'.[14]

Thinking about a sleep plan is a fine first step.

2. Caught Napping?

Our natural cycle, our circadian rhythms, differ by person, but generally cause a dip in alertness mid-afternoon. Robert Cialdini, psychologist and author of 'Influence – the psychology of persuasion', calls this 'the post prandial alertness dip'. By the way, when food is provided at a lunch time 'power meeting', we unconsciously make a positive association between the luxury food and the proposal. This 'appetiser' is proven to increase the likelihood of your proposal being approved.[15]

After lunch, with our natural cycle on a low ebb and the burst of energy exhausted by eating and approving so-so proposals, it is not that surprising that we enter the 'graveyard session'.

Don't be caught napping. Do it on purpose!

*Power naps restore alertness,
enhance performance and reduce errors*

James B Maas

There are those, including Walker who advocate 'biphasic' sleep, i.e; two sleeps a day, one at lunchtime and one at night. This aligns more with prehistoric rhythms and of course still prevails in some communities, such as Spain or Greece, which is probably why Greek Islands, like Ikaria, are sometimes described as places where people 'forget to die'. An Inhabitant of Ikaria is four times as likely to reach the age of ninety as an American.

In most societies, sleeping in the day is not that practical, yet extensive research by NASA

Seymour Timing

Timing of that nap of course has an impact and Liz Seymour proposes that your personal nap zone is optimised by reference to your sleeping patterns, with a range of 1.5 hours either side of 12 hours from the midpoint of your main sleep. So, if you sleep 10pm till 6am, the midpoint is 2am and you should nap at some time between 12.30 and 3.30pm.[17]

---

has taught their leadership that 26-minute naps increase task performance by 34% and alertness by 50%, resting their case for the NASA nap culture.[16]

The Federal Aviation Authority (FAA) too are very active in exploring and optimising nap times, especially critical for long haul pilots, who may have long shifts with short nap opportunities– the nap buys some time. Once you are deprived, there is no way back.

Of course, napping is better than not sleeping at all, but not a great replacement. Long naps which upset your circadian rhythms are likely to leave you feeling groggy and unsettled.

Try using Seymour's guidelines, and remember that we are all unique -knowing what best suits you is inevitably a matter of trial and error, the key (again) is to 'know thyself'.

US aviation findings

68% of 'hull losses' occur at the end of a long shift – called 'top of descent to landing'. The FAA have found that if you have to be awake for up to 36 hours, napping at the early phase, at the front end of a bout of sleep deprivation, is more effective than later.[18]

For all of us, our drive for sleep is strong. The wide base of Maslow's 'Hierarchy of needs' pyramid includes our basic physiological needs - food, water, warmth and rest[19]. Sleep squeezes into the 'warmth and rest' category, although in fact our bodies actually need to be cooled by a couple of degrees to optimise the conditions for sleep.

A word of warning though; if you sleep a lot more than the 8 hour recommendation, there is some evidence of increased mortality rates, cardiovascular disease, diabetes, stroke, obesity etc...[20] Although it is not clear if this is a causal relationship or due to other factors relating to long-sleepers. In any case, it is always advisable to note what Granny says about moderation.

3. Seek Expert Advice

Sleep deprivation is personal and critical to well-being so, if in doubt, expert counsel is advisable.

There are pills of course, but they wipe out many of the benefits of natural sleep.

Cognitive behavioural therapy for insomnia (CBT-I) is generally accepted to be an effective option, being aimed at addressing anxieties which might inhibit sleep. There are also an increasing number of apps available that monitor sleep patterns and can infuse you with restful sounds, and tailor for you an AI based plan of self-improvement, should you be unable or unwilling to secure specialist treatment. (e.g; Sleepio, Sleepspace...)

Walker's 12 point plan

Matthew Walker provides a twelve-point plan: keep to a schedule, exercise, but not too late, avoid nicotine and caffeine, and alcohol before bed. Don't drink or eat too much too late, avoid sleep medicines, don't nap after 3pm (so use the earlier part of your 'nap zone'), relax, unwind, take a hot bath, have a dark, cool, gadget-free bedroom, get some sunlight during the day and if that doesn't work, don't lay in bed awake – do something distracting, as sleep anxiety is the enemy of sleep.[21]

Remember those Israeli judges denying parole because they were hungry and tired? What's the worst decision your fatigue could help you make?...

REFLECTION TIME

Sleep		
Mens Rea	Actus Rhesus	Guilty? ☑
1. Sleep is the third corner of the Well-Being triangle	Are you getting enough?	☐
2. It is possible to avoid excessive fatigue.	Do you nap when you want to, or when you need to, or neither? Do you have a plan to ensure you get sufficient rest to perform at your best?	☐
Knowing yourself is a useful starting point. Time to learn more about self-reflection...		

When we take the time for thought, we can better shape our actions

Chapter 5:
Reflection

It is time to look at ourselves a bit more. It's time to reflect on reflection. And if we are too busy for that, well it's when we don't have time for a timeout that we surely need it most.

Self-Reflection

Looking at 'the person in the mirror', as Michael Jackson might have put it, can be a bit frightening! It goes beyond the 'bad hair day'. Sometimes we don't particularly like what we see, and yet we are afraid to take steps to change. Perhaps it's better not to look at all?

Some of us are more narcissistic than others, but none of us can help looking at ourselves. When we see a group photo, we scan it for our own image, and if we are in the picture, we check that out first. From Electroencephalograph (EEG) studies we know that we 'preferentially deploy attentional resources to facial recognition'[1] (we tune in to people's faces very rapidly), and markedly more-so to our own. However humble, we have a great personal significance to ourselves. We also recognise our past selves, quickly. Even if we have changed behaviourally and emotionally, we are still us.

And yet we may or may not have a strong sense of who we are. We may or may not have created a very clear story of our lives. We may or may not be living up to that ideal.

Before we make any change, as Stephen Covey says, we would be wise to 'seek first to understand'[2]. If you don't know where you are, then it is much harder to direct yourself towards your goal.

How thick are you?

You are a flawed individual, we all are. And the thinner your frontal cortex, the thicker you are. Your cortex, the Latin word for 'rind', is thicker if it is worked hard and thinner if neglected. Likewise, the girth of your corpus callosum, the densely packed body of neurons splitting your two brain hemispheres, like the body of a butterfly between its wings, reflects your cognitive strength. Generally, a thicker corpus callosum correlates with higher intellect, using a wider metric of intelligence than mere IQ.

Whilst this is true, Howard Rosen in 2009, observed 40 neurodegenerative-diseased patients finding that a less accurate self-assessment correlated with lower quantity of tissue in the right ventromedial prefrontal cortex[3], which (as any fool kno') is associated with processing and manipulating complex information.

Sshh!!!

FMRI scans show that the pre-frontal cortex is quietest in those with highest fluid intelligence. So, if we are looking for the brainiest person, we shouldn't look for the one with the most activity, (the noisiest brain), but the quietest. It turns out that empty vessels really do make the most noise!

One day, if you are so inclined, you will probably be able to get a brain scan and, by adding your rind thickness and the dimensions of your caterpillar-like corpus callosum, award yourself a definitive intelligence score. In the meantime, we can wrestle with the alternative measures if we really must keep score.

Let's say you score 100 points, you could target 110 for your next annual brain reading.

But we should beware of Goodhart's Law...*

*Goodhart's Law

Charles Goodhart, the economist, said that 'when a measure becomes a target, it ceases to be a good measure'. Any measure is only helpful if it is treated as one piece of feedback, one part of the overall system.

If the idea of getting to 110 appeals, you had better devise a plan. **You will need to do some cognitive reflection...**

Beware. Sometimes we feel a great urgency to act, and to do so quickly and decisively. Quick-witted, decisive people are perceived as more charismatic and more persuasive. Most of us want to be thought of in this way.

Hmm...If I stop and think about this, people won't see me as decisive, quick witted, persuasive...

The Beautiful Game

The success of soccer goalkeepers can be directly measured.

When facing a penalty shoot-out, they know the statistics. They know that they have a 33% chance of saving the shot if they don't move, far greater than the chance if they move. They stay put only 6% of the time nevertheless[4].

Goalkeepers need to act, and they need to be seen to act. They avoid 'losing' by showing they have put in maximum effort. It is not always the most effective approach.

And yes, we are all like this.

The answer is to do both, to think well, **and** act decisively - the secret of this conundrum lies in our timing.

The Japanese Hansei, meaning self-reflection, is a core tenet of the Japanese culture.

The Toyota production system[8] uses this principle, and it is favoured by lean practitioners across the globe. It advocates regular self-reflection. Even when things go right. We do well to consider how they might have gone wrong. In doing so, we avoid the extraordinary power of 'outcome bias' (see *Some Other Substantial Reason*).

Reflections from a Call Centre

Research by Giada di Stefano et al concluded that 15 minutes reflection by call centre workers at the end each day (at the Indian IT giant WiPro, prompted by high staff turnover and staff disenchantment) resulted in a 23% improvement after just 10 days.[5]

In another study, commuters in London, who thought about and planned their day whilst in transit, were found to be happier, more productive and less burned out.[6]

Jennifer Porter in Harvard Business Review advocates self-reflection in order to give conscious consideration to a given task, for the purposes of learning. It is in doing so that we can sort through the tangled web, consider the possible interpretations of each situation and create meaning for ourselves.[7]

Follow effective action with quiet reflection. From quiet reflection will come even more effective action

Peter Drucker

Hansei or self-reflection is central to the very notion of continuous improvement. In this world, no problem is itself a problem. It applies equally to the individual as to the corporation.

Quick-witted, Decisive, Persuasive

> *Time past and time future,
> what might have been and what has been
> point to one end which is always present*
>
> TS Eliot (Burnt Norton – from Four Quartets)

Where did that burst of poetry come from?!

When confronted with a difficult situation, it is human nature to panic; the flight or fright reflex kicking in at low levels prevents us from thinking clearly, feeling (and staying) calm and doing our best in that moment of pressure.

Success demands that we have the Presence of Mind to think quickly enough to be able to do the right thing at the right time.

Presence of Mind
The ability to make good decisions and to act quickly and calmly in a difficult situation or an emergency

Presence of Mind, like wit, comes from making rapid connections, and it is a skill that can be learned Verbal wit comes from connecting unusual words and ideas. Quick and high-quality actions derive from depth of knowledge in the area concerned and are enhanced by our access to connections across other spheres of knowledge.

Quick wit

Saying the right thing at the right time is also more important than some realize. A famous Norman Miller study found that you are considered more persuasive if you speak quickly. Those speaking at the higher end - 195 words per minute, were perceived as more confident, intelligent, knowledgeable and objective. We even link in charisma – fast talking suggests an exceptional ability to think on your feet.

If you speak at just 100 words per minute, the opposite applies.

According to Adi Gaskill at Forbes, charisma is judged by speed. Which explains the success of many confidence tricksters with motor mouths and silky tongues.

Note: Fast talkers may be better at blagging it, without real knowledge, but it doesn't make them any better at handling conflict or showing empathy.

Presence of Mind is about Feeling, Thinking and Acting, which are most rapid when the three operate in harmony. It's about impulse control, it's about our ability to consider the multiple alternatives before taking action. Sometimes it is about running away from and sometimes it is about running towards the fire.

In his book, *I Have the watch – becoming a leader worth following*, John S Rennie, trained firefighter and nuclear submarine US navy veteran explains that it is vital to know when to counter the natural instinct to run away; in a submarine, you don't have much time[9]. The same applies in a home or business situation; attacking the flames before there are fires burning all around is key to success.

As the climate has warmed, the incidence and scale of forest fires has leapt to new heights. Sometimes the heroes who tackle the fires can be encircled. A surging tide of flames can travel at 20 mph and lay waste anything that stands in its way. Current advice is to seek escape routes, roads, natural firebreaks, assess the dryness of the terrain, the direction of the wind, the direction of the smoke, go downhill as fire causes hot air masses which tend to rise. Yet sometimes there is no respite, and experts recommend digging a trench and lying face down with feet facing the flames, covering yourself with dirt and waiting for the fire to travel over you, rather like assuming the brace position in a diving aircraft. Good luck with that!

Living in a fire zone...do you run or stay?

In Victoria, Australia, University Professor, Ian Thomas chose to stay; his house and gardens were surrounded by great pines and the eucalyptus forest of Kinglake National Park. He was living in a tinderbox, the ground was crispy underfoot, temperatures rose to over 50C, and a single spark in a remote hillside pasture coupled with strong, blazing hot winds triggered a web of chain reactions, devastating 1500 square miles of forest, taking 210 lives and destroying 2000 homes.

Clearly, with most presence of mind, we make the most rational decision. Professor Thomas had calculated the odds of survival from leaving or staying, went with the percentages and was lucky. Many perished as they chose to leave their homes.

Professor Thomas was a survivor.

Of course, these situations are complicated, and full of unknowns. So are many of our own unusual experiences, and a rational decision is often far from easy.

True presence of Mind means living your life in a multiverse. Taking the best choice on every move like the chess computer which establishes best option from the trillions, not just for short term, to win the latest pawn, but for the long term, to save your King or Queen. Of course, in the same way that making more jokes, more spontaneously demands practice (Jerry Seinfeld's unbroken chain), improving the quality and speed of our actions requires knowledge that is deep and broad, and practice, practice, practice, in those 'difficult situations or emergencies'. Like all things, we must resort to dedication and conscientiousness. We can't always get it right, but we can always try!

Another Perspective

Terry Pratchett wrote a minimum 400 words a day, for many years – "I was fixated on the idea that if you have not got work in progress you are not a writer at all, you are a bum."[10]

Reflective Competence

As we learned from Philip Tetlock and his 'superforecasters', brilliant puzzle solvers may have the raw material for forecasting, but without an appetite for questioning, and challenging their emotionally charged beliefs they tend to be less effective than a person of lower intelligence but with a greater capacity for critical thinking[11].

Of course, we are not always interested in forecasting major world events, but the same process applies at all levels of decision making.

If we want to increase our reflective competence, we benefit from exploring all our feelings and intuitions and identifying our biases, some of which if left unchecked can cause us, and others, harm.

It's not just about what we don't do; if we are aware of what tickles our Mesolimbic dopaminergic/reward pathway, we can plan and act accordingly.

> **Brain porn**
>
> Our Ventral Tegumental Area (VTA) along with the Nucleus Accumbens (NA) vet our inputs, reinforcing the pathways - if we love that crème patisserie, and vomit at the first sight of sour milk, that neuronal 'etching' potently reminds us what to do and what not to do.
>
> The VTA and NA link with the amygdala and hippocampus to ensure our memory has strong emotional resonance and promotes in us those most desirable behaviours.

Three Pillars

Academic success is often marked by General Intelligence, Curiosity and Conscientiousness. Our reflective competence might use the same measures.

We know that General intelligence constitutes a wide range of traits and skills. Let's look a little further at curiosity and conscientiousness.

A high level of curiosity fits the superforecaster mould.

When it comes to promoting curiosity* in the young, the 'do as I say, not as I do' approach doesn't work. You are being watched!

William Hazlitt, the 18th century sage and literary critic said that *'hypocrisy is the setting up of a pretension to a feeling you never had and have no wish for'*. If you do not act in a manner consistent with your words, adults may be deeply offended, whereas children's brain are not so disturbed. They simply tune into what we do and pretty much ignore what we say[12].

In *The Stupidity Paradox*, Mats Alvesson and Andre Spicer tell us that, despite the billions of pounds or dollars our most well-known organisations spend, they remain 'engines of stupidity'[12].

---

*Promoting curiosity

In *The Hungry Mind*, Susan Engel observes nursery children as they watch their parents from behind a screen. Where the parents studied the objects on a table, the kids did the same, and vice versa.

Curiosity is transmitted this way. Parental curiosity bleeds across into their children. Those whose parents opened up on topics when questioned saw a chain of questioning with as many as 26 questions per hour at home, and far greater learning and curiosity than those whose parents were not so open, leaving them asking just 2 questions per hour.[13]

Notably techniques like smiling encouraged questions, but beware; any hint of anxiety seems to kill children's curiosity stone dead.

Our organisations 'fail to reflect on their base assumptions, fail to show curiosity around their purpose and fail to consider the wider consequences of their actions'. Alvesson and Spicer present a convincing argument that organisations actively promote this stupidity, with excessive specialisation and division of responsibilities, and with a demand for loyalty and unyielding optimism, which stifles natural curiosity.

It is indeed a shame to stifle that curiosity as we know that our dopaminergic system, our reward pathway, which fires when we are curious, (when we are finding novelty) is the same network of brain regions that fire as adults when we want food, drugs or sex...or chocolate.

To satisfy the third pillar, to meet Yoda's expectations and the spirit of Nike's Swoosh, calls for our conscientiousness. This means discipline, sometimes sheer, bloody-minded determination and resilience in the face of persistent set-backs, and a resolve to do what you have committed to do. This is the grit of champions, as Angela Duckworth would describe it[15].

Ageing or Asian

There is growing evidence that wisdom grows steadily with age. At least in WEIRD countries - WEIRD being an acronym for Western Educated Industrialised Rich Democratic...

Research in Japan shows no such pattern of wisdom with age as a typical Japanese person at 25 is calculated to be as 'wise' as a 75 year old American![16]

East and West

94% US professors think they are better than average, which means deploying Dunning Kruger logic, probably only 6% really are! And anyone who has been to a 'speed awareness course' will know, and independent statistics verify, 99% of car drivers are better than average.

*In East Asian countries, there is not this blind spot bias.

The difference may be because, from early age Japanese children are taught to think from the perspective of others, to be open minded and intellectually humble, as are many of their role model literary characters. Indeed, their very language requires relative status to be defined, your name changes depending on who you are speaking with, and whilst we say there is no I in team, there really is no 'I' in Japanese!

Globalisation does however appear to be starting to push Western individualism Eastwards.

Another language, another soul

Our ability to reflect and reason is affected by our language. A second language, which lacks the subtle emotional resonances of our native tongue, prevents some of the typical somatic markers. In a second language we are less likely to be influenced by emotion. In a second language we are more prone to reflective reasoning because we are forced to open our minds a little wider.

Some words are untranslatable, providing a benefit in the same way as those invented words for our emotional states (like 'hangry'). Linguists tend find it easier to tolerate ambiguities and perceive the world from alternative perspectives.

> **The Interactive Brain Hypothesis**
>
> When we engage socially, our brains engage different neural and cognitive processes.
>
> For example, live monitoring during interactions (using fNIRS – functional Near Infra-Red Spectroscopy) saw poker players' neural pathways opening to assess other persons perspective, not opening when playing against a machine.[17]

Creating a Thinking Environment

No matter how articulate we may be, we all think faster than we can speak. We have time to listen. We don't always use that time wisely. When we listen well, we are opening our minds so that we may be changed by what is being said. We tend to forget that thinking is often a social process.

Nancy Kline is the notoriously inspirational pioneer of the 'Thinking Environment', in which she promotes a different way of listening which frees the speaker to think[18].

First, ask yourself this question… Are you a KY kind of person?

KY – Kuuki Yomenai, Japanese: **'One who cannot read the air'**

Not to be confused with the New Yorkers' abbreviation KY for 'Know Yuse'. They were rather more successful with OK, based on the equally poorly spelt 'Oll Korrect'.

We may have two ears and one mouth for a reason, but it is probably more about survival than about listening to conversation. There are two schools of opinion regarding our listening skills. Some believe that we have one attention and can listen to one person at a time. Others suggest a quantity of attention that can be shared out so we can listen to many if we divide our overall attention capacity between them.

In the 'one person at a time', or 'bottleneck' scenario, one stream effectively blocks the other.

Two Ears

Tests of our 'dichotic listening' skills suggest that it is not possible to do twice as much listening because we have two ears. In fact, if we are focused on the input to one ear, we can barely tell the gender of the person talking into the other. In the famous Colin Cherry tests back in 1953, our predecessors couldn't even discern the language spoken by the person talking in the 'other ear'. This is now known as the 'bottleneck effect'.

A little later, in 1975, Von Wright found that our 'other ear' could hear shock inducing words – in other words, only those sounds which might invoke a response to ensure our survival.[19]

This 'bottleneck effect' is disputed by the likes of Daniel Kahneman whose 'Cocktail party effect' claims our one amount of attention can be divided, and our working memory seems to dictate its size.

Both are probably true. I know personally that when I am focused on one person, I am simply unaware that the other (probably almost always my wife) has spoken at all. This appears to be a common complaint from wives the world over and perhaps suggests, without any definitive evidence, that women and men do divide up their attention differently. It seems certain there is a spectrum on which we all fall, with me on one end and the likes of Nancy Kline on the other...

A really good listener doesn't do anything

In *Time to Think*, Kline listens to an Italian speaker. Kline doesn't speak a word of Italian, and yet the speaker feels liberated. Kline gives 100% attention. She creates a setting where her speaker can feel and think freely for themselves, without passing judgment or promoting magic bullets.

Brad Stone's *The Everything store* documents the early life of Amazon's Jeff Bezos. Bezos' mother, who was only 17 when Jeff was born, talks about his childhood, his infectious enthusiasm for his latest project, for example his magic mirror box. She always believed that... 'it was not necessary that I understood. It was only necessary that I listened.'

Most of our listening comes with strings attached, as we either attempt to solve the other person's problem, solve our own problems whilst they are talking, or impress them with our knowledge and/or wit. True listening actually **frees the speaker to think** not just to talk. When Nancy Kline listens, the speaker is liberated to solve their own problems, they keep responsibility and own their issues.

Arthur Dent was lucky not to pay the price for not listening. We don't all have the benefit of Douglas Adams' rather unlikely infinite improbability drive![20]

Of course, we have long established that we all benefit widely from listening to the wisdom of our mothers, and grandmothers (provided they behave accordingly!).

Perhaps I am a KY kind of person. Perhaps you are too? A KY person is not a good listener. A KY person is not good at 'reading between the lines'. The Japanese language demands a lot of reading between the lines. Those who do not excel at this are termed KY – Kuuki Yomenai, literally 'one who cannot read the air'. Erin Meyer in *The Culture Map* suggests that Japanese people think all Americans are 'KY' guys[21]. I am sure they would think the same of me.

It is not a failing that is reserved for the less intelligent. On the contrary, we have already seen that an illusion of superiority can affect judgement. It affects the desire to listen too. Other factors do not help. Sometimes intelligent people are feared because of the sense that they are superior, and they represent an unknown quantity and perhaps a threat. Sometimes they are resented because that sense of superiority affects their ability to connect. They know it all already, so why would they need to? Sometimes they are resented because their superiority affects their willingness to give the other party the chance to think for themselves. Sometimes, as Douglas Adams put it, we just don't like a smart ass!

Our brain, which uses what it knows as the baseline for what everyone else knows, sometimes struggles to bridge the gap in an effective way. Luckily, as in all things, using the wisdom of Carol Dweck's *growth mindset*, we can improve if we are prepared to put in the effort, and conquer our fears...

Fear of Change

Marianne Williamson was probably right when she said in her 1992 self-help book *A return to Love*, that 'our biggest fear is that we are powerful beyond measure'.

---

*Metathesiophobia

The persistent, abnormal and unwarranted fear of change.

Perhaps we all think we suffer from sporadic metathesiophobia?*

Perhaps we all fear change from time to time. Perhaps our fear of change is not that abnormal. Maybe it's not all that unwarranted either. We are hard-wired to resist uncertainty, to fear the unknown. We want to create a story for our lives because we fear impermanence – we are afraid that change might be bad for us, we fear that too much change will mean we don't recognise ourselves, but we also fear the pressure of being a better person. Does this mean we should settle like winter snow, and leave ourselves vulnerable to our environment, or do we decide to take control…?

Gustavo Razzetti: 'We fear failure because we consider it our story, rather than just a chapter which needs to close in order to open up the next'. We try to control all the characters when we'd be better letting them grow organically.

Ernest Hemingway: 'the first draft of anything is sh*t'. We have infinite chapters, we can embrace impermanence, create our own plot twists, recognise that failure is not the destination, and we don't have to control everything. We can envision a chapter or the whole story but leave plenty of scope for change.

Improvement Actions

As always, with conscious effort, we can take actions to improve…

1. Know yourself

Our reflective competence is based on a combination of our general intelligence, curiosity and conscientiousness. We should focus on those areas we can control.

It is important that we get to know ourselves. By reflecting on our actions, we extract learning from things we do right and even more from our mistakes.

If you, like everyone else, wants to be quick witted, decisive and persuasive, you do well to be aware of what you do, the curiosity to understand why you do it and how you could do it better, and the conscientiousness to practise, practise, practise.

2. Improve your listening skills

There are probably as many benefits to good listening as there are techniques to improve. It is the only sure way to resolve conflicts, it can enable others to help us solve problems that we cannot, and it can help enable us to solve those same problems for ourselves. If we allow ourselves the humility to listen, we may also be liberated from our natural biases.

If all else fails, let's agree that rather than talking over each other like, I imagine, at a big Italian family dinner, the only person allowed to talk is the one holding the wooden spaghetti serving spoon.

Listening Tip 1

Listen to yourself – Are you solving their problem, or thinking about your own? Stop it! If you are thinking about your own problem, then you are not listening. If you are solving their problem, don't! They don't want your advice! Try supporting without judging instead.

Listening Tip 2

Can't seem to settle a conflict? Try agreeing to listen to each other – two minutes with commitment to absolutely no interruption - works wonders as finally you are forced to understand their point of view.

Listening Tip 3

Can't solve a problem? Ask a couple of friends to discuss it for five minutes – you must listen but do not intervene. They may fix your problem. More likely you will solve it whilst listening, using the new connections they create for you.

3. Ask Better Questions

The best listeners learn to ask the best questions. Asking the right questions applies to ourselves as much as to others. An expert mentor will ask us empowering questions that stimulate us to think, stretch our comfort zones and push us to new heights. As Adam Grant puts it, 'Ask how, not just why'.

Catherine Tinsley, Professor of Management at Georgetown University, Washington DC specialises in corporate catastrophes and our outcome bias. Her experience is that 'functional stupidity' usually arises due to lack of curiosity and reflection. The better companies ask better questions. They ask What might have happened? as well as What did?

In high-risk industries, about a thousand near-misses un-addressed will result in one serious injury or fatality. A true safety-first culture focuses on detection and prevention of these near misses.

Do our organisations ask the right questions?

* Sometimes

And do they listen to the answers?

* Shortly before the Deepwater oil spill disaster, an engineer described the well as, 'a nightmare well that has everyone all over the place'. It appears that no-one listened.

* At Enron, it was well known that you had to 'drink the Enron water' to succeed. The senior team refused to listen, instead demanding relentless, blind optimism.

* Nokia executives shouted 'at the top of their lungs' if they were told something they didn't want to hear about the inferiority of their Symbian Operating System – a middle manager explained to researchers that the mindset was 'if you criticise the product, then you are not genuinely committed to it'. The senior team failed to listen.

* A senior member of the Quartet, Saddam Hussein's senior committee, was asked 'what does Saddam do when people bring bad news to him?'. He could not answer. No-one had ever brought bad news to Saddam. He created an environment where questioning was a no-no. The chance to listen never arose.

Carlene Roberts of the Center for Catastrophic Risk Management, University of California, says that 'often when organisations look for the errors that caused something catastrophic to happen, they look for someone to name, blame and then train, (or get rid of). But it's rarely what happened on the spot that caused the accident. It's often what happened years before'. Chernobyl provides another classic example of the failure to heed warnings, preferring to pursue a policy of blind hope. The warnings signs and system breakdowns preceded the final meltdown in 1986 by many years.

Our biases, like the tendency to blind optimism, are exaggerated by a sense of time pressure, so it is all the more important in highly critical environments to encourage regular breaks to take a pause and ask reflective questions like, if I had more time and resources, would I make the same decisions?

Alongside the usual post-mortems after an incident, we should promote a culture where pre-mortems are deployed (asking every conceivable what went wrong question is an effective way of preventing it from happening), and a tenth man or devil's advocate may be employed to critically question and hunt out flaws in the base logic. Whilst Spicer observes that this can lead to a slight increase in the number of dissatisfied people at work, it is far outweighed by the higher quality decisions made. In the failing organisations, or indeed failing countries, the tendency not to ask those uncomfortable questions prevails. In some cases, people are happier...until they are not.

Rewarding good questions

Dr Weick with Kathleen Sutcliffe explain that safety critical organisations need to be preoccupied with failure, rewarding error reporting. They need to have a deep reluctance to simplify interpretations, rewarding the questioning of assumptions and received wisdom.

We'd all prefer that our nuclear power stations have a deep commitment to resilience, deploying systems like the US Navy SUBSAFE system, with a collective mindfulness and a culture in which juniors can challenge seniors and indeed are encouraged to do so.

What is more, if you don't ask, or don't listen to the answers, then you fit Alvesson and Spicer's definition of stupidity. In the end, Saddam Hussein may even still have believed he had Weapons of Mass Destruction, and the invincible Nokia found that they did lack the technology and products to compete with Apple, and so Iraq fell, and the 150-year-old Finnish paper milling company was quietly consumed into the somewhat successful Microsoft.

Predicting the present

The idea of pre-mortem of course assumes we are concerned to prevent the worst. The opposite could be an even greater gift – by asking the right questions we can increase likelihood of best-case outcomes too – many successful companies actively deploy this approach – notably Pixar have used their famous 'Notes Day' to secure thousands of ideas from their employees. These employees have been challenged to imagine they are reporting on events four year in the future, assuming phenomenal success has occurred. When asked questions amounting to 'how did we do it?', the resulting idea generation has significantly enhanced both creativity and cost effectiveness, according to Pixar co-founder Ed Catmull, who can cite myriad successful movies that make the case!

Back at the level of the individual, our lives and relationships benefit immeasurably when we ask the right questions and listen to the answers. If in doubt, we might follow the advice of Edith Eger, the inspiring Auschwitz survivor, who suggests that part of our reflection should be to take responsibility for our own actions, and before acting ask three simple questions:

- Is it kind?
- Is it important?
- Does it help?

4. Seek the Truth

Should I wear a face mask to protect me from airborne bugs? As King Cnut shows, communication is difficult; messages get twisted, even when they are clear, which is so often not the case. When we get mixed messages, we tend towards listening to those we respect, those closest to us first. We look for 'truthiness'. We are all susceptible to this bias.

When Jonathan Swift said that 'falsehood flies, and the truth comes limping after it', he was not wrong. We think it is true if it passes our test of familiarity and fluency. If something is familiar, it instinctively feels right, (especially if it is dressed up in a pithy little ditty, like Jonathan Swift's) making it is easy to process and therefore clearly more credible. This plays to our laziness, or more accurately, our efficient brains, which do not want to do unnecessary work. Our mental shortcuts fuel our biases and leave us open to manipulation. Yet without them we could not function.

Weirdly, the priming effect appears to affect our judgement of truthiness. The MMR vaccination message successfully did its worst as it presented as truth and showed the spiralling effect of relying on an initially credible source, rather like the FBI fingerprinting error. It is easy to see that once you believe, you can prove almost anything, with terrible impact when malice is added to the pot.

Familiarity Effect

We can see the effect in many celebrated cases, for example at Theranos. Elizabeth Holmes, the founder claimed to have a cutting-edge blood testing system, raised $6m venture capital by age 20 and had built a stock market valuation of $10bn by 2013. In 2014 she claimed sales of $100m when sales were in fact just $100, and the company was dissolved in September 2018, losing some major investors over $1bn (including Rupert Murdoch $121m), making the recovery from the £94m hole at Patisserie Valerie seem like a piece of cake. All because one believable lie about her testing kit was repeated enough, and Holmes had attracted some highly credible names to build the foundations of her house of cards.

Norbert Schwarz and Eryn Newman at University of South Carolina in Los Angeles have found that the most effective way to boost a statement's 'truthiness' is to repeat it. By 'accidentally' duplicating the same statement on a political pamphlet, the recipients' opinion of the statement was altered as if it was expressing more people's views. Schwarz also found that a statement said by one person over and over again was as convincing as the same statement made by many people. 'We just don't take proper account of who has said it'.[22]

Hence, the more we see someone, the more familiar they become and the more trustworthy they become, which is presumably why a clerk who regularly paid in checks at a local branch of a business whose finances I was responsible for was not challenged at the bank when she started (fraudulently) withdrawing money on checks for which she had no authority, apart from a recognizable face.

If you read Mein Kampf, you will see that Hitler understood our cognitive flaw of familiarity. He noted that 'the most brilliant propagandist technique will yield no success unless one fundamental principle is borne in mind with unflagging attention. It must confine itself to a few points and repeat them over and over'.

Sometimes the tendency proves fatal as we prefer friendly to expert advice – psychologists (for example, Dr Karl Weick, professor of organisational behaviour and psychology at University of Michigan notes that in times of crisis we have a tendency to be more rigid in our thinking, seeking help from those most familiar to us.

Communication is challenging because our 'information deficit model' assumes that we need to be given the information to

---

In the heat of the moment

When a logging fire in Geraldton, Ontario Canada went wrong, eight men were encircled by flames. One was a local fire technician but not familiar to the others and when he explained that their only means of escape was to run through the high intensity flame front, they failed to listen. Even though they knew he was a fire expert, they did not know him well enough to trust him. Whilst he suffered some minor burns, the other seven died that day in August 1979.[23]

fill our knowledge gaps…but that is not our reality. Whether we like it or not, we are unconsciously selective about what we take on board. It may seem to make sense to say that this is your belief, and this is why it is wrong, but the so-called 'debunking approach' reinforces our false belief. We readily dismiss sound reasoning and thus an error or lie (like MMR link to autism) gets spread further and deeper, in the same way that cigarette warnings encourage smokers to light up.

Try 'steel-manning'. In the reverse of 'straw manning', where we aim to make our 'opponent's argument seem flimsy and there is a tendency for them to dig their heels in, now we firstly take an extra effort to strengthen our opponent's argument. Then when we have done so, we can show why, with even further reflection, they can refine their reasoning. This encourages deeper thought and allows our opponent to change their opinion without losing face. As for whether we should use a mask, the general consensus is that our masks protect other people from us. Its for you to decide for yourself whether that makes them worth wearing!

5. Mind your language

Never say to yourself, something you wouldn't want to hear others saying to you, or about you. The 'sapir whorf hypothesis' tells us that our language affects our thoughts. This can be seen in macroeconomic terms. Some languages, like Finnish and, even to some extent English, have a language with a convoluted future tense. We do not think about the future as much if we do not have a language structure that makes it easy to do so. In the same way, we do not think about our failings as much if we do not put them into words. Of course, if we do not reflect on our failings, we cannot take actions to improve. As ever, it is a question of balance.

No Future

Countries with a less defined future tense actually save less and are more 'irresponsible' in their behaviours.

e.g; smoking habits, sexual protection habits etc..)

6. Accept you are not always in control

King Cnut was the son of Sweyn Forkbeard and ruler of England (and Norway and Denmark) about a thousand years ago. We know that, contrary to popular opinion, he was a wise Viking king, although, like a naïve politician he may have given the press free fuel for abuse and criticism.

Is he or isn't he?

Cnut perhaps didn't take charge of the optics. Perhaps we shouldn't take too much notice of legend, although we can't always predict what will live on in our memories, like Ed Miliband and that bacon sandwich or former labour MP Neil Kinnock stumbling on the beach. These images give lie to the desired message of control. Of course, if we allow for the incorrect but more popular understanding of his intention, we are all surrounded by too many 'King Cnuts', especially in the workplace.

King Cnut

King Cnut couldn't control the actions of others, any more than he could control the tides; that was his point. But he could control his own actions. And so can we.

We don't always do our best. Sometimes our thoughts allow our performance to suffer, as Matthew Syed describes in his book, Bounce. Even the highest echelons, those closest to the top choke under pressure, demonstrating behaviours we lesser mortals suffer from equally but on a less public stage. Choking belongs in the same camp as the famed tennis academy's Nick Bollettieri's 'Centipede effect'[24]– if we think about moving all our 100 legs in the right order, our conscious attempt at control disrupts the smooth working of our brilliant, subconscious minds.

Desmond Morris deliberately insulted us by calling us 'naked apes', 50 years ago[25]. Today, perhaps we are thicker-skinned, (even if some of us do still have little hair), but maybe he was provoking us to self-distance and reflect.

I thought I had Impostor Syndrome. It now turns out I really was just sh*t at my job!

Daft Apeth (suffering a crisis of confidence, or is it enlightenment?)

Don't worry DAFT Apeth; there are other jobs that you are much better at!

Anais Nin said that 'we see the world not as it is, but as we are', and of course the ability to see things from others points of view becomes harder as we move away from the middle and towards the extremes of any spectrum. Yet we know that third party reflection, that is; pretending to ourselves that we are a third party, maybe a celebrity, maybe a superhero, elicits a more considered response, with reduced tendency to listen to our biases.

7. Be aware of your environment

We don't always do what is in our own best interests. Behavioural economists, like Kahneman, and probability specialists like Taleb demonstrate that, instead of facts and data we err towards what is 'in our face' (What You See is All There Is – WYSIATI[26]). We mistake local for national, we follow the law of small numbers rather than big data, and our brains are influenced by our myriad prejudices and biases. We are egocentric and hopelessly influenced by what other people think. If our waiter puts eyes on our bill, we pay a bigger tip, as if we are being watched! If they add a smile or kisses, we pay even more.

As an example of the impact of the priming effect on our reflective thinking, Viren Swami in 2014 at University of Westminster found that the participants in a cognitive study who had been playing word games including words like reason, ponder, rational, performed better in cognitive tests than those participants whose word games included more physical words like hammer and jump. Their reasoning was better. Their more logical thinking was beneficial for non-related thoughts too, suggesting we will think better if we 'prime' ourselves appropriately.

We have the power to be aware of our environment and, most times we have the opportunity to use that awareness to change that environment if it is not helping us...

8. Step into the Light

We are all different, start from a different place, travel a unique course, and end in a different, if equally undesirable place. As John Kerr described in his leadership book, Legacy, Suvorov categorised our states of control as 'the dark' and 'the light'. In the 'dark' state, we are 'red headed', by which he means tight, inhibited, results oriented, aggressive, over-compensating and desperate. In this state we focus on the negative, what can go wrong, why it will happen to us. In the 'light state', when we are 'blue headed', we feel loose, expressive, in the moment, calm, clear and on task.

With self-reflection, we can see 'the light', control our attention, control our thoughts, govern our emotions; from which we control our behaviour. This is what meditation or mindfulness can do for us.

We benefit from gaining greater awareness of all our senses (see power of five). When we understand ourselves best, we can create plans, which encourage habits that have the most positive effect and promote optimal patterns of mental and emotional behaviour.

When we do this effectively, we naturally maintain the appropriate acetylcholine levels to promote our alertness without the surfeit of cortisol and other stress related hormones.

> **Stay out of the red**
>
> In *The Real McCaw*, Richie McCaw (The All Black rugby star) observes that at times of stress, having a system that recognises the red v blue or dark v light helps to manage the fight or flight type triggers by preventing wallowing in the area of concern by keeping our attention on the present.[27]

9. Navigate the multiverse in your head

Over the years, Jorge Tejada, the pathologist we met in the introduction, has examined over 10,000 brains, slicing them into slithers for examination and research. He has earned the right to muse at our wonderful machine. In the spirit of the work of the psychologist K Anders Ericsson, made even more popular by Malcolm Gladwell in Outliers, it may be fair to say that Jorge has achieved mastery in slicing and dicing the brain. 10,000 brains probably equates to more than 10,000 hours practice which is the rule-of-thumb effort required for a talented person to achieve expertise.

Of course, Gladwell originally misinterpreted Ericsson and would probably concede that it is also possible that Tejada has not achieved such expertise; 'time served' does not always equal 'practice'. Repetition without learning, like at least some of the many years I spent in Finance churning out the same monthly and annual financials, may not bring mastery – it may rather fit the definition of arrested development.

Assuming though that he has achieved mastery, his mastery is in slicing and dicing the inert object, not in truly understanding the live beast. The slivers and shavings of brain matter surely help to pinpoint abnormalities and provide evidence of sources of anomalies, they may even give some indication of the areas most used and hence most rich in tissue, yet they reveal scant evidence of the life and genius of their owner.

With PET scans, FMRi, EEG, fNIRS and Artificial Intelligence we now have the ability to hone in on our patterns of synaptic behaviour. This is not accessible to every individual yet, but it will soon come!

Man v Machine

The great battle for machines to surpass humans has been long won by the machines, with IBM's Deep Blue smashing the stronghold of humans at the game of Chess to Stockfish and Alpha Zero achieving mastery within 24 hours and currently able to operate 400x as fast. Machine's superhuman ability is such that we humans cannot even quantify the scale of their superiority.

As the centenarian science genius, James Lovelock described, from AlphaGo's use of machine learning and tree-searching using human input, combined with computer ability to teach itself, Alpha Zero and AlphaGo Zero used an Artificial intuition, rather than brute force, with just 80,000 positions reviewed per second, compared to Stockfish's 70 million[28]. Machines are far cleverer and so much more efficient too!

The pace and extent of AI intuitive reasoning surpasses the human capacity, of course. However; before we face 'singularity', we can explore our own ability to assess all our options prior to making our decisions, lest we are left like Bolletieri's Centipede or Buridan's ass, paralysed with inability to do so.

As pattern seekers we rely on intuitive reasoning rather than brute force. In Blink, Malcolm Gladwell suggests 'thin slicing' as our means of taking information and editing it so that we can recognise patterns and take quick decisions. Clearly, we do not wish to overload ourselves with data that might paralyse our decision-making processes. We know that when we are so 'paralysed' our emotions will nudge us forward, like the physical nudge given to a catatonic patient in the Dr Oliver Sacks recounting of 'The Awakenings'[29].

Thin slicing is like 'bacon slicing', the business tool used to hedge risk, like foreign currency fluctuations, so that over time the organisation builds up a composite rate, matching the external environment and providing optimal protection by incorporating a large portion of the most common factors as well as a smaller element of extremes. Perhaps the best measure of our reflective intelligence is our ability to do the same, to consider the options at the critical steps on our journey through life and make the optimal decisions by, in effect weighing up the expected value of each outcome, and building up the slithers, in the way a chess playing computer can.

Of course, with infinite decision points, we would be as paralysed as Dr Sacks' patients with Encephalitis Lethargica, if we didn't allow the majority of our actions to run on auto-pilot, having provided it with a framework based on our belief systems and our dreams and desires. The trick is to understand which are your critical steps. Do you spend your time focusing on the thick or the thin? Do you sweat the small stuff?

Focus only on your priorities, those activities that are truly meaningful, your life will be uncluttered, rewarding and exceptionally peaceful

Yogi Roman from Robin Sharma's best seller
The Monk who sold his Ferrari

REFLECTION TIME

Reflection		
Mens Rea	Actus Rhesus	Guilty? ☑
1. You don't have time for all this...	This is when you need it most. Can you allocate a five minute slot each day for reflection? Something to think about...	☐
2. General Intelligence, curiosity and conscientiousness are key	Are you embracing all three to ensure that you GROW	☐
When you know yourself, you are ready to understand others...		

We help ourselves by helping others

Chapter 6:
Empathy

With our brain's strong egocentric bias, we are so desperate to look good at all costs that we do not naturally see how others look, except in comparison to us. **The more like us they are, the more we empathise.**

> **Empathy**
>
> The ability to understand and share the feelings of another.

> **The Empathy Circuit**
>
> Studies show this circuit to be most complex with at least 10 brain regions and various components[1], including **affective empathy** - the drive to respond with appropriate emotion to another's mental state, and **cognitive empathy** which is also known as theory of mind.

I don't care if you live or die, but I do empathise with you

But perhaps surprisingly, **the more we empathise the less we sympathise.**

> **Sympathy**
>
> Feeling pity and sorrow for someone else's misfortune

When the other person, who we understand well, hits upon hard times, we are less forgiving than we are to a stranger. It may sound counter-intuitive but, because we tend to feel like masters of our own destiny, we think that people who are like us should be masters of theirs too!

The 'just world perspective' is a cognitive bias (yes, another one) that tells our brain to assume that the world is fair, which probably seems like a good thing, as to think of the world as random may lead us to conclude that it is also meaningless. It may seem to be a good thing but perversely it enables us to justify or tolerate inequities; we simply adjudge that when something bad happens, you had it coming to you. You must have, otherwise the world is unfair...

Bias Correction
Our 'Right Supramarginal Gyrus' works to correct this natural bias. It does so with variable success.

Life is not fair; we may as well accept it. We live in a world where never a good deed goes unpunished, as was recently pointed out to me by a man who saw that I was rewarded with an intensive airport customs search for offering a stressed traveller my see-through bag for her cosmetics.

The less like us another person is, the more we instinctively sympathise. However, when you are experiencing pleasure, it is much harder to recognise that someone else is experiencing pain.

Our default state helps explain the societal gap between rich and poor, as each simply does not appreciate the other's perspective, and so does not even begin to consider showing the kind of level of sympathy that might level the playing field. Conscious action is needed to move the dial.

Hear this...

John Paul Getty III was the grandson of American oil tycoon J.Paul Getty, once the richest man in the world. While living in Rome in 1973, he was kidnapped by the 'Ndrangheta and held for a $17 million ransom. The wealthy grandfather was reluctant to pay, until his grandson's severed ear was received by a newspaper, and he negotiated release for a payment of just over to $2million.

It must have been hard for J.Paul to empathise with his grandson's captors, the poor and disaffected.

It is ironic that it took a chunk of his grandson's ear to make him sit up and listen.

Go West

I may have some compassionate empathy and cognitive empathy but do not extend to emotional or affective empathy. I do not sympathise with your desires, although I sympathise with you for having them. I am aware of your thoughts and perspective but do not feel the same way, although I don't know why I am telling you this as I know that, as an evil psychopath, you don't give a damn what I think or feel.

So goes my imaginary conversation with Fred West, famed serial killer, before not putting on his jumper in case I catch something.

Of course, all psychopaths are not evil killers and vice versa. As Thomas Erikson explains, they live among us. Estimates range from around 1 to around 3 people in every 50 fitting in this category, although with considerable regional and gender variations[2]. These manipulative people, mostly Western males, are not short of empathy; they can read our feelings and perspectives rather well, but they stand above us, happy to use this skill to manipulate us. They simply don't feel anything for us themselves and therefore they do not care.

Let's put psychopaths to one side and assume that you are one of the 47 or 49 who isn't one, as otherwise you would be far too busy manipulating people to read this. Let's consider toddlers instead...

Out of the mouths of babes

Two-year-olds don't have it at all.

Oscar can hide behind the same sofa cushion twenty times in a row and each time show the same shock and surprise..."How the earth did you find me?!"

Thankfully, Hide and Seek becomes somewhat more challenging as children age.

By four, we are well on our way to development of a Theory of mind. By four, a deficit of such awareness is an early indicator of certain mental disorders like autism spectrum disorders or ADHD. By four most children will have their whole body behind the tree, even if they do still keep their eyes closed, for extra stealth.

Theory of Mind

By the age four, most children know that you will look for an object where you last saw it rather than where they last saw it.

Theory of Mind is the field of psychology deployed to assess capability for empathy and understanding of others, their beliefs, intents, desires and emotions, their knowledge and perspectives. This is cognitive empathy.

Other people's emotions

Our ability to read the emotions of others is so important that the subject is never taught in schools, and as a result, in order to improve our interactions our relationships and our lives, it is an area for easy gains.

Other people's emotions are on show, as Charles Darwin attested in his *Expression of the emotions in man and animals*[3], identifying our three principles of expression.

Firstly, 'serviceable associated habits'; which are direct or indirect actions to relieve or gratify desires. If we use our will-power to suppress these habits, we invoke other (involuntary) actions. Leonard Keeler's polygraph or lie detector test relies on this principle – measuring blood pressure, pulse and skin conductivity, the same somatic markers that showed how we can integrate a table into our body image.

Dr Paul Ekman, in *Emotions Revealed*, the psychologist and world leading adviser on the subject of emotions and how to manage them, describes the basic emotions, anger, fear, disgust sadness, and happiness, how they 'cascade across our faces' enabling us to read the emotions of those around us. In *Telling Lies*, we see techniques (later deployed by law enforcers) for identifying micro-expressions or 'tells', those barely visible tics or behaviours which may reveal if you are being honest, if you have two faces or four aces.[4]

Secondly, Darwin points to the 'antithesis' where the opposite triggers provoke the opposite reaction, whether desired or not; 'A vulgar man scratches his head when perplexed...another rubs his eyes or gives a little cough when embarrassed.'[6]

Darwin's third principle identified the 'direct action of the nervous system (autonomic)', for which we have no control. Together these three principles help us to understand how, with the right effort, we can all improve our ability to understand others better. We can build a bridge to help us see other perspectives, and there is good reason to try...

> **People Watching**
>
> Desmond Morris dedicates a significant portion of his so named book to this topic. Even if we cannot read faces, the leakage from other body parts (hand rubbing, knee shaking, foot tapping etc...) will reveal much to the observant eye.
>
> The general rule is the further from the face the less the concealer is conscious of its movement and so the more 'honest' that movement is[5].

Relationships

Whilst having good relationships has to start with ourselves, it is also worth remembering John C Maxwell's observation that 'with one minor exception, the entire population of the world is composed of other people'[7]. In the Chinese proverb, if you want happiness for a lifetime, help others. We can't help others if we don't first understand them.

> **Importance of Relationships**
>
> A recent piece of research explored the major effects on our life expectancy...
>
> Whilst Exercise, Nutrition and Sleep feature highly, the top spots go to (the quality of) our close connections and our relationships.[8]

Robert Rosenthal, psychologist at Harvard University, devised a test of empathy called the 'Profile Of Non-verbal Sensitivity' or PONS, in which he applied a series of recordings of a young woman expressing the spectrum of feelings all the way from loathing to love. Those who performed best at correctly identifying their emotions were found to be more popular, more outgoing, and yet more sensitive.[9]

Actions for Improvement

Try these three steps...

1. Understand your own biases

Lasana Harris, a neuroscientist and experimental psychologist at UCL, with Susan Fiske at Princeton has found that when we feel disgust, we exhibit prejudices linked to our fears, and we allow ourselves to dehumanise others. It is in fact surprisingly easy to stop ourselves having empathy for the plights of others. But we can regulate this bias, by changing our brain's learned patterns. To do this we have to undo our flawed learning and re-learn. We can find out what our biases are (with or without the help of the Implicit Association Tests we mentioned earlier), and we can make ourselves accountable for over-riding these biases[10].

It starts with awareness, then we undo, then we resist categorisation which creates a 'them and us' mentality. If our bias is a racial one for example, we benefit most by interacting more with the specific racial group we instinctively treat differently.

It was Robert Jones Burdette who first said that 'the world doesn't owe you anything - it was here first'. Jean Twenge, the psychologist behind Generation Me and The Narcissism Epidemic conducted many studies before concluding that the younger generations do have an increased desire to have more, and to work less. She states that the more recent self-esteem focus has indeed fuelled an inflated belief about our self-importance. This sense of entitlement (sometimes called affluenza) is not helpful as it can lead us to overestimate our abilities and expect fast results. It can lead to disillusionment when we aren't as successful as we expect, or a tendency to accept failure as not our responsibility. Or it can lead us to take ill-advised short-cuts.

2. Increase your self-awareness

To increase your empathy, you can coach yourself, monitor your behaviour, regulate your emotions and think about your thoughts. We know we can change our mindset. We can also change our focus. If we are competitive, we can remind ourselves that winning isn't everything.

We can take example from the Olympic sailor, Lawrence Lemieux, in Seoul in 1988 who sacrificed his medal position to rescue and probably save the life of one of the Singapore two-man team who was clearly distressed and drifting away from his upturned boat. Lemieux fell back to 22nd place. He was recognised by the Olympic Committee and awarded the Pierre de Coubertin medal for sportsmanship. In the end, the latter medal will almost certainly provide a greater source of inspiration[11].

Which medal would you rather show your children or grandchildren?

3. Focus on others

If we remember that a sense of personal control is vital to our well-being, we can work to reframe our relationships such that we help to optimise that sense of control for others. As we have established, good listening is about allowing the other party to find their own solution.

If you are the kind of person who would rather park someone's car than show them the size of the gap with your hands so they can park for themselves, perhaps it is worth considering whether you follow the same approach in other interactions. Do you leave the other party feeling engaged or disempowered?

As the Canadian Astronaut, famed for his International Space Station rendition of the David Bowie classic, 'Space Oddity', Chris Hadfield, put it, 'do you make all your interactions +1 or at worst 0, or are too many of them -1's?'[12]

People will forget what you said, they will forget what you did, but they will never forget how you made them feel

Maya Angelou

If, like me, you sometimes struggle to read people's faces, or even if you are closer to the extreme like Dr Oliver Sacks, who famously 'mistook his wife for a hat'*, the good news is, and the Rosenthal study confirmed it, that empathy scores can be improved and as Rosenthal put it, if nothing else, those who improve most do end up with 'better romantic relationships'.

Remember the advice of Maya Angelou, and you won't go too far wrong.

*Actually it was one of Dr Sacks' patients who mistook his wife for a hat, but the brilliant Doctor did coincidentally suffer from prosopagnosia – the inability to recognise faces.

REFLECTION TIME

Empathy		
Mens Rea	Actus Rhesus	Guilty? ☑
1. I understand my own biases so I'm ready to focus on others	Do you observe other people's biases? How do you help them?	☐
2. When I focus on others I understand myself better	When does helping others help you?	☐
When you know yourself and understand others...success is in your grasp...		

We will do our best and be
our best if we direct our minds
appropriately

Chapter 7:
Achievement

> *Men are born soft and supple, dead they are stiff and hard... The hard and the stiff will be broken, the soft and supple will prevail*
>
> Lao Tzu from the *Tao Te Ching*

When we know ourselves, we are better positioned to truly know others. In knowing others, we build better relationships and when we build better relationships, we learn to know ourselves.

We have been daring to know since the Enlightenment, the Age of Reason. Yet, the more we know, the more we realize how little we know.

Albert Einstein declared once that the more he learnt, the more he realized how much he didn't know.

The Socratic Paradox:

All I know is that I know nothing.

Ironically Socrates never said it. The saying comes from Plato's account of the Greek philosopher, his teacher.

Like Daniel Keyes' brain enhanced Algernon, it is easy to wonder sometimes if ignorance really is bliss...

The Socratic paradox does seem a little negative. We surely all agree that the more we know, the better decisions we can make, assuming our emotions are in-tact? I prefer to think so anyway, don't you?

Neuroplasticity

In 1890 William James informed us that the human brain can change over time. In 1948 Jerzy Konorski coined the term 'neuroplasticity', and in 2000, Erik Kandel won the Nobel prize for describing nerve cell communications using electrical and chemical signals, and how they change the structure of the connections between the cells.

In children we see 'experience dependent' neuroplasticity. Then, by our early 20's we move to the 'experience expectant' (mature brain) neuroplasticity phase. Parts of the brain will atrophy, like a muscle, if it is not tested with new learning. Thinking makes the brain sculpt itself.

Neuroplastic for life

Evidence shows that although our brain cells die as we age, we never stop producing new ones. What is more, our exercise and nutrition impact this 'neurogenesis'.

Specifically, generation of new cells in the hippocampus; such generation can be hindered by poor exercise and nutrition. This has a direct impact on our rate of cognitive decline.

Old dogs, when kept well exercised and fed can and do learn new tricks. It is the tricks, or skills, that we do not feed and water that we lose the fastest.

Learning in depth increases our perceptions and as we learn more, we see more. It is not only the devil that is in the detail; it is everything.

If we feel a task is routine, giving it our conscious attention may make it novel again. A soccer expert will see the match and observe the off-the-ball machinations, an arborealist will see a picture of a woodland and understand the life patterns of the trees. When Craig Foster, the 'Octopus Teacher' studied the ocean bed, he not only saw depths which few others have seen, he was able to share some of this detail with us as he formed his mystical friendship with the eight independently intelligent armed*, three-hearted mollusk[1].

---

*Eight Minds

An octopus is considered the smartest of the invertebrates – each of its eight arms has its own 'mind'. An octopus can recognise individual humans and when its arms combine forces, it has even been known to open 'child-proof' bottles.

Taking Control

Psychoanalysts are trained to be acutely aware of the associations they make, their chains of thought. We can do the same, and enhance our own connections, creating new networks by practice, by deliberate practice, for example selecting random pictures and establishing links between them. If we do this regularly, we enhance our brain's internal networking skills.

Our brain works best when problems are shared across all areas, rather than focused in one. If you are being bombarded with phone calls, a written note rather than another verbal message can help to prevent overload in one area. We can select our tasks so that we balance out our usage.

Our brain cells are plastic, and high neuronal turnover reflects the dynamic nature of the brain. Our actions sculpt its structure and functioning. Learning Braille is a classic example as the delicate finger stimulation increases the number of neurons, enabling the fine touch sensitivity required to make words from the barely raised dots. The inactive areas associated with sight will degrade accordingly. Learning languages demands similar sculpting, with additional perspectives.

But brain encoding takes time and rushing it can be detrimental to efficiency. We must be patient and disciplined to enable change.

With FMRI we have witnessed the anterior cingulate cortex, part of the neocortex associated with executive function, actively switching off the superior colliculus to take control. Of course, our brain is multi-channelled so tasks not requiring executive function can be processed simultaneously. But recall from *Thinking Fast and slow* - try multiplying three-digit numbers whilst out walking and you'll soon be left standing.

Going nowhere, never?

Robert Maurer in his book, One small step can change your life: the Kaizen Way, advises we take small steps to **'tiptoe past our amygdala'**[2]. If we slowly increase our comfort zone, we do not feel threatened, we do not feel fear, our emotional centre doesn't get over-aroused. We do not feel trampled on.

We should be wary of overload. As Steven Kotler, Pulitzer Prize-nominee says in *The Rise of Superman*, 'trying to improve performance by being everywhere, every when, ends up nowhere, never'.

Perhaps you add new tasks without taking old ones away. Do you try and do it all?

Multi-tasking, or task switching costs effort. When we send signals one way then another and then back again, we waste around half a second and use extra energy to reorientate ourselves. We can take 20 minutes to get fully back on track after a distraction and we take a full 50% longer to complete a task, with 50% more errors[4]. We keep on doing it though as we have an innate attraction to novelty, we are unable to acknowledge that it is ineffective, and we have a belligerent desire to do more. And when we do, we deploy the same flawed instinct that leads us to pull all-nighters to get work done. As Stanford University's Clifford Naas puts it, 'habitual multitaskers are suckers for irrelevancy'. Harvard psychologists who gathered data on students' moods at random times found that their minds wander on average 47% of the time…that is a lot of wasted effort![5]

Mars or Venus?

Some people claim to be able to multi-task, but scientifically this is a misnomer. They may be better at task switching, traditionally a female attribution, although without any scientific evidence. We do know that when we have reached unconscious competence, when the tasks are set in the basal ganglia, they demand little conscious effort, so lots of hamsters can be running at once. Women, it is said, are 'from Venus', so they tune into emotional tasks more intuitively and with less apparent effort.

Curiously though, Swedish experiments recently have suggested that working memory and spatial ability are the two key factors in 'multitasking' ability, with spatial ability tending to be superior in males[3]. The jury is still out.

We need strategies to change habits, taking bite sized chunks and giving ourselves bite sized rewards. Unlearning requires 'long term depression'; we weaken old networks to make way for the new ones. Oxytocin helps to erase old bonds - we know this from the sheep-birthing findings. Old skills will fade with lack of use due to 'competitive neuroplasticity'. The blind will learn to hear better and to read braille as their sight fails. Yet, the vestiges of many old skills are held inside us, ghost images ready to be re-awoken. We will rapidly be able to balance on a bicycle even after many decades out of the saddle.

We can take control by making our actions conscious. We recognise and describe a trigger for the habit we want to change. We then distract ourselves by setting an alternative action. I keep my fruit bowl next to the fridge. I start juggling oranges rather than chocolate oranges. I keep doing this until a new pathway is formed. I sharpen my hand-eye coordination and I no longer feel the compelling urge to tap and unwrap. As Egan says, we have the power to exercise choice...

We can choose to continue to 'go with the flow' and let circumstances lead us wherever they might or, if we finally accept that we may be as daft as a brush, but we truly want to be twice as useful, we can take a conscious decision to 'Grow with the Flow'...

Creating the 'FLOW'

Mihaly Csikszentimihalyi, the founder of this concept, identified an optimal state for performance, learning and contentedness. He termed the almost zen-like state where you are so focused on the task that time ceases to exist, 'flow'. When in this state the world passes around you as if you were on an entirely different wavelength and, for that focused time, nothing else matters. This is the way we bring attention to one challenge. When we find flow, we are totally focused, our attention is on our goal, and that goal is so clear that nothing stands in our way. Some of us achieve this state easier than others, but the great news is that anyone can get into this state, whether you are a free diver invoking the mammalian dive reflex to explore the unseen beauty of the ocean, a BASE jumper, checking your parachute cords before leaping from the Christ the Redeemer statue, or a regular householder, sweeping the fallen autumn leaves from your backyard.

FLOW

Four steps to induce and exploit **F.L.O.W**, are as follows:

Focus - concentrate on one task above all else, it may be for 5 minutes, or five hours.

In the same way that meditating clears the mind, use your powers of concentration to channel your entire focus in one direction, the direction of the task. Sweep all the distractions away, funnel all your thoughts to that single point of focus. For this period of time, everything else becomes such a blur that nothing else exists. For Steven Kotler's daredevils this is easy, because one wrong move means instant death. For the rest of us we need our own clear goal, to return this one serve, to write this one brilliant sentence, to flatten more molehills than your three-year-old playmate.

As we approach a flow state, we may reach a fork; one tongue leading us into the 'fight or flight' urge, the other into peak performance. Our brain builds up those neurochemicals like cortisol for our survival. We feel the pre-match nerves, the butterflies and then for the performance. We either flump our lines, flounder and retreat, or we take a deep breath, find our way into the zone, follow the path we have practised and away we go.

---

way into the zone, follow the path we have practised and away we go.

Liberate yourself – for this period of time, stop judging yourself, just let it happen, let the wave take you and send you wherever it wants. Again, you must believe in yourself; it may be hard, but you can do this. If you naturally have a fixed mindset, it is even more difficult. When you open your mind to your possibilities, when you find your growth mindset, you will believe in yourself. And, if all doesn't go according to plan, there is always time for reflection afterwards. We learn at least as much when things don't go to plan, and this reflection is essential for the next phase of improvement.

Output – the output of your efforts can and should be scrutinised and lessons learned to improve future performance. This regular and deliberate feedback is vital to self-improvement, but it can't happen whilst in flow.

When you shift focus to output you have exited your state of flow. This is the time to adjust your bike spokes!

Work – achieving this state does not come without effort. In Steven Kotler's, *The Rise of Superman*, he describes flow as a state of 'effortless effort'[6]; in this state we can accomplish all that we need without fear, tension, or anxiety. We feel incredible, creative, and empowered. We give ourselves our best chance for success.

We always have to work hard to achieve our goals. Although sometimes hard work is not as hard as we might fear.

The cumulative data suggests that a challenge of about 4% above 'normal peak' is needed to keep us in flow – to prevent boredom setting in. This is the real summit of our performance v stress curve (see Yerkes-Dodson curve below). If you usually juggle 100 oranges, juggling 104 will get you into FLOW.

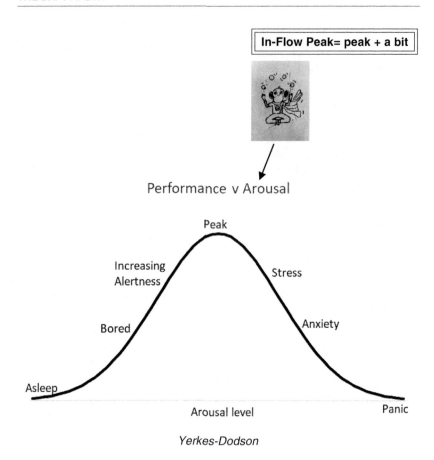

In-Flow Peak= peak + a bit

Performance v Arousal

Yerkes-Dodson

More realistically,in other words, if you play tennis against someone who is 4% better than you, (whilst perhaps hard to measure) then you will play your current absolute best; you will hit your 'sweet spot'. If your opponent is closer in ability, they will provide insufficient challenge. More than 4% greater skill and ability level however and they will most likely sweep the floor with you, perhaps leaving you humiliated and demotivated...

Or, talking of sweeping the floor, if it took you ten minutes to clear that last fallen maple leaf from your backyard last time, can you do it to the same standard in 9 minutes 36 seconds this time?

Now bear in mind what we said at the beginning about impact of 1% improvement each day for a year. That would mean nearly 38x better over a year. At 4% improvement, our performance would have increased by more than 1.6 million times. Now, whilst making daily improvements is not easy, surely that is a goal worth chasing!

Danger: Comfort Zone Ahead

And we already saw that if we deteriorate by 1%, then after 365 iterations we are left with just 2.5% of what we started with. ($0.99^{365}=0.025$).

This decline might mean one service return every ten games – a rather poor return rate, which shows the danger of 'settling' into a comfort zone - the only way is down.

Yet, it's not all about winning or being the best. Mihaly's initial research was a series of studies into our happiness. When we are in flow, we are at our happiest, and the more we devote ourselves to our flow state, the more fulfilled and the happier we are. We grow our peaks of performance when we have a rich source of intrinsic motivation. And if all we want is to reflect better, then daily practice will similarly accelerate us along that path. That is the essence of the enlightenment journey.

Isn't this 'FLOW' state rather selfish - I thought you said that I was my best when I help other people to be their best?

In a way, this is true. But the two are not mutually exclusive. When we are our best at what we do, we bring others with us. It is why Abraham Lincoln told us and why it is oft found amongst the slogans on pithy bar room placards somewhere, 'whatever you are, be a good one', and 'whatever you do, do it to the best of your ability'.

What is more, FLOW is not just a solitary state; it applies to groups, or teams too*.

When we work together 'it was almost like we were playing in slow motion', says Bill Russell, Hall of Fame basketball player with Boston Celtics. 'Everything seemed to click'[7].

> *Solitary FLOW feels good, social FLOW feels even better.
>
> The phenomenally successful Boston Celtics team was like a Swiss watch; a marriage of precision and harmony,

Dr Keith Sawyer of 'Group Genius' lists 10 conditions for group flow including those above, alongside collaboration, meaning just the right level of interaction between team members, the kind of interaction which makes every member peak simultaneously, sparking off each other like the engaged and motivated workers who designed and created the 'Ralpholator' in William C Byham and Jeff Cox's, *Zapp, the Lightning of Empowerment*, (so named after Ralph, one of the shop workers)[8].

We might think of the Harlem Globetrotters running rings round their opponents, in flow, and having fun, but in real life, to get into this enhanced state, our Group also needs to be pushing itself, having some skin in the game, something at stake.

So, what makes a really successful team?

Robert Sternberg, Yale University psychologist explains that a group can be 'no smarter than the sum of the specific strengths of the group', but they can be much dumber, if everyone cannot fully share their talents*.

---

*The Wrong Type of Talent

A study by Robert Kelley and Janet Caplan at Bell Labs looked at their highest performing engineers (academically).

In their task of designing and creating electronic switches for phone systems, these 'superior' groups showed no superiority in performance compared to other groups.

On a wide range of cognitive and social measures, from standard IQ tests to personal inventories, academic talent of the group was not a good predictor of on-the-job productivity.[9]

In fact, too much talent in a team can have adverse effect, even result in catastrophes. Enron is a classic example where subordinates fear to challenge the senior executives. Those who 'do', the Ralphs of this world, have their opinions discounted due to the illusion of superiority held by the senior team. Studies by Angus Hildreth at Cornell University have shown that groups of highflyers find it harder to reach agreement. In 'high power teams', status conflicts and individual's over-riding interest in being 'top dog' abound. These individuals willingly withhold critical information, which unwittingly makes consensus less likely and impairs productivity.

FMRI scans of members during abstract reasoning tests shows many instances where the emotional centre, the amygdala, lights up with activity at the same time as showing a corresponding reduction in the pre-frontal cortices. This suggests that, for some of the high-flying team members conflict results in emotional states which disable

The Right amount of Talent

Boris Groysberg of Harvard Business School used five years of data and found that teams with more stars do perform better, up to a certain point. For Wall Street equity analysts, 45% of the team as star performers proved to be the tipping point. More stars than 45% resulted in less success, although this increased to 70% where the members' areas of expertise did not overlap.[10]

some of their natural problem-solving capability - in other words, during a conflict situation, some of the team literally become less smart.

The fixed mindset also appears to play a part. A company that believes it has a certain amount of talent and can't really change that may affect a 'collective fixed mindset' which shapes their thoughts and actions. They assume that having all the smartest people means achieving the best outcome, and they fail to challenge themselves.

Of course, the contributory factors in Enron's demise are not clear-cut, but elements of the above certainly were at play as the company grew from $10bn to $65bn market capitalisation over 16 years, before its ultimate and rapid collapse.

> **The Right amount of Challenge**
>
> David Ulrich in *The Why of Work* attests to the benefit of FLOW. A degree of desirable difficulty is beneficial. '**We learn better when it is hard than when it is easy**'.

The single most important factor for maximising the excellence of a group's product is consistently found to be the degree to which the members are able to create a state of harmony[11]. A state of harmony allows full advantage of the full value of all its members. The primary factor for creating harmony is the building of a rapport with a network of people. Those who do this well find that things go more smoothly. They put time into cultivating good relationships with people whose services might be needed in a crunch, and consequently have instant ad hoc teams available to call upon to solve a problem or handle a crisis.

> **Collective Intelligence for Team Building**
>
> Anita Williams Wooley at Carnegie Mellon University, Pittsburgh, designs tests to capture the full range of thinking required of a group, with five hours of tests on generating ideas, choosing solutions, negotiating and general ability at execution.

Average IQ accounted for just over 2% of the 'collective intelligence', and just under 4% impact of the highest IQ individual. Far more significant was the member's **social sensitivity**. And the better groups allowed all to participate relatively equally with the worst being dominated by one or two individuals. Who hasn't attended management meetings where a loud and sometimes even rude voice dominates, resulting in a poor outcome or, more often, no outcome at all, apart from the dejectedness of the other parties?!

Interestingly, in line with most evidence of the benefit of greater diversity in the workplace, a greater proportion of women seems to change the dynamic and contributes to a higher collective intelligence, encouraging greater cooperation from all. In a world where there are still more CEO's called Dave or John, than there are female CEO's, female leaders stand out mostly for good reasons, and rarely for bad.

There is always the odd exception...

Exceptions prove the rule

Elizabeth Holmes, founder of Theranos, established Wellness Centres in Walgreens and Safeway with $105m in investment and loans, a close relationship with Pfizer and widescale significant investment including the $121m from Rupert Murdoch and $150m from Walmart Brothers.

She made sure that all employees knew it was her way or the highway. As at Enron, not committing to the product meant lack of loyalty and you would be kicked unceremoniously off the bus. Her aspiration was to be a billionaire, to be the next Steve Jobs. She was determined to change the world, although her focus on the outcome over-rode any focus on the process, which she compromised along the way with deceit, manipulation, charm and flannel.

She was so convincing that she reeled in these big hitters, giving the company the illusion of creditworthiness, and to an extraordinary level.

Holmes' brass neck only rivalled her turtleneck (she even took to dressing like Steve Jobs). Her success was on account of her ability to sell snake oil, to imitate The Turk, (the 18th Century Chess playing automaton -an elaborate box hiding a human chess-player). Holmes became a convincing, influential member of the highest US society, schmoozing at the highest political levels, with a theoretical personal net worth of $5bn.

Her product offering started as a patch to test blood samples for many conditions, became a 'rapid test kit', called the Edison machine, which in the end she pretended to use when secretly using her rivals' full-scale, and more importantly, actually functioning equipment. Her testing kit only provided 12 of the 250 tests she claimed it could and even these were entirely unreliable. It was quite literally a box of tricks. A luxury box of false promises.

In the beginning, Holmes probably never intended to put lives at risk, however her self-justifications, her self-comparisons to Steve Jobs, her desire to be a visionary world changer, led her to do just that. One senior member of her team, who tried to speak up, is known to have committed suicide.

The outcome could have been much worse for many more, and only the weight of the truth prevented more catastrophic misdiagnoses, adverse health impacts and deaths.[12]

So, why on Earth does Holmes earn a place in a section on 'achievement'?!

Doing the Right Thing

Holmes is an exception that proves the rule. Women in the workplace normally have a positive, performance enhancing effect. They naturally possess more of the qualities that make a strong leader in the 21st century. Holmes is a standout exception among women. Not so much among men, for whom such malpractice is commonplace and indeed arguably often encouraged (just look at Adam Neumann's WeWork[14], or the leadership team at Enron).

Holmes does provide us with a prime example of the slippery slope we might all fall down,

> **Chain Reaction**
>
> Clayton M Christensen shows this effect in his classic How will you measure your life as do Carol Tavris and Eliot Aronson in their brilliant Mistakes Were Made (but not by me)[13].
>
> They describe our 'pyramid of choice', and how small decisions can vastly alter our direction, with our brains then finding ways to justify our decisions, triggering a chain reaction or a slippery slope...

if we allow ourselves to make that one small decision, to be dishonest, that one little white lie to 'prove the truth'.

Holmes knew her tests didn't work, but she was so convinced that she was prepared to lie until she could prove her truth, much like DCI Jones and all the detectives who were so convinced of Ben's guilt (a born criminal for sure) that they planted evidence accordingly (see Some Other Substantial Reason). The fact that she dismissed her CFO after he questioned her and failed to recruit one for the next seven years surely should have given the game away. Yet, even when her Board challenged her, she used her persuasive skills to get them to reverse their decision to remove her. Holmes and her partner-in-crime, Sunny, a deceitful, intimidating, controlling, trigger-happy bully fired anyone who raised concerns. They routinely repeated the Enron style mantra, 'if anyone here does not think we are working on the best thing that humans have ever built, or if you are cynical, then you should leave'.

She stepped off the wrong side of the pyramid and slid rapidly to the bottom and so deep that her blood has poisoned the soil, exploiting the illusory bias, repeating lies enough so they were believed, exploiting the illusion of authority by reeling in renowned medical experts, exploiting our optimism bias, because she was selling something which would be of great value to the world, if only it wasn't a hollow shell.

Contrast Holmes with the CEO of Biocon, Dr Kiran Mazumdar Shaw. She is India's first female brew-master, and the country's richest self-made woman.

The Right Side of the Pyramid

Mazumdar-Shaw's driving force is what she describes as 'affordable innovation'. She champions the principle of universal access to all of her company's life-saving medicines.

Her company was founded in 1978 with just 1000 rupees ($130). As is common, she struggled for financial backing at first, due to age, gender and politics, but she persevered and found a first significant financial backer at a chance social encounter. Despite an unstable infrastructure with unreliable water and power supplies and restricted equipment and skills, her strong sense of purpose drove the company to success.

The company, which now has billion-dollar revenues focuses on treating cancer, diabetes and auto-immune diseases including arthritis and psoriasis. It is Asia's largest insulin producer having supplied more than two billion affordable doses of biosimilar insulins to patients globally. Mazumdar-Shaw deploys her affordability criteria to ensure maximum access to the benefits of the company's developments. The company also ploughs back 10% of its revenue into Research and development, with around 1000 pharmaceutical/bio-pharmaceutical patents.

Her corporate social responsibility extends to her Medical Foundation which includes a 1400 bed cancer care centre, and despite her corporate success, she is best known for putting patients before profits.

Far from the empty promises of Holmes, Mazumdar-Shaw has used her background in brewing and fermentation sciences to guide her biotechnology company to myriad life-changing developments. She has committed her life to improving the health, education and welfare of millions of people. And she continues to use her company's discoveries to benefit others. In 2014 her company, Biocon was India's first biotech company to go public. On its listing, it was valued at more than a billion dollars, only the second Indian company to meet that landmark.

In 2020, she earned the title of World Entrepreneur of the Year in the renowned EY business awards, as well as securing her place on the Forbes' 100 Most Powerful Women list. In 2016 Mazumdar-Shaw signed 'The Giving Pledge', committing three quarters of her wealth to philanthropy, or compassionate capitalism as she prefers to label it.

Of course, Dr Mazumdar-Shaw and Elizabeth Holmes represent extremes. One of them thinking, feeling and acting with the benefit of others as her core purpose, the other, not so much.

Holmes scores a solid 100% on any standard test for psychopathy, notably unconcerned about the feelings of others, except for the weaknesses they reveal and how to use those for personal gain.

For the rest of us, non-psychopaths, our brains are still remarkably adept at explaining our actions and making them seem acceptable. But as we know only too well, our brains get it wrong, sometimes surprisingly so.

Verbal Overshadowing

In the same way that our brains create stories to justify our actions, Jonathan W Schooler describes a 'verbal overshadowing effect', where the words we use actually affect our understanding.

Our left hemisphere translates the pictures we see into words. Oddly, applying these words can actually displace a picture in our minds; in a police line-up we may identify a criminal, but if we have tried to describe them in words first, it impairs our picture - we are then less likely to spot them!

> When I was being trained to teach a leadership programme, I felt that I knew the content and understood the message, until I tried to put it into words. I bungled the words and then found that I no longer understood the message. I then had to re-learn the message in words, before I could understand it.
>
> Sometimes learning is an iterative process as the two halves of our brain come together to make a whole.

We know instinctively what our values are, yet when we see our actions, we have the power to frame them accordingly, reluctant to admit that we are doing wrong.

Given this innate skill for reinvention and self-justification, it is indeed wise to make every effort to stay on the right side of the slope. As Christensen explains, 100% of the time is easier than 98% of the time.[15]

The Pythagoric letter two ways spread, shows the two paths in which Man's Life is led

Carlos Cardoso Aveline
The Pythagorean Y

A snake with a forked tongue can chose to lick pleasure or virtue. Pleasure may have steps and a handrail but there is a precipitous drop at the end, however; virtue is less comfortable, but at least you don't plunge to your death! Aveline's two paths of course, provide a false dichotomy.

We are not restricted to two, and have infinite choices, but like Buridan's Ass or Elliot, the unfortunate patient of Antonio Damasio, we cannot make that choice if we do not have a 'why'. Why; our raison d'etre, is usually clear and simple, but is sometimes more complex than the sum of the square of the other two sides.

Simon Sinek in his, itself inspirational TED Talk, 'How Great Leaders Inspire Action' watched 53 million times as I write this, explains that we are looking for meaning, we seek to connect at an emotional level. It is the reason the Wright Brothers succeeded in getting airborne, with scarce funding, but Samuel Pierpoint-Langley, despite substantial institutional financing and support had to leave the 'race to the skies' with his tail between his legs.

Why?

As Sinek repeats, 'people buy why we do something before the what and the how'. It accounts for the success of Apple but doesn't guarantee that anyone who wants to can 'change the world', as Elizabeth Holmes found to her discredit.

Some may argue that Steve Jobs was lucky; his blags and bluster came good, whereas Holmes not so much. History is still written by the winners.

Having a purpose seems to be a fundamental human desire; as we age, we tend to perceive ourselves less useful, and as a result our cognitive decline accelerates. Remaining useful prolongs youthful cognitive abilities (alongside the drug, ISRIB - Integrated Stress Response Inhibitor![16]). The essence of our dreams usually involves 'being useful' in some form; DAFT as a brush we maybe, but we still aspire to being twice as useful.

Of course, we can be more than twice as useful. So why don't I push for more?

A third brush is one too many as I only have two hands! Seriously though, our potential is so much greater than we can even imagine - we set our own limits based on our self-belief and our dreams. We can decide how much we Grow with the Flow...

GROW with the FLOW

The GROW model, a tool for goal setting and problem-solving, asks that we assess the gap between where we are and where we want to be. When we maximise our quantity and quality of flow, and continually define and refine our Goals, Reality, Obstacles and Way forward, we GROW as we FLOW. This way we enjoy the best of ourselves for the moment and continue to develop for the future. We savour the short term as well as relishing what's to come.

In business, when we focus on short term profits, we compromise the long-term prospects for the organisation. In politics, the same applies with profits exchanged for popularity. When we focus on the processes, we let profits (or popularity) take care of itself. We set ourselves up for long term success. As individuals we face the same trade off. We increase our overall value by getting that balance right and by doing the right thing.

Fifty Anyhow

Tho' we are not now that strength which moved earth and heaven, that which we are, we are

Tennyson (said of Ulysses, the great warrior, explorer)

In the long term we will grow older, whether we like it or not. Whether we grow wiser is up to us. If we choose a positive path, our wisdom will at some point surpass our talent.

'Let's hope our contribution will not be forgotten as wisdom and understanding spread outwards to embrace the cosmos,' as James Lovelock put it.

Our successors look to us to impart our wisdom so that they can grow and achieve their potential, a potential which becomes far more important than ours. As they watch and learn, their neurons fire like Dr Rizzolatti's chimpanzees, whose 'mirror neurons' sparked hot debate since the day one of his students noticed them firing in a group of chimps as they watched another chimp licking an ice cream[17]. Our successors, like the other chimps, may gain from us so much neurological pleasure, without the calories.

We are being watched and mimicry and imitation are fundamental for learning. Why else would we be so fascinated to watch other people on-line? Watching fires the neurons (almost) as if we were doing the thing ourselves, from shopping to game playing, to being smart, funny, wacky and definitely not sad losers locked away in our teenage bedrooms watching other people having fun and creative lives!

> **The Joy of Watching others**
>
> When 17 year old Nick Baily from Detroit broadcast himself opening up his Nintendo Wii in 2006, scoring 71,000 Youtube views within a week, the craze for gratification through watching others in the internet age was born.

It is also why, when I took a dinghy out of the harbour on a holiday in Spain, my middle son, Lucas, age 6 at the time, showed no signs of fear until I started to panic, suddenly realizing the size of the waves and my relative incompetence in the water. As I feigned calm, I watched Lucas's fears dissolve. His expressions mirrored mine almost exactly. I now understood why people don't react to smoke in a crowded room... unless others do.

> **You are being Watched**
>
> Children copy us, and the quality of our communication bears great significance....Dr Steve Roberts suggests four ways to ensure effective communication: ensure it is the right time, the right place, the right agenda and delivered in the right way.
>
> It is helpful to communicate with facts not feelings, in a calm manner, deploying our best listening skills. Where there is potential conflict, it is most effective to seek first to understand, take time to reason well, to find common ground, to graciously compromise and accept differences. It pays to be aware of our body language, our intonation, the speed volume and emphasis we place on our words and to ensure the right ambience.
>
> And when all that fails, take a chill pill – they are only kids for chrissakes!

It is commonly known now that it is most effective to praise children for effort rather than achievement; we cannot change innate talent, but we can change effort, and effort is what develops our talents and breeds our confidence, whatever our starting point. Studies show that children praised for intelligence will chose to look at the papers of lower scorers in a test to bolster their self-esteem, whereas children praised for effort chose to look at those higher scorers so they could learn from their mistakes. The short-term profit from a self-esteem boost is far outweighed by the long-term erosion of confidence and further development[18].

We should also be wary of giving excessive praise as Carol Dweck explains in *Mindset*, it can be detrimental, especially if we focus on the outcome rather than the process.

Pygmalion

Robert Rosenthal and Lonore Jacobson in 1965 introduced the 'Pygmalion effect'. Average children, when treated as if they were gifted and talented and taught accordingly, actually performed better, as well in fact as if it were actually true!*

Those who have been trained to think that the result is everything, that all their abilities are innate, do not respond well to negative feedback. FMRI imaging shows less activity in the temporal lobe, the area associated with conceptual processing, suggesting a reluctance to learn from errors[20]. This is why so many of those hares, who leapt away from the starting gun, starting so far ahead, are often overtaken later in the race by the more steadfast tortoises.

*Pygmalion in Greek myth was the talented sculptor, who fell in love with Galatea, his own ivory sculpture. His belief in its perfection brought her to life. The name was later borrowed by George Bernard Shaw's Henry Higgins to reflect the same 'belief-making-it-so' for Eliza Dolittle.

Dweck points to her friend Sara Blakely, founder of the major US clothes company, Spandex and now a demonstrably generous employer (First class flight tickets and $10,000 to every employee upon the company's stock market listing, being a fine example). Blakely's father used to routinely ask, 'what did you fail at today?' With the right intonation, and follow-up support, failure was embraced and demonstrably defined as evidence of learning.[19]

The most important determinant of personal success is our 'interpersonal intelligence'. The socially aware child observes first and then finds a way to connect by imitating, and only then do they talk their way in. It is this ability to take a pause and see the other child's perspective that enables them to excel.

Interpersonal Intelligence

Thomas Hatch and Howard Gardner identified four key components; organising groups, negotiating solutions, personal connection and social analysis.

When taken together they reflect the ingredients of charm, social success, even charisma. Some children are more naturally aware of these ingredients, even if they couldn't articulate them.

Children who lack this interpersonal intelligence struggle to fit in. Studies show that the socially-inept child, desperate to join in with a group, makes it hard for themselves by forcing their way in where a more socially aware child is more circumspect.

As in children, so in adults. But beware of social chameleons; what Helena Deutsch, the psychoanalyst calls 'as-if personalities', those who try to fit in everywhere. They can become highly effective at impression management and well suited only to a career in politics!

The great Isaac Newton for example, was no social chameleon. He founded modern mathematics, described the duality of light, and gave us the immutable laws of physics. He notoriously 'stood on the shoulders of giants'. And yet, he lectured to empty theatres. His Emotional Intelligence apparently trailed his IQ somewhat.

Perhaps at the other end of the spectrum, Rhonda Byrne. In *The secret*, purports to give us the answer to Douglas Adams 'ultimate' question, the Meaning of Life, the Universe and Everything.

This is 'the law of attraction'[21] – whatever is going on in your mind, you are attracting to you. Knowing our Reticular Activation System, the filter that helps provide our focus, it is hard to argue with her conclusion. Byrne says that believing is the first step to having. In the way of Zen, the Universe will provide.

As Christine Mansfield, The Living Leader, leadership guru says, 'change your thinking, change your day. Create the day you want and repeat to create the life you want'.

And, if you want to change, why not start with something small, perhaps reflecting over a nice hot cup of coffee. As ever, to prevent scalding, and to prevent going nowhere never (the Steve Kottler way), may I advise you to take small sips...

Our actions define us, not our intentions. Think about it, then do it!

ACTUS RHESUS

To a large extent our culture will impact our definition of achievement – in the Western world, we tend to consider our personal successes first. In other cultures, it is all about our relationships.

How you undertake an improvement journey will depend on your starting point. The middle-aged man in T.S. Eliot's poem '*The Love Song of J. Alfred Prufrock*' has measured out his life with coffee spoons[1]. He has enjoyed his coffee but rues his excessive control in every day decision making. He was careful and considered, but on reflection, just occasionally he should have drunk hot chocolate – with whipped cream, marshmallows and chocolate sprinkles!

When Bronnie Ware, the Australian writer, divulged the deathbed regrets of the elderly, 'I wish I had made budget' did not feature very highly on her list. It is easy to be caught up in the minutiae of the moment and that is essential if we are to perform at our highest levels and enjoy ourselves in that moment, yet it is in the bigger picture that we will assess our lives.

If we are afraid of failure, then our human instinct is not to expose ourselves to the potential for such an outcome. Until recently I am a little ashamed to admit that I believed, genuinely, that evidence of effort is a sign of weakness. I wanted to be judged for my potential. I wanted people to say, 'if he put in the effort, he could be amazing'. 'Could do better' always featured on my school report cards. I ws happy with that. In many ways, I had a fixed mindset, I had certain innate talents (and many more innate no–go areas). The school system seemed to reinforce this with the annual reports to the parents, grading A for achievement and 1 for effort, in that order. The smart, funny, lazy guy is a better friend than the lazy, smart, funny one. So, no-one cared about the number – the effort grade. Worse still, who was ever awarded an A2 or A3?!

In the same way, a person with 'all the gear, but no idea' may be ridiculed, so I feared, all the effort but none of the achievement. Hence minimum effort to get by makes perfect sense. This way we only do what we know we can do. We have none of the gear and still no idea. We shrink into our shells and slither away, smearing our path with the glimmering slime of unfulfilled potential.

Where Yoda says 'do or not do, there is no try', The DAFT Apeth says 'there is try and there is do not try; there is do, and there is also do-do. BUT OK THAT IS!'

'I wish I had the courage to live a life true to myself, not the life others expected of me', was high on Bronnie Ware's list, a list which might never have reached the public, might never have guided millions of people, might have stayed with Bronnie Ware and her immediate contacts, but for her persistence, having been rejected by all 25 targeted publishers. Ware chose to self-publish, hit that gap in the market, between where we are and where we want to be, and was soon swooped upon by global publishers and the rest is history[2].

When LS Lowry, one of my favourite artists, was finally recognised by the powers that be late in his life, he chose not to make the great trip South from his Greater Manchester home to Buckingham Palace. He said that there was 'no point collecting his OBE as his mother wasn't there to see it'. His brushstrokes were masterful, his subtle use of bleak colours amazing, but did he really live his best life?

Do you work too hard, lack the courage to express your feelings, lose touch with friends and not allow yourself to be happier? You are in good company, according to Bronnie Ware. Instead, why not aim to bow out like Frank Sinatra or Sid Vicious, able to sing, I did it my way? And if you do want a philosophy and are not satisfied with that of Eric Idle's waiter in 'The Meaning of Life', hungering for more than just one 'wafer-thin' mint[3], you might recall the oft-quoted Victorian poem, Invictus:

'It matters not how straight the gate; how charged with punishments the scroll. I am the master of my fate; I am the captain of my soul.'

Whether or not we assume the Haka stance, we can ask ourselves, are we heading in the direction of our Dreams, with Actions, Feelings and Thoughts all aligned? If we are going to live our DAFT 'hero's journey', we will take time to 'find our way', we will take sudden and unexpected detours, we will experience promising adventures and severe perils. Our character will be tested alongside our skills, and our strength of will. We will make mistakes throughout our journey, we will push ourselves out of our comfort zone, sometimes too far out, and will need to rein back in for the time being, we will struggle to find the balance of challenge and safety to suit our personality, we will encourage others to do the same, helping them to expand their comfort zones lest they wither and wane, and we'll let them know for sure that we have faith in them, giving them the sense of safety to explore and expand. We will look back on our lives and celebrate how far we have come and what we leave in our wake.

That is what I call achievement, and most importantly, when you can't achieve what you want on your own, it is perfectly sensible to go out and get yourself a jet pack!

As we go, let's take the time to laugh a lot, it produces more serotonin than anti-depressants, enhances cognitive strength, and most importantly boosts our sense of happiness and fulfilment. Let's be grateful for all that we have. Let's look after ourselves so that we can also look after others. Let's eat from the tree of knowledge and occasionally from a branch of Patisserie

Valerie (other cake shops are available). Let's keep trying, to remain soft and supple as long as possible so that, when we do become stiff and hard, we feel like that inimitable German joker, Till Eulenspiegel, who sat up in his coffin, put his thumbs in ears and waggled his fingers and tongue to the world, before laying back down for the last time yelling 'it's been a good life'.

That, my friend, is what it means to be a DAFT Apeth.

The best DAFT APETH in town!'

FINAL REFLECTIONS

Achievement		
Mens Rea	Actus Rhesus	Guilty? ☑
D Know your dreams, your passions and your purpose?	Do you?	☐
Know what you want? What are your desires?	Can you articulate them to yourself?	☐
Who do you want to be?	Have you defined your identity. Do you act like that?	☐
Are your desires guiding you towards your dreams?	Are you satisfied you are moving in the right direction?	☐
Do you want it?	Have you made what you really want attractive enough to you?	☐
Are your aware of your need for Novelty and Risk?	Do you know your risk preferences?	☐
Do you seek novelty?	Do you find ways to make the old new?	☐

Achievement		
Mens Rea	Actus Rhesus	Guilty? ☑
A — Do you want to get closer to your dreams?	How are you changing the way you act?	☐
A — Change is chaLLEnge made simpler	Take Little steps on Light feet, Everyday. We can tiptoe past our amygdala and humbly achieve greatness. What little steps are you taking today?	☐
F — Do you understand your emotions?	Do you use this knowledge to change the way you act?	☐
F — Can you control your emotions?	Are you acting differently to take control of your emotions?	☐
T — Thinking is hard	Are you using this most precious resource wisely?	☐
T — Thinking creates your reality	Are thoughts still hijacking your dreams? Can you practise changing those thoughts?	☐
Biased Beyond Belief — Are you aware of the signal to noise ratio when making decisions?	Have you asked yourself what decision you would make tomorrow, next year, in many different environments?	☐
Biased Beyond Belief — Can is not the same as do. Do you always exercise humility?	Can you avoid 'Hot Emotions'? Have you tried self-distancing?	☐
M — You can choose your frame of mind	Choose positivity, choose optimism, choose life*	☐
M — You can take control. You can make Happiness happen.	Have you found meaning? - it's on your path to well-being...	☐
E — Mind and body work together...or not at all.	Are you keeping the cogs well-oiled...so your chain doesn't seize up?	☐
E — It is not great to take everything sitting down	What exercise are you doing today?	☐

Achievement		
Mens Rea	Actus Rhesus	Guilty? ☑
N	Good food creates good mood - Eat what you like, when you like...	Do you choose to like to eat food that nourishes you, at times that suit your circadian rhythms?	☐
	Do you know your personalised dietary need? Your body and mind will tell you if it is right for you	Do you feel your energy levels remain stable? Do you feel good physically? What can you do to increase your stable energy levels?	☐
	Treat yourself but don't spoil yourself - seldom pleasures bring the sweetest joy	Do you ask yourself – do I need the whole cream donut, or will one bite do? Are you asking NOT what the donut can do for you...?!	☐
S	Sleep is the third corner of the Well-Being triangle	Are you getting enough?	☐
	It is possible to avoid excessive fatigue.	Do you nap when you want to, or when you need to, or neither? Do you have a plan to ensure you get sufficient rest to perform at your best?	☐
R	You don't have time for all this...	This is when you need it most. Are you allocating five minutes each day for reflection?	☐
	General Intelligence, curiosity and conscientiousness are key	Are you embracing all three to ensure that you GROW?	☐
E	I understand my own biases so I'm ready to focus on others	Do you observe other people's biases? How do you help them?	☐
	When I focus on others I understand myself better	When does helping others help you?	☐

Achievement		
Mens Rea	Actus Rhesus	Guilty? ☑
A	When you know yourself and understand others... success is in your grasp...	See DAFT APETH'S Top Ten Action Plan	☐
ACTUS RHESUS You are the best DAFT APETH in town!		

DOUBLE YOUR USEFULNESS - TOP TEN TIPS TO MAKE YOU THE BEST

DAFT APETH

You are you! In the same way that Theseus's ship is the same ship despite all parts having been swapped out, and Trigger's broom is still Trigger's broom despite having its head replaced seventeen times and its handle fourteen.

So, from the ship of Theseus to the ship of fools, from Plutarch to Peckham, we are all DAFT but LOVABLE characters - throughout our lives our cells are constantly dying and being replaced, our heads may literally change seventeen times, and our handles (or nicknames) certainly change many times too. We remain the same but different.

We don't control everything, but there are actions we can take, principles we can follow to be the best we can be. Here's my top ten + 1:

1. **B**elieve in your dreams; there is no lie in belief; mind you there is also no truth in our thoughts − dream big and keep doing it. This is what gives meaning to our lives; meaning we will be happier than if we chase happiness itself.

2. **E**xercise your acting skills to become the person (or ape) that you want to be.

3. **Y**outhful enthusiasm is yours by reframing your feelings and experiences. Finding the new in the old will invigorate you and enhance your experience of life.

4. **O**bjectively challenge your own thinking and become more aware of the flaws in your own logic than you are of the flaws in others. And flaws make you human so...

5. **U**rge yourself to be at least as compassionate with yourself as you are with others and remember, whether your glass is half full or half empty, the liquid in the glass sure tastes good.

6. **R**un, walk or crawl – any regular physical activity releases those precious neurotransmitters.

7. **B**etter diet leads to better life balance - listen to your borborygmus, and listen to your granny - a little bit of what you fancy really doesn't do any harm.

8. **E**motions need a rest too – press pause when you can and switch off often.

9. **S**top and Think – are you inclined to agree? Can you question more? Our astronauts see our little blue planet and our daily conflicts and challenges seem a mere trifle. Can you think more like that?

10. Take time to see others' perspectives. If you are playing black, walk around the chess board and imagine you are white.

11. Friend – are you your own bestie? Remember to laugh - **at** yourself, and **with** others.

And vice versa.

END

Bibliography

REFERENCES

DREAM

1. https://www.newyorker.com/books/page-turner/the-mystery-of-s-the-man-with-an-impossible-memory, Reed Johnson, April 2017 - Neuropsychologist Alexander Luria's case study of Solomon Shereshevsky

2. Moore's Law states that the number of transistors on a microchip doubles about every two years, though the cost of computers is halved. Investopedia Sep 2021

3. Jessica Hamzelou, interviewing Jorge Tejada, I slice up human brains for a living, New Scientist 24 September 2016

4. Desmond Morris, The Naked Ape, Penguin 2017, p19

5. Desmond Morris, The Naked Ape, Penguin 2017, p29

6. Ken Robinson, Finding Your Element, 2014

7. Dr Daniel Amen, TED-X Orange Coast https://www.bing.com/videos/search?q=daniel+amen+youtube&cvid=cf5b496bab574343a928e2f8187680a2&aqs

8. Brad Stone, The Everything Store, Jeff Bezos and the Age of Amazon, 2013

9. Ken Robinson, Finding Your Element, 2014, p60

10. Barry Schwartz, Success DNA, https://workplacestars.com. September 2021

11. Desmond Morris, The Naked Ape, Penguin 2017, p 31

12. Charles Andrew, The Neuroscience of Desire, Charles Andrew, New Scientist, 17 June 2015; https://lsa.umich.edu/psych/research&labs/berridge/publications/nueroscience of Desire and Desire Regulation, C h6, Motivation and Pleasure in the Brain, Morten L. Kringelbach Kent C. Berridge

13. Martin Lindstrom, Buy-Ology, 2009, p108

14. Clayton.M. Christensen, The Innovators Dilemma, 2006, p260-1, disruptive technologies.

15. James Clear, Atomic Habits, 2018 20, p49-51

16. James Clear, Atomic Habits, 2018, p105=108

17. Rizzolatti, Giacomo; Sinigaglia, Corrado (2008). Mirrors In The Brain: How Our Minds Share Actions and Emotions. New York: Oxford University Press. ISBN 978-0-19-921798-4.

18. Tom Butler Bowden, 50 Psychology Classics, (2017) Ch38, Walter Mischel,

19. https://www.genecards.org/cgi-bin/carddisp.pl?gene=DRD4, September 2021

20. Desmond Morris, Human Zoo, Vintage, 1994, Chapter 2, Status and Superstatus

21. Dr Angela Duckworth, Grit,2017, p190

22. Joseph Campbell – The Hero with a Thousand Faces, New World Library, 2008, p210

23. Atul Gawande, Being Mortal – Illness, medicine and what matters in the end, Wellcome Collection, 2015,

ACT

1. Malcolm Gladwell, Blink, 2005, The Power of Thinking without Thinking, 'the statue that didn't look right', p3-17

2. https://www.brainvoyager.com/bvqx/doc/UsersGuide/MVPA/ MultiVoxelPatternAnalysis, MVPA. Html 23 Sept 2021

3. Tom Stafford – Choice Engine, New Scientist 6 April 2019

4. James Lovelock, Novacene, Allen Lane, 2019, p19

5. Friederike Fabtritius and Hans W Hageman, The Leading Brain, 2018, p181-4

6. Friederike Fabtritius and Hans W Hageman, The Leading Brain, 2018, p183

7. Dr Carol S Dweck, Mindset, Robinson, 2017, Jim Marshall, Defense for Minnesota Vikings, p31-2

8. James Kerr, Legacy, Constable, 2013, Clive Woodward and David Brailsford espouse benefit of marginal gains, p64-6

9. Geoff Calvin, Talent is over-rated, Nicholas Brealey Publishing, 2010, Ch5-6

10. K Anders Ericsson, Ralf Th.Krampe, Clemens Tesch-Romer, The Role of Deliberate Practice in the Acquisition of Expert Performance, Psychological review 100, no.3,1993 (p363-406)

11. John P Kotter, Leading Change, Harvard Business review, 2012, https://www.kotterinc.com/8-steps-process-for-leading-change/ 23 Sep 2021

12. https://history-biography.com/taiichi-ohno/ 22Spetember 2021

13. Stephen Pinker, Enlightenment Now: The Case for Reason, Science, Humanism, and Progress, Penguin 2019

14. Thich Nhat Hanh, The Art of Communicating, 2013, The Cake in the Refrigerator, p162-4

FEEL

1. Nassim Nicholas Taleb, Fooled By Randomness, 2007, p223

2. Antonio Damasio, Descartes Error, Emotion, Reason and The Human Brain, New York, Avon Books, 1994

3. Daniel Goleman, Emotional Intelligence, Bloomsbury 1996, p9

4. Desmond Morris, The Naked Ape, Penguin 2017, p103

5. Desmond Morris, The Naked Ape, Penguin 2017, p114

6. http://news.bbc.co.uk/1/hi/magazine/8035540.stm, Tom Geoghagen, May 2009,

7. Desmond Morris, People Watching, Vintage, 2002, Pupil Signals, p250

8. Desmond Morris, The Naked Ape, Penguin 2017, p121

9. https://www.scientificamerican.com/article/the-me-effect/ Nicole Branan on November 1, 2010, The emotional contagion effect https://positivepsychology.com/emotional-contagion, Geoffrey Gaines, 18 August 2021

10. Robert Maurer, One Small Step can change your life, the kaizen way, New York Workman Publishing Company, 2014 (kindle edition), preface

11. Matthew Walker, Why We Sleep, Penguin, 2018, p208-214

12. Daniel Goleman, Emotional Intelligence, Bloomsbury 1996, p48

13. https://www.child-encyclopedia.com/sites/default/files/textes-experts/en/892/temperament.pdf, Nov 2019, Daniel Goleman, Emotional Intelligence, Bloomsbury 1996, p215-9

14. https://www.researchgate.net/profile/Miguel-Kazen,

15. Daniel Goleman, Emotional Intelligence, Bloomsbury 1996, p266

16. Daniel Goleman, Emotional Intelligence, Bloomsbury 1996, p75-77

17. https://www.ted.com/talks/mark_rober_the_super_mario_effect_tricking_your_brain_into_learning_more

18. Edith Eger, The Choice, Rider, 2018, p204

19. https://albertellis.org/rebt-cbt-therapy/ Rational Emotive Behaviour Therapy

20. Edith Eger, The Choice, Rider, 2018, p114

THINK

1. The Secrets of Houdini, JC Cannell, Dover Publications Inc, New York,1973

2. Robert J Shiller, Irrational Exuberance, 2000, Princeton University Press

3. Jon Ronson, The Psychopath Test, Picador, 2012, Ch2, The Man who Faked Madness

4. Dr Carol S Dweck, Mindset, Robinson, 2017, p117

5. Amy Cuddy, Presence, Orion, 2016,

6. David Robson, BBC, LinkedIn 18 August 2020 'What would batman do?'

7. Daniel Kahneman, Thinking Fast and Slow, Chapter 4, The Associative Machine. eg; Florida Effect, p53 https://uxplanet.org/5-examples-of-how-priming-influences-behaviour – Eugene Esanu 15 Nov 2019, 16 June 21.

8. https://www.acefitness.org/education-and-resources/lifestyle/blog/548/do-mini-workouts-throughout-the-day-provide-the-same-benefit-as-one-continuous-workout

BIASED BEYOND BELIEF

1. Friederike Fabtritius and Hans W Hageman, The Leading Brain, 2018, p

2. E.g;2520youtube%26sc%3d044%26sk%3d%26cvid%3d14B5674BAFC
   14852AC986ED6CC79718F&view=detail&mid=647089DAF1C2565C46
   79647089DAF1C2565C4679&&FORM=VDRVRV

3. E.g;Tom Cutler, The Pilot Who Wore a Dress, published by Harper
   in 2016, yes 2016, with this and other 'Dastardly Thinking Lateral
   Mysteries'!; Francesca Gino, Rebel Talent, Pan Books 2019, P249

4. Neuroscience News, A Ten Minute Run can Boost Brain Processing,
   Naoko Yamashina, University of Tsukuba, 7 December 2021

5. Nassim Nicholas Taleb, Fooled By Randomness, Penguin 2007, Gird
   Girenzeger p200,287

6. Nassim Nicholas Taleb, Fooled By Randomness, Penguin 2007, p68,
   90, Daniel Kahneman, Thinking Fast and Slow, ch26, Prospect theory,
   p286-8

7. Nassim Nicholas Taleb, Fooled By Randomness, Penguin 2007, p160

8. Julian Baggini, Do They Think We're Stupid? Granta 2010, Ch100,
   Complacent Superiority,p312-314

9. David Robson, The Intelligence Trap, Hodder, 2020, part 1

10. Nassim Nicholas Taleb, Fooled By Randomness, Penguin 2007, p197
    Steven Pinker, 1997, How the Mind Works, New York, WW Norton,
    1997, The Blank Slate, New York, Viking, 2002

11. Penrod and Cutler, (1995) 'Witness Confidence and Witness Accuracy:
    Assessing their Forensic Relation', Psychology, Public Policy and Law 1
    (4), 817–45

12. JC, Some Other Substantial reason, Daniel Kahneman, Olivier Sibony,
    Cass R. Sunstein, Noise, Harper Collins, 2021

13. Jeff Bezos – https://www.princeton.edu/news/2010/05/30/2010-
    baccalaureate-remarks

MEANING AND WELL-BEING

1. Douglas Adams, The Hitchhikers Guide to the Galaxy series, Pan, 1985

2. Tara Swart, Kitty Chisholm, Paul Brown, Neuroscience for Leadership, Palgrave Macmillan, 2015, p57

3. Daniel Kahneman, Thinking Fast and Slow, Chapter 27, The Endowment Effect

4. Dr Steve Peters, The Chimp Paradox, Vermilion, 2012, p128

5. https://learnsomethinginteresting.com/2021/03/23/the-harvard-university-hope-experiment/Curt Richter

6. Daniel Goleman, Emotional Intelligence, Bloomsbury 1996, p173/1777

7. https://www.gallup.com/cliftonstrengths/en/strengthsfinder.aspx, 21 Sept 2021

8. Tom Wolfe, The Right Stuff, Farrar, Straus and Giroux, 1979

9. HPA axis refers to the Hypothalamus, Pituitary and Adrenal glands - a complex feedback system of neurohormones that regulate the physiological mechanisms of stress reactions, immunity etc....

10. Ian Dury - Reasons to Be Cheerful, Part 3 Lyrics

11. https://gretchenrubin.com/books/the-happiness-project/about-the-book/21Sep 21

12. Douglas Adams, The Hitchhikers Guide to the Galaxy, the ultimate question of life the universe and everything, the answer is of course 6*9 in base 13. IN ASCII language 42 is designation for * and * means "whatever you want it to mean", which is both convenient and useful.

13. Dr Steve Peters, The Chimp Paradox, Vermilion, 2012, CH5, The Guiding Moon (Part 2)

14. Amy Morin, 13 Things Mentally Strong People Don't Do, Harper Thorsons

15. Martin Gore, Depeche Mode, Get the Balance Right, January 1983

16. Dean Burnett, The Idiot Brain, Faber and Faber, 2016, Richard Restak, Mozart and the Fighter Pilot, The River Press , New York, 2001, p117

17. https://www.scn.ucla.edu/pdf/AL-UCLAToday.pdf, 19 Mar 2010

18. Amy Morin, 13 Things Mentally Strong People Don't do, Harper Thorsons, 2015, Chapter 8, The Hershey's Story and Reese's Peanut Butter Cups

19. https://paulineroseclance.com/impostor_phenomenon.html 23 Sept 2021

20. https://pubmed.ncbi.nlm.nih.gov/24769739/Gillian Sandstrom and Elizabeth Dunn Pers Soc Psychol Bull 2014 Jul;40(7):910-922. doi: 10.1177/0146167214529799. Epub 2014 Apr 25,

21. UK Channel 4's Goggle Box Star, Andy Michael, who died in August 2021.

22. K Carrie Armel and VS Ramachandran, Projecting sensations to external objects: evidence from skin conductance response – The Royal Society published on-line 29 Jan 2003

23. https://people.com/human-interest/valery-spiridonov-head-transplant-backs-out/ Jason Duaine Hahn April 10, 2019, Mr Canevero may have come across a few hurdles, but he has not given up!... https://www.sciencenatures.com/2021/08/the-worlds-first-human-head-transplant.html, https://www.wikigrewal.com/human-head-transplant/ "Zac Efron", 21 Sept 21

EXERCISE

1. Linda Geddes, Happy New You, New Scientist 5 Jan 2019, Arash Javanbakht – The Conversation, Neuroscience News, How exercise keeps your brain healthy and protects it against depression and anxiety. 26 Feb 21.

2. https://www.mind.org.uk/information-support/tips-for-everyday-living/nature-and-mental-health/how-nature-benefits-mental-health/Sep2021, Harvard Health Publishing July 2018 – Sour mood getting you down? Get back to nature. 24nov2020

3. Asst Professor Kristine Williams, University of Copenhagen, Neuroscience News 3 Aug21

4. Tom Vanderbilt, https://nautil.us/issue/73/play/raising-the-american-weakling, 4 July 2019

5. https://www.thelancet.com/journals/lancet/article/PIIS0140-6736(14)62000-6/fulltext, Prognostic value of grip strength, Dr Darryl P Leong et al, 13 May 2015, Helen Thomson , Discover your inner strength, New Scientist 18 April 2020

6. Desmond Morris, The Naked Ape, 2017, p103

7. Caroline Williams, Move, New Scientist 17 July 2021

8. Friederike Fabtritius and Hans W Hageman, The Leading Brain, 2018, Regulate your emotions, p42

9. Frontiers in Psychiatry Sept 21- Skiiing reduces anxiety – Copenhagen Study

10. Herman Pontzner, Burn, New Scientist 2 February 2021 – metabolism myths

11. https://bigthink.com/21st-century-spirituality/what-western-people-stand-to-gain-from-squatting-more-often extracted 3 Aug 21.

12. https://news.usc.edu/166572/squatting-kneeling-health-sitting-usc-research/Squatting and kneeling may be better for your health than sitting.

13. Emily Gersema, "A new USC study of human evolution finds that spending more time in a position where your muscles are somewhat active could reduce the health risks of sedentary behavior". 9 March 2020

14. https://www.bhf.org.uk/informationsupport/heart-matters-magazine/research/blood-pressure

15. Alain de Botton, How Proust can change your life, 1997, p14-18

NUTRITION

1. https://www.who.int/news-room/fact-sheets/detail/obesity-and-overweight, 9 June 2021

2. https://www.who.int/news-room/fact-sheets/detail/obesity-and-overweight, 9 June 2021 – population in 1975 was 4bn , in 2021 it is 7.8bn

3. David Raubenheimer, Stephen Stimpson, In Perfect Balance, New Scientist, 23 May 2020

4. Amelia Tait, Why can I never be bothered?, New Scientist 29 May 2021, Clare Wilson, Junk Food, Dangerously delicious, New Scientist, 12 June 2021

5. https://www.who.int/dietphysicalactivity/publications/f&v_promotion_initiative_report.pdf, https://www.nhs.uk/live-well/eat-well/why-5-a-day/21Sept2021

6. Amelia Tait, Living by the Numbers, New Scientist 11 September 2021

7. Kerry Torrens, https://www.bbcgoodfood.com/howto/guide/health-benefits-fasting nutritionist. https://centerfordiscovery.com/blog/the-dangers-of-intermittent-fasting

8. http://personalnutrition.org . Prof. Eran Segal and Dr. Eran Elinav Weizman Institute, 21 Sep 2021

9. Graham Lawton, Precision Nutrition, New Scientist, 12 September 2020

10. https://joinzoe.com/21 Sept2021 - Test your gut, blood fat and blood sugar responses with our at-home test kit

11. Claire Dayle, Patricia Payton, Physical Intelligence, Simon and Schuster, ICAEW Business and Management, Sept 2020, http://personalnutrition.org . Prof. Eran Segal and Dr. Eran Elinav

12. https://www.bbcgoodfood.com/howto/guide/what-are-health-benefits-drinking-water 17sep 21

13. ACSMs Health Fit J. Author manuscript, PMC 2014 Nov 1.

SLEEP

1. https//www.aaafoundation.org/acute-sleep-deprivation-and-crash-risk,AAA Washington DC survey (>7000 drivers), 2016

2. Dean Burnett, The Idiot Brain, Guardian Books, 2016, p20

3. Amelia Tait, Living by the Numbers, New Scientist 11 September 2021 Ying-Hui Fu at University of California found that mutations in genes ADRB1 and NPSR1 seems to allow people to thrive on 4 hours sleep

4. Matthew Walker, Why We Sleep, Penguin, 2018, p136

5. Carmen Chai, Global News, 15 June 2015, Why the WHO is warning about poor sleep and heart health

6. K Matthew Walker, Why We Sleep, Penguin, 2018, p239-40

7. Matthew Walker, Why We Sleep, Penguin, 2018, p53

8. Dean Burnett, The Idiot Brain, Guardian Books, 2016, p20-22

9. Matthew Walker, Why We Sleep, Penguin, 2018, p124

10. Matthew Walker, Why We Sleep, Penguin, 2018, p204

11. Matthew Walker, Why We Sleep, Penguin, 2018, p139

12. Matthew Walker, Why We Sleep, Penguin, 2018, p187-88

13. Matthew Walker, Why We Sleep, Penguin, 2018,p301-2

14. Matthew Walker, Why We Sleep, Penguin, 2018,p333

15. Robert Cialdini, Influence, First Collins Business Essentials, 2007, Matthew Walker, Why We Sleep, Penguin, 2018, p69

16. Matthew Walker, Why We Sleep, Penguin, 2018, p304

17. Dr James B Maas, Power Sleep: The Revolutionary Program That Prepares Your Mind for Peak Performance, Harper Collins 1998, Liz Seymour, Power Napping,

18. Matthew Walker, Why We Sleep, Penguin, 2018, p143

19. https://www.oxford-royale.com/articles/5-levels-maslows-hierarchy-needs-affect-life/23 Sep 2021

20. Amelia Tait, Living by the Numbers, New Scientist 11 September 2021

21. Matthew Walker, Why We Sleep, Penguin, 2018, Appendix, 12 Tips for Healthy Sleep, originated from National Library of Medicine (US) 2012, https//www.nim.nih.gov/medlineplus/magazine/issues/summer12/articles/iussues/summerl2pg20.html

REFLECTION

1. https://www.sciencedirect.com/science/article/abs/pii/S0092656608001347, Goal-directed attentional deployment to emotional faces and individual differences in emotional regulation, Journal of Research in Personality, Volume 43, Issue 1, February 2009, Pages 8-13

2. Stephen Covey, The Seven habits of Highly Successful people, Free Press, 1989, Habit Number five.

3. https://ieeexplore.ieee.org/document/6789450, Characterization of Empathy Deficits following Prefrontal Brain Damage: The Role of the Right Ventromedial Prefrontal Cortex S. G. Shamay-Tsoory;R. Tomer;B. D. Berger;J. Aharon-Peretz, 2003 MIT Press https://en.wikipedia.org/wiki/Ventromedial_prefrontal_cortex, 22 Sept 2021

4. https://digest.bps.org.uk/2007/11/28/dont-jump-advice-for-goalkeepers-from-economic-psychology/ https://thesefootballtimes.co/2020/05/19/the-psychological-warfare-behind-every-penalty-the-numbers-the-dark-arts-and-the-odds/Edd Norval

5. Giada di Stefano et al, Making Experience Count: The Role of Reflection in Individual Learning by Giada Di Stefano, Francesca Gino, Gary P. Pisano, Bradley R. Staats

6. https://papers.ssrn.com/sol3/papers.cfm?abstract_id=2414478

7. Jennifer Porter, Why you should make time for self-reflection (even if you hate doing it) - Harvard business Review 21 March 2017

8. https://global.toyota/en/company/vision-and-philosophy/production-system/22Sept 2021

9. John S Rennie, I have the Watch, Amazon, 2019

10. Terry Pratchett, A Slip of the Keyboard, 2015, p78

11. Philip Tetlock and Dan Gardner, Superforecasting: The Art and Science of Prediction, Crown, 2016

12. Adele Faber, Elaine Mazlish, How to Talk so Kids will Listen, and Listen so Kids will Talk,Picadilly Press, 2013

13. Mats Alvesson and Andre Spicer, The Stupidity Paradox: The Power and Pitfalls of Functional Stupidity at Work, 2016

14. Susan Engel, The Hungry Mind, Harvard University Press, 2015

15. Angela Duckworth, Grit, why passion and resilience are the secrets to success, Ebury Publishing, 2017

16. Dan Jones, How WEIRD are you?, New Scientist 5 Dec 2020, Erin Mayer, The Culture Map, PublicAffairs, 2015

17. Ezequiel Di Paolo and Hanne De Jaegher. Neurosci., 07 June 2012 https://doi.org/10.3389/fnhum.2012.00163The interactive brain hypothesis

18. Nancy Kline, Time to Think: Listening to Ignite the Human Mind, Cassell, 2002; Angela Duckworth, Grit, why passion and resilience are the secrets to success, Ebury Publishing, 2017, p111

19. https://www.simplypsychology.org/attention-models.html, Theories of selective Attention, Dr Saul McLeod, 2018

20. Douglas Adams, The Hitchhikers Guide to the Galaxy, Pan, 1985

21. Erin Mayer, The Culture Map, PublicAffairs, 2015, Ch1, Listening to The Air, Mayer explains the low context Eastern v high Context Western communicating tendencies, further detailed by Richard E Nesbitt, The Geography of Thought, Nicholas Brealey Publishing, 2005.

22. https://behavioralpolicy.org/wp-content/uploads/2017/05/BSP_vol1is1_Schwarz.pdf Lenin Norbert Schwarz, Eryn Newman, & William Leach

23. "A lie told often enough becomes the truth" Vladimir Ilyich

24. ME Alexander – 'You are about to be entrapped or burned over by a wildfire – what are your options?' -Science Direct, Forest Ecology and Management 2006 (S6).

25. James Kerr, Legacy, Bolletieri Centipede effect. Mathew Syed describes playing table tennis in the Sydney Olympics. He became barely able to hit the ball "Instead of just doing it using the subconscious part of the brain, which is a very efficient deliverer of complex task [people who choke] exert conscious control and it disrupts the smooth working of the subconscious"

26. Desmond Morris, The Naked Ape, 2017, p237

27. Daniel Kahneman, Thinking Fast and Slow, Chapter 7, A Machine for Jumping to Conclusions, p85

28. James Kerr, Legacy, Constable, 2013, The Real McCaw: The Autobiography, Aurum Press, 2015

29. James Lovelock, Novacene, The Coming of Hyperintelligence, Allen Lane, 2019, p80

30. Oliver Sacks, Awakenings, Picador, 2010

EMPATHY

1. Simon Baron Cohen, New Scientist 3 Dec2020, from Pattern Seekers, a new theory of Human Invention

2. Thomas Eriksson, Surrounded by Psychopaths, Ebury Publishing, 2020, p9/10

3. Charles Darwin, The Expression of the Emotions in Man and Animals, Ch1, General Principles of Expression, Oxford University Press USA, 2009

4. Paul Ekman, Telling Lies, Clues to Deceit in the Marketplace, Politics, and Marriage W. W. Norton & Company, 2009

5. Desmond Morris, People Watching, Vintage, 2002, Contradictory Signals, p162-9

6. Charles Darwin, The Expression of the Emotions in Man and Animals, ch1, p3

7. John C Maxwell and Les Parrott PhD, 25 Ways to Win with People, Thomas Nelson, Nashville, 2005, p87

8. Daniel Goleman, Emotional Intelligence, Bloomsbury 1996, Ch8, The Social Arts, p118, https://www.health.harvard.edu/mental-health/can-relationships-boost-longevity-and-well-being June 1 2017, https://thedivest.com/the-importance-of-relationship-in-life-and-why/Max Abraham 2018

9. Daniel Goleman, Emotional Intelligence, Bloomsbury 1996, Robert Rosenthal PONS – Profile of Non-Verbal sensitivity, Ch 7 The Roots of Empathy, p97

10. Lasana Harris, (neuroscientist and experimental psychologist at UCL) told Daniel Cossins in New Scientist 29 Aug 20

11. Amy Morin, 13 Things Mentally Strong People Don't Do, Harper Thorson, P251

12. Chris Hadfield, An Astronaut's Guide to Life on Earth – Audible, 2015

ACHIEVEMENT

1. https://www.netflix.com/title/81045007 My Octopus Teacher, Craig Foster, 2020

2. Robert Maurer, One Small Step Can Change Your Life: The Kaizen Way, Manjul Publishing House Pvt Ltd, 2015

3. https://bmcpsychology.biomedcentral.com/articles/10.1186/2050-7283-1-18, Are women better than men at multi-tasking? Gijsbert Stoet, Daryl B O'Connor, Mark Conner & Keith R Laws BMC Psychology volume 1, Article number: 18, October 2013, Mäntylä T: Gender differences in multitasking reflect spatial ability. Psychological Science. 2013, 24: 514-520. 10.1177/0956797612459660.

4. https://www.businessnewsdaily.com/4019-multitasking-not-productive.html, Matt D'Angelo, 6 Feb 2019, https://www.verywellmind.com/multitasking-2795003, Kendra Cherry, 30 july 2021

5. https://news.stanford.edu/2009/08/24/multitask-research-study-082409/ Adam Gorlick, Aug 2019

6. Steve Kotler, The Rise of Superman, Quercus, 2015

7. Sam Walker, The Captain Class, Ebury Press, 2017

8. William C Byham, Jeff Cox, Zapp, The Lightning of Empowerment, Random House Business, 1999

9. Daniel Goleman, Emotional Intelligence, Bloomsbury 1996, p162

10. Daniel Goleman, Emotional Intelligence, Bloomsbury 1996, p162

11. Daniel Goleman, Emotional Intelligence, Bloomsbury 1996, p161

12. John Carreyrou, Bad Blood, Secrets and Lies in a Silicon valley start-up, Picador, 2019

13. Clayton M Christensen, How Will You Measure Your Life, Thorsons, 2019;Carol Tavris and Eliot Aronson, Mistakes Were Made (but not by me) Why We Justify Foolish Beliefs, Bad Decisions and Hurtful Acts, Pinter Martin Ltd, 2015, Pyramid of Choice

14. https://en.wikipedia.org/wiki/Adam_Neumann, 22 Sep 2021

15. Clayton M Christensen, How Will You Measure Your Life, Thorsons, 2019

16. https://en.wikipedia.org/wiki/ISRIBSRIB, 22Sept 2021

17. Rizzolatti, Giacomo; Sinigaglia, Corrado (2008). Mirrors In The Brain: How Our Minds Share Actions and Emotions. New York: Oxford University Press. ISBN 978-0-19-921798-4

18. Dr Carol Dweck S Dweck, Robinson, 2017, Ch1 Inside the Mindsets

19. Dr Carol Dweck S Dweck, Robinson, 2017

20. Angela Duckworth, Grit, why passion and resilience are the secrets to success, Ebury Publishing, 2017, ch2, Distracted by Talent, p287

21. Rhonda Byrne, The Secret, Atria Books, 2006…

ACTUS RHESUS

1. T S Eliot, The Love Song oF J Alfred Prufrock, Amereon Ltd, 1976,

2. https://bronnieware.com/regrets-of-the-dying/22 Sept 2021, https://indiebookwriter.wordpress.com/2012/03/01/bronnie-ware-from-self-published-author-to-international-best-seller-and-a-contract-with-a-traditional-publisher/Keith Gorek, March 2012

3. Monty Python, The Meaning of Life movie 1983, with Terry Jones as Mr Creosote and Michael Palin as the abruptly disillusioned Maitre D' " Not much of a philosophy I know, but fxxk you!"

BOOKS AND OTHER REFERENCES

BOOKS

Clayton M Christensen, How will you measure your life, Harper Collins, 2012

John Carreyrou, Bad Blood, Picador, 2019

Steven Pinker, Enlightenment Now, Penguin Books, 2019

James Geary, Wit's End, WW Norton, 2019

Helen Thomson, Unthinkable, John Murray, 2018

Joshua Foer, Moonwalking with Einstein, Penguin Books, 2012

Adrian Furnham, Backstabbers and Bullies, Bloomsbury, 2016

Dave Ulrich and Wendy Ulrich, The Why of Work, McGraw Hill, 2010

Jim Collins, Good to Great, Harper Collins, New York, 2001

Lolly Daskal, The Leadership Gap, Portfolio/Penguin, New York, 2017

Mark H McCormack, What they don't teach you at Harvard Business School, Profile Books, 1984

Yuval Noah Harari, Homo Deus, Vintage, 2017

Yuval Noah Harari, Homo Sapiens, Vintage, 2015

Eileen Shapiro, Fad Surfing in the Boardroom, Capstone Publishing, 1998

Matthew Walker, Why We Sleep, Penguin Books, 2017

George Orwell, 1984, Penguin Books, 1989

Robin Sharma, The Monk who sold his Ferrari, Thorsons, 2015

Dr Richard Shepherd, Unnatural causes, Penguin Books, 2019

Ralf Dobelli, The Art of Thinking, Clearly, Sceptre, 2014

Dear Leader, Jan Jin Sung, Rider, 2014

Anne Rooney, Think Like a Philosopher, Arcturus Publishing, 2019

Deborah Tannen, You Just don't understand, Virago Press, 1992

Sandra Newman, Howard Mittelmark, How Not to write a Novel, Penguin Books, 2009

Daniel Goleman, Emotional Intelligence, Bloomsbury Publishing, 1996

Martin Lindstrom, Buy-ology, Random House Books, 2009

Martin Lindstrom, Small Data, Hodder and Staughton, 2016

Clayton M Christensen, The Innovators Dilemma, Collins Business Essentials, 2006

Clare Cherry, Douglas Goodwin, Jesse Staples, Is the Left Brain always Right? A guide to whole child development, Fearon Teacher aids, California, 1989

Dale Carnegie, How to Win Friends and Influence People, Simon and Schuster, 1981, P91-3

Nassim Nicholas Taleb, Fooled by Randomness, Penguin Books, 2007

Kitty Chisholm, Tara Stewart and Paul Brown, Neuroscience for Leadership, Palgrave MacMillan, 2015

Robert Cialdini, Influence – the psychology of persuasion, First Collins Business Essentials 2007

Amy Cuddy, Presence, Orion, 2016

Angela Duckworth, Grit, Vermilion, 2017

Edith Eger, Choice, Rider, New York, 2018

Richard Restak MD, Mozart's Brain and the fighter pilot, Three Rivers Press, New York, 2001

Ken Robinson, Finding Your Element, Penguin Books, 2014

Steve Peters, The Chimp Paradox, Vermilion, 2012

Thomas Erikson, Surrounded by Idiots, Vermilion, 2019

Thomas Erikson, Surrounded by Psychopaths, Vermilion, 2020

Scott Galloway, The Four, Bantam Press, 2017

Thich Nhat Hanh, The Art of Communicating, Rider, 2013

Ram Chara, What the CEO wants you to know, Random House, 2017

Usha Goswami, Child Psychology – A Very Short Introduction, Oxford University Press, 2014

Dawn E. Holmes, Big Data - A Very Short Introduction, Oxford University Press, 2017

Richard Passingham, Cognitive Neuroscience– A Very Short Introduction, Oxford University Press, 2018

Desmond Morris, The Naked Ape, Vintage, 2017

Desmond Morris, The Human Zoo, Vintage, 1994

Desmond Morris, People Watching, Vintage, 2002

Daniel Keyes, Flowers for Algernon, Millennium, 1994

Naoki Higashida, Fall Down 7 Times, Get Up 8, Sceptre, 2017

Naoki Higashida, The Reason I Jump, Sceptre, 2014

Sam Walker, The Captain Class, Ebury Press, 2017

Julian Baggini, Do they think you're Stupid? Granta, 2010

Andrea Petersen, On Edge, Broadway Books, 2017

Adele Feber and Elaine Mazlish, How to talk so kids will listen, and listen so kids will talk, Piccadilly Press, 2013

Adam Jacot de Boinot, Toujours Tingo, Penguin Books, 2007

Kevin Cashman, Leadership from the Inside Out, Berrett Kochler Publishers, California, 2018

Friederike Fabritius, MS and Hans W Hageman PhD, The Leading Brain -Neuroscience hacks to work smarter, better, happier, Tarcher Perigree, 2018

James Lovelock, Novacene, Allen Lane, 2019

Carol Dweck, Mindset, Robinson, 2017

Steven Kotler, The Rise of Superman, Quercus, 2015

Stephen Kotler, The Art of Impossible, Harper Collins, 2021

Dean Burnett, The Idiot Brain, Guardian Books, 2016

James Clear , Atomic Habits, Random House Business Books, 2018

Penny Ferguson, Living Leader, The Infinite Ideas Co Ltd, 2015

David Robson, The Intelligence Trap, Hodder Staughton, 2019

David Robson, The Expectation Effect, Canongate Books, 2022

Amy Morin, 13 Things Mentally strong people don't do, Harper Thorsons, 2015

Daniel Kahneman, Thinking Fast and Slow, Penguin, 2011

Rhonda Byrne, The Secret, Atria Books, 2006

Ben Goldacre, Bad Science, Fourth Estate, 2009

Douglas Adams, The Hitch Hiker's Guide to the Galaxy series, Pan 1985

Emily Alison and Laurence Alison, Rapport, Vermilion, 2020

Jon Ronson, The Psychopath test, Picador, 2011

JC Connell, The Secrets of Harry Houdini, Dover, New York, 1973

Joseph Campbell, The Hero with a Thousand Faces, New World Library, California, 2008

John C Maxwell and Les Parrott PhD, 25 Ways to Win with People, Thomas Nelson, Tennessee, 2005

Atul Gawande, Being Mortal – Illness, medicine and what matters in the end, Wellcome Collection, 2015

Adam Grant, Think Again, WH Allen, 2021

Ray Dalio, Principles. Simon and Schuster, New York, 2017

Alain de Botton, How Proust can change your life, Picador, 1998

Richard E Nesbitt, The Geography of Thought, Nicholas Brealey Publishing. 2019

Shankar Vedantam and Bill Mesler, Useful Delusions, WW Norton and Co, New York, 2021

Christopher Chabris and Daniel Simons, The Invisible Gorilla, Harper Collins, 2011

Tom Butler Bowden, 50 Psychology Classics, Nicholas Brealey Publishing. 2017

Terry Pratchett, In his Own Words – A slip of the Keyboard, Transworld Publishers, 2015

Stephen Blake and Andrew John, Shite's Unoriginal Miscellany, Michael O'Mara Books, 2003, p50

Guy P Harrison, Think, Why You Should Question everything, Prometheus Books, 2013

Ian McGilchrist, The Master and his Emissary, Yale University Press, 2019

Andrea Petersen, A Journey through Anxiety, Broadway Books, New York, 2017

Erin Meyer, The Culture Map, Public Affairs 2015

Malcolm Gladwell, Blink, Penguin Books, 2006

Malcolm Gladwell, Outliers, Penguin Books, 2009

Julian Baggini, Do They Think You're Stupid, Granta, 2010

James Kerr, Legacy, Constable, 2015

Charles Darwin, the Expression of the Emotions in Man and Animals

Allen and Barbara Pease, Why Men Don't Listen and Women Can't read Maps, Orion Books, 2001

Geoff Colvin, Talent is Over-rated, Nicholas Brealey, 2013

Tom Cutler, The Pilot Who Wore the Dress, Harper Collins, 2016

Antoine d'Exupery, Wordsworth Editions, 1995

Steve Radcliffe, Leadership plain and simple, Pearson Education, 2012

Timothy D Wilson - Strangers to Ourselves, Harvard University Press, 2002

J Pool, Nature's Masterpiece: The Brain and How it Works. Walker, New York,

Antonio Damasio - Descartes' Error, Vintage, 2006

Sigmund Freud, Civilisation and its Discontents, Penguin Classics, 2002

Joseph LeDoux, The Emotional Brain, W and N, 1999

Howard Gardner, Frames of Mind, Fontana Press, 1993

Shane Snow, Dream Teams, Piatkus, 2018

James Surowiecki, Wisdom of Crowds, Abacus, 2005

Luke Jackson, Freaks, Geeks and Aspergers Syndrome, Jessica Kingsley Publishers, 2002

Daniel Coyle, The Talent Code, Bantam, 2009

Daniel Pink, Drive, Canongate Books, 2018

Manfred Kets DeVries, The Leader on the Couch,

Susan Smalley, Diana Winston, Fully Present: The Science, Art and Practice of Mindfulness, DeCapo Lifelong Books, 2010

Annie Murphy Paul, The Extended Mind, HMH Books, 2021

Tom Wolfe, The Right Stuff, Vintage Classics, 2018

Daniel Lieberman, The story of the Human Body, Penguin, October, 2013

David Raubenheimer and Stephen Simpson, Five Apetites, Eat Like the Animals, William Collins, 2020

James B Maas, Power sleep, The Sleep Advantage: Prepare Your Mind for Peak Performance, Villard Books, 1998

Matthew Syed, Bounce, Fourth Estate (GB), 2011

Susan Engel, The Hungry Mind, The Origins of Curiosity in Childhood, Harvard University Press, 2018

Dr Oliver Sacks, The Mind's Eye, Picador, 2010

Dr Oliver Sacks, The Man who mistook His wife for a Hat, and Other Clinical Tales, Simon and Schuster, 1968

Nancy Kline, Time to Think, Cassell, 2002

Brad Stone, The Everything store, Bantam Press, 2013

Mats Alvesson and Andre Spicer, The Stupidity Paradox, Profile Books, 2016

Screw It, Let's Do It: Lessons in Life and Business, Virgin Books, 2007

David Rock, Your Brain at Work, Collins Business, 2009

Stephen Kosslyn, Top Brain, Bottom Brain: surprising insights into how you think, Simon and Schuster, 2015

Philip Tetclock, Superforecasting – The Art and Science of Predicting, Random House, 2016

Richie McCaw,The Real McCaw, The Autobigraphy, Aurum Press, 2015

Jean Twenge, Generation Me, The Free Press, 2006

Jean Twenge, The Narcissism Epidemic, Living in the Age of Entitlement, Atria Books, 2010

Bronnie Ware - The Top Five Regrets of the Dying, Hay House, 2019

Robert Maurer,'One small step can change your life: the Kaizen Way', Manjul Publishing House Pvt Ltd, 2015

Jon.S.Rennie, I Have the watch – becoming a leader worth following, ind, 2019

Daniel Kahneman, Olivier Sibony, Cass R. Sunstein, Noise, Little Brown and Co, 2021

Simon Baron Cohen, The Pattern Seekers, A New theory of Human Invention, Allen Lane, 2020

Carol Tavris and Eliot Aronson, Mistakes Were Made (but not by me), Pinter and Martin Ltd, 2020

TS Eliot, The Quartets, The Love Song of J. Alfred Prufrock', Penguin 1998

Francesca Gino, Rebel Talent, Pan Books, 2019

OTHER

Tom Stafford, Sphex - New Scientist 6 April 2019

Jessica Hamzelou, I slice up human brains for a living –- New Scientist 24 Sept2016

Pragyar Arwal, New Scientist Aug 2020

'You're Welcome' by Dwayne Johnson, as Maui from Moana, Disney, 2016

Enron: The smartest guys in the room, Magnolia Pictures, 2005

The Big Short: Paramaount Pictures, 2015

Loren W Jeffries, Mayan End of the World miscalculated by 75 years, 2018 - see article for a simple explanation for the calculation error.

David Adam– weird illusion makes you think objects are lighter than nothing - New Scientist, 2020

Susie Cranston, and Scott Keller at McKinsey, Increasing the Meaning Quotient- website Jan 2013

Richard M.Ryan and Edward I.Deci, Self-determination theory and the facilitation of intrinsic motivation, social development and well-being – American Psychologist Jan 2000

Linda Geddes, Happy New You - New Scientist -5 Jan 2019

Xenia Taliotis – ICAEW Business and Management October 2020

David Raubenheimer and Stephen Simpson, In Perfect Balance, New Scientist 23 May 2020

Tom Vanderbilt, Raising the American Weakling - there are two different interpretations of our dwindling grip strength –Nautilus on-line, Sept 21

Graham Lawton - Precision Nutrition –New Scientist, 12 Sept 2020

Julia Naftulin, What is hangry?, https://www.health.com/nutrition/what-is-hangry - June 13, 2018

Jeff Wise – Surrounded by wildfire, should you run or fight? Psychology Today 3 Aug 2010

Adi Gaskill - Forbes, 3 Dec 2015

Rhea Wessel - BBC psychology of work – the secret to a quick-witted comeback, 8 April 2016

Ephrat Livni – L'esprit de l'escalier Quartz on-line Nov 14 2018

Miguel Rubianes - Are we the same person throughput our lives? – Neuroscience News 30Nov20

Jennifer Porter, Why you should make time for self-reflection (even if you hate doing it) - Harvard business Review 21 March 2017

Gustavo Razzetti, How to Overcome the fear of change – become the author of your own life - Psychology today 2018

ME Alexander – 'You are about to be entrapped or burned over by a wildfire – what are your options?' -Science Direct, Forest Ecology and Management 2006 (S6).

James Duffy, MorethanAccountants.co.uk 'Malcolm Gladwell's 10000Hours rule explained' 15Dec2018.

Erik Hoel, Dream Power, New Scientist 7 November 2020

Richard Woods and Nick Rufford, Sunday Times 10 Oct 2004

Carlos Cardoso Aveline, The Pythagorean Y – A choice between two paths - FilosofiaeEsoterica.com 3 Dec 20.

Drug reverses age-related cognitive decline – Neuroscience news 3 dec 20

Janet M Gibson, Laughing is good for your mind and your body, The Conversation – 4 Dec 20Richard Woods and Nick Rufford, Sunday Times 10 Oct 2004

Simon Baron Cohen, Our Restless Minds, New Scientist 5 Dec 2020

David Robson, Warm Inside, talking to Kari Liebowitz, New Scientist 5Dec 2020

Charles Arthur, The Independent, were-Einstein-and-Newton-afflicted-by-an-obscure-form-of-autism? 1 May 2003

Keith Chen, The Effect of Language on Economic Behavior: Evidence from Savings Rates, Health Behaviors, and Retirement Assets - American Economic Review Vol. 103 No. 2 April 2013

Printed in Great Britain
by Amazon